EXPLORING
THE MULTIAGE
CLASSROOM

EXPLORING THE MULTIAGE CLASSROOM

■

Anne A. Bingham

with

Peggy Dorta

Molly McClaskey

Justine O'Keefe

STENHOUSE PUBLISHERS

York, Maine

Stenhouse Publishers, 226 York Street, York, Maine 03909

Library of Congress Cataloging-in-Publication Data

Bingham, Anne A.
    Exploring the multiage classroom / Anne A. Bingham with
Peggy Dorta, Molly McClaskey, Justine O'Keefe.
        p.   cm.
    Includes bibliographical references.
    ISBN 1-57110-013-X (alk. paper)
    1. Nongraded schools—United States.   I. Title.
LB1029.N6B56   1995
371.2'54—dc20   95-12556
                                                              CIP

Cover and interior design by Joyce C. Weston
Cover drawing by Timothy Plante
Typeset by Octal Publishing

Manufactured in the United States of America
on acid-free paper
99 98 97 96 95 8 7 6 5 4 3 2 1

To—

Liz Farman
Marilyn Johnson
Susan Mahony
Phyllis Murray
Jane Perry
Carol Wheelock

*—for their support and friendship
on a shared multiage journey*

CONTENTS

∎

FOREWORD

———————————————■———————————————

T H E hand-wringing in America continues as politicians and parents struggle with ongoing signals that America's schools remain troubled. Declines in achievement have slowed, but we are far from seeing the reversal of trends first noted by presidential and philanthropic commissions more than fifteen years ago.

Our knee-jerk reaction has been one of policy making. We seem to want to mandate and legislate a return to the good old days. Days when children came to school well fed, ready to attend, and anxious to learn the lessons of democracy and the skills of reading, writing, and arithmetic.

Times have changed. Not only are more children of increased diversity coming to school, but they are entering at a time when entry-level jobs have decreased precipitously, and the jobs demand problem solving and collaborative skills never before required in the history of this country. The fast-moving service sector has emerged as a major employer in this country. Graduates have to adapt, adjust, retrain, communicate, and meet the challenges of societal change at rates unprecedented in our history.

Our children are remarkably unready to face this new set of circumstances. Ask any teacher in America and you will be told that an increasing number of children are coming to school unsettled, unable to concentrate or cooperate. They are filled with television images of how life is lived and unused to knowing what it is to be interested in something for more than twenty minutes at a time. Play—the activity that taught most of us the values of persistent activity and cooperative companionship—has been replaced for most of America's kids with either highly organized, stressful sports or persistent and passive viewing of TV programs. Is it any wonder school seems irrelevant to and disconnected from the lives of many children? Is it any wonder

· ·

school achievement standards are at risk? Is it any wonder we worry once again about the next generation's chances of success?

A second look at the good old days provides hope. Child-responsive teaching and learning is an enduring strand in the history of America's schooling. Starting with Freiderich Froebel's ideas for early education in the 1800s and continuing through the progressive era to our current interest in constructivist pedagogy, we know there is a way of teaching that builds from children and expands to the world we live in. Children's interests are the center point of teaching activity. Their natural impulses are the connecting point for learning the dispositions of democracy, equity, and social interest. We know the tradition of child-responsive teaching produces learners who are independent, capable, collaborative, and well-informed. By disposition and education, learners will be able to address the challenges our day and age presents.

In a body of work begun in *Multiage Portraits,* Anne, Peggy, Justine, and Molly illuminate the most recent version of this responsive tradition. Where *Multiage Portraits* gives us a picture of how responsive teaching and learning looks, *Exploring the Multiage Classroom* suggests how other teachers might pursue a similar style of responsive teaching and how parents might come to understand it. *Exploring the Multiage Classroom* is not a cookbook for developmental practice, but it comes as close to a manual for child-centered teaching as any book I have ever read. Because the authors are learners at heart, they know other teachers can't be given a prescription to pursue their kind of teaching. Their approach is as it might be with students: they describe, model, suggest, and illustrate, trusting that readers will adapt their own methods and strategies.

What is most powerful in this book is the interplay between explanation and illustration. With Anne taking the lead, she calls upon a career of working with children to skillfully show how children learn through interesting questions and curiosities. Anne opens her classroom family to us and invites us to share her thoughts and decisions, moment-to-moment, day-to-day. We see her organization and skill from two perspectives: from her own, through her decision making, and from the children's, as they respond to her decisions. Teaching and learning are revealed as one piece. Anne the teacher becomes Anne the learner as she watches what happens within her classroom family. The children become teachers as Anne assesses their moments and thinks about what to do next. The classroom thus constructs itself, providing the students with the skills necessary to emerge from school confident, powerful, and effective citizens of that community.

Exploring the Multiage Classroom is the best writing to date on the multiage classroom. Grounded in the wisdom of Piaget and Vygotsky and the knowledge of superb classroom practitioners, the commentaries on language, classroom as family, open-ended Explore Times, literacy learning, real mathematics, and the assessment of authentic learning are ground breaking in what they offer.

At its core, *Exploring the Multiage Classroom* is a book about how children learn and what teachers need to know and be able to do to ensure that children learn. It challenges us to alter several fundamental characteristics of education that remain firmly in place for most teachers in America. Anne, Peggy, Justine, and Molly suggest that in order to graduate children from our classrooms who are ready to take on the needs of our workplace and our democracy, we need to effect at least three structural changes in our schools. Time and curriculum must be made flexible so learning is not held hostage to inappropriate schedules of coverage. Classroom talk must shift from being dominated by teachers to being dominated by children so intentional conversation and activity become the medium through which thought and learning occurs. And finally, school organization must move away from a graded structure to a multiage structure to lessen the damaging effects that grade-related status attributions have upon an increasing number of learners. The authors' practices are ample evidence that these changes can be accomplished.

The work of this gifted quartet reminds us once again that children come to school needing continuity of experience and activity and congruent thoughts and feelings in their school lives. The classroom is person-centered. It opens the door to every child's most essential confirmation as learner, it accepts play and fun and eavesdropping as essential elements in learning, it makes school a place where children love to go, and it is a place where research affirms that children become powerful achievers.

Anne Bingham and her colleagues give us hope for our schools. The goals they set for improving education will require strong commitment and a unified effort from parents, policy makers, school administrators, and teachers. At least we have a direction now. For this, our children can be grateful.

Charles Rathbone, Ph. D.
Burlington, Vermont

PREFACE

———————————————— ■ ————————————————

I N 1990 the teachers on my team at the Shelburne Village School decided to
come up with a new name for our grouping of four multiage classrooms.
We chose "Explorers" because we felt that it defined our expectations for children in school and for their productive lives beyond it. "Explore Time" was a
central part of the school day, but our exploring continued throughout the
day through themes, numbers, problems, stories, and writing.

The name "Explore Time" had a history, too. It is a time each day when
children can choose their own activities. In the beginning, we called it "activity time," and then, because the children were allowed to "float" from one
room to another during that time, they came to call it "floating time." The
more we used this term, the more we realized that it conveyed the wrong
message. Floating—drifting about from room to room—was not our purpose or our expectation for the children. We expected focused work and play,
and self-directed active learning. So when I heard the name "Explore Time"
on a visit to the nearby Williston Central School, we adopted it, since it better
defined what we wanted to see the children doing.

Most of the years I was a part of that team, from 1972 until 1993, our
grade-level configuration was either kindergarten through third grade or
first through third grade, and the children's ages five through eight, with
some nine-year-olds. Over the years we explored different ways of organizing
classrooms for this range of ages and found answers that seemed to work for
us and for the larger community.

In 1987 I spent a half-year sabbatical visiting multiage classrooms, mostly
in my own state of Vermont. Each was unique, like each teacher and each community. The small number of books about multiage classrooms also presents

different models. Because there are such varied approaches to this exciting way of teaching, I offer this book as one example. I hope that by seeing what others have done teachers will find ideas, support, and inspiration.

How you read the book depends on what you need right now in your own professional journey. If the development of interdisciplinary themes is your goal this year, turn to Chapter 8. If assessment is your current concern, you may want to dive into Chapter 11. I have tried to address particular concerns teachers have about multiage classrooms.

The classroom stories, the activities described, and the children's projects in this book are based on real happenings, either recorded in notes I have made from time to time or remembered. In the interest of confidentiality, however, I have made the children themselves composites of real children. Stacie, Jason, and the others are doing things real children did, but they represent more than just one boy or girl who has spent time in my classroom over the last twenty years. Some children are shown at different ages in different vignettes, since most of them spent more than one year with me.

Part One, Chapters 1 and 2, provides background: a definition of a multiage classroom; advantages teachers have found in this approach; and research, theory, and beliefs related to learning in multiage environments.

Part Two examines the underlying structures of space and time that must be addressed before school starts and during the school year.

Part Three shows the children exploring in all sorts of ways—through themes, language, and math—and addresses ways of organizing multiage classrooms for such work.

In Part Four other teachers join me to bring other voices and other experience to bear on the subject. In Chapters 9 and 10 Justine O'Keefe introduces math in September to a group of six- and seven-year-olds; Peggy Dorta finds ways to introduce math topics "individually all at once" to her eight- to ten-year-olds; and Molly McClaskey weaves the thread of literacy through an entire day in her K–2 classroom. In those two chapters I add expanded descriptions of math and literacy in my own classroom.

Chapters 11 through 13 present further details from the classrooms of these three teachers. In Chapter 11, Molly and Justine write about their personal experience in the search for more authentic forms of assessment. In Chapter 12, Peggy presents a recipe for "Moving into Multiage," and in Chapter 13 we share the experience of "total immersion" teaming with Justine. Here are real teachers dealing with contemporary issues.

Today the "Explorers" in Shelburne are off on a new adventure. In September 1994 they moved into a brand-new space in a wing built onto the Middle School, now the Shelburne Community School. The old Village School and the classroom described in this book stand empty, but the new space is animated by the vibrant voices of six-, seven-, and eight-year-old children. Their bright pictures and projects are everywhere.

I hope you will enjoy exploring the possibilities of the multiage classroom with me and come to agree that these and classrooms like them are exciting places to learn.

ACKNOWLEDGMENTS

—————————————————— ■ ——————————————————

Many people are responsible for my growth through the years as a teacher and for the opportunity to do what I have wanted to do since I was ten years old: write a book. I feel lucky to have been able to do both.

Some of the greatest joys of teaching come from the challenges the children themselves provide. A teacher learns first of all from the children, from constant day-to-day interaction and from watching as they go about absorbing information and acquiring the tools they will need throughout life. To all the children who have found their way to Room A, I am grateful. Special thanks go to the following children whose drawings or poetry have been used to illustrate the text: Mae Agna, Elizabeth Drumheller, Maxime Grangien, Annie Grover, Emily Liebowitz, Timothy Plante, Daniel Schillhammer, Julienne Stiller, Fischer VanGulden, Nicki Whitney.

The team of teachers with whom I have worked has been extraordinary in their support of one another. Some members of the team have changed through the years, but always it has remained a group of friends I can count on and from whom I learn constantly.

Marilyn Johnson, who was my companion through the entire journey, read the description of our beginnings and assured me that it was accurate. Liz Farman and Jane Perry helped me with the bibliography and perused the materials list for Appendix A. Phyllis Murray never allowed us to get so serious that we could not see the humor in a situation. Conversations with these friends during our years of working together underlie all that is written here.

Marion Stroud, my guide and teacher in the early years of our program, also confirmed that my brief description of our move into multiage was accurate.

Our principal, Gus Mercaldo, contributed the gift of trust, so that developing our own program, methods, and curriculum was possible.

In 1990 Charles Rathbone, from the University of Vermont, joined us in Room A during a spring semester. His keen observation and insight enabled me to see with fresh eyes what was happening around me. He also contributed valuable insight through his review of the manuscript.

Through his grant from the Ford Foundation, Charlie established a small teachers' writing collaborative during the summer of 1990. This group of teachers worked together with him through a summer of writing and talk about teaching and learning in multiage settings. The same teachers became contributors to this volume, and I have valued our many conversations during the process of planning and writing.

Philippa Stratton at Stenhouse has been extremely helpful to a new writer, answering questions patiently and providing needed support.

My own children—Larry, Rick, and Robin—now grown, were some of my best teachers. They were there during the early years of my multiage experience as part of a loving family that both stretched and supported me. My husband, Dick, was the first reader of these pages and made many needed suggestions. He was always encouraging and never complained about the many meals of spaghetti and pizza in the last weeks. I am immensely grateful.

PART ONE

---■---

OUR
DESTINATION

CHAPTER ONE

■

MULTIAGE CLASSROOMS:
WHAT AND WHY

"WANT to see my walking stick?" Alex greets his friend, Wally, at the classroom door. The two boys cross the room and huddle over a screen-topped aquarium, where the insect Alex has brought in emerges from a cluster of twigs it closely resembles. They both watch, wide-eyed.

"Did you hear what happened to Jerry's praying mantis?" asks Mike, who is passing by. It fell out of the jar when he was about to show it to us. But . . . but he didn't see it and he sat on it. Gross!"

"Yeah," adds Alex. "We thought it was dead. But it started to move. Mrs. B. said 'Let it go,' so we took it out at recess and pushed it through the fence. That's so no one else would get it."

"It needed a rest," Mike suggests, snickering.

"Do ya think it's OK?" asks Wally.

"Yeah."

A GROUP of children works around a table heaped with materials, some natural—leaves, twigs, pinecones—and some not so natural—pipe cleaners, beads, and buttons. They are creating fantasy insects. For the insect body: three linked sections of an egg carton. Betsy holds hers up for inspection. She has given it maple leaf wings. "A maple fly, a maple syrup fly."

"Hey, you're supposed to stick the legs all in the middle part." Patty points to the picture. "The thorax."

"Oh well," says Betsy. "It's going to fly away anyhow." She swoops across the room and lands the butterfly on a low table where Beth and Suzie continue listening through earphones to *Frog and Toad* (Lobel 1970) stories.

. . . .

AT THE easel a giant ladybug is emerging on one side, a rainbow with a ragged row of flowers on the other. "Got any yellow?" asks Jill, and Polly, her partner, passes a cup of yellow paint around the corner as she counts the spots on her ladybug.

IN THE block area a bridge is under construction. The children have made massive supports by taping several blocks together. They are measuring a string to represent the cable between the towers. "Hey Chuck, will you hold this end?" Ron asks.

"Wait!" Jerry stops everything. "We need it to hang down in between the parts. It's gotta be longer."

"We need a sign," states Mark, who is not involved in the measuring. "Where does it say 'Golden Gate Bridge' here?" Jason points to the caption under a picture in the book propped up nearby.

ON THE rug Kate and Adam are playing Mancala, an African pebble game, while another child watches. Nearby three children, two boys and a girl, are constructing a marble maze. In one corner Wendy is writing at a computer, and at a desk tucked against the wall Mac is making designs with pattern blocks.

FROM a table in one corner, the teacher announces: "Who still needs to make an insect catcher?" A couple of hands go up. "OK, come on over. We need these for tomorrow. And could somebody find Sarah? She hasn't finished hers." Stacie whispers in her ear and goes off, returning shortly with Sarah in tow. On the table the "insect catchers," yogurt cups with little plastic covered windows and holes in the lids, sit ready for use.

EMMA and Cindy hold hands as Emma reads aloud from the bulletin board labeled "Partner Poems." Vertical strips of paper intermingle with colorful drawings of butterflies and caterpillars, ants and bees, and a large, carefully drawn grasshopper. Books on insects are heaped on the shelf below.

Twiggly	Bee-e-e-es
It walks	Bees
all day long.	Buzz
It feeds	All day
on leaves.	Long
It never jumps.	On flowers
The walking stick	
changes colors	Making
When it hatches	Honey

it is green.
As it gets
older it
turns brown.

For us,

Getting
Pollen
To feed
Their babies

They never
Get paid
And they never
Get to
Play.

What is happening here, in this busy classroom? It is obvious that a theme study is in progress. The children have been reading and writing about insects, and drawing and collecting insects. Because this is also "Explore Time," a free-choice period, not everyone is involved with the theme. Sarah was working on an activity in the multiage room across the hall. Wally was visiting from another room and got involved in observing the caged walking stick.

Wally is six and Alex is seven. They live in the same neighborhood and have lately been stalking insects together as well as building a "fort" in Alex's backyard. Mike, who joins them at the aquarium, is eight. The interaction among children of different ages is as natural here as it is in the neighborhood.

Variations in size give some indication that this class of children contains six-, seven-, and eight-year-olds, but it is not easy to determine the ages of some of them, even after observing them for a while.

This surprised me when I first started visiting other multiage classrooms. Each child is on an individual developmental path, and each "internal time clock" is a little different, so it is possible to have the "mature" first grader and the "young" eight-year-old in the same classroom. Because children grow in spurts and then plateau, these labels may not even fit the same children next year. Mac, over in the corner creating a design with pattern blocks, and Wendy, writing at the computer, could be six, seven, or eight years old. Jason, the tall child helping Mark make a sign for the bridge in the block area, might be a second or a third grader. In actuality, Mac is seven and Wendy eight. Patty, constructing fantasy insects, is a careful and precise seven-year-old. Betsy, with the "maple syrup fly," is six, as are Beth and Suzie with the earphones. Jill and Polly at the easel are also six and seven.

In the block area, a cluster of boys embodies the three-year age span of the class. It was the eight-year-olds who discovered the construction method of taping blocks to make strong bridge supports, and they are supervising the measuring. Seven-year-old Jason helps Mark with the sign.

Although Jason and Mark are both seven, neither meets grade-level expectations when it comes to reading: Jason can read complex chapter books, while Mark is a beginner. Yet both are comfortably accommodated within a class where the the age range means that children work at a variety of levels.

Anna, six, is learning to play Mancala by watching two older friends. At the bulletin board eight-year-old Emma is reading to Cindy, who is also six. We will meet some of these children again.

Grouping children by grade level is an idea introduced into the United States from Prussia in the mid-nineteenth century by Horace Mann. Before that time it was common for children of different ages to learn together. Multiage classrooms are very different from what most of us have experienced in our own schooling. Our preconceived ideas about grade-level expectations and our twentieth-century view of education may make a multiage classroom seem a strange concept. I believe, however, that multiage classrooms are one good way to best provide the kind of education current theory suggests, and to respond to the changing and varied world in which today's children find themselves.

In this book I want to consider both the "whys" and the "hows" of multiage teaching, to take readers inside multiage classrooms and to describe specific programs, the spatial organization of classrooms, and schedules—some of the "nitty-gritty" of working in this kind of setting. We will move from the underlying philosophical ideas (why multiage?) to the hows of space, time, and curriculum, and finally to some reflections on planning for change. I also want to try to convey some of the joys of living and learning in such a community. I have taught a primary, multiage class for over twenty years and have asked other teachers with multiage experience to help me present material I hope will interest those involved in multiage classes or contemplating a change to such classes. If teaching in a multiage classroom seems like a journey into a foreign land, I hope this book will serve as a guide for those who would venture there.

WHAT IS A MULTIAGE CLASSROOM?

A multiage classroom is one in which the developmental range is wider than that in a single-grade classroom: it might include first and second graders, or third through fifth graders, for example. (Other terms—ungraded or non-graded, family, vertical, or mixed-age grouping—are sometimes used.) But not every classroom that combines grade levels will be a multiage classroom by our definition. In a multiage classroom, children's developmental diversity is

- celebrated
- valued as part of a natural community of learners
- harnessed in subtle ways to support learning

Uniform grade-level norms tend to exclude those children who don't fit in, intensifying the experience of success or failure. In a multiage classroom, in contrast, the varied experience, development, and learning style of each child is *celebrated*. For the teacher, the students, and the parents, the family nature of this kind of grouping provides positive support and challenge, and interactions within that mix become a source of power and joy.

A multiage class is a *natural community of learners,* which incorporates some of the learning that happens daily outside of school, in families and neighborhoods. What children learn in the larger world, from language to games, may be both positive and negative, but it is effective learning. And such learning is a dynamic process we can incorporate into life at school. Single-grade classrooms, by comparison, are small, segregated societies. The diversity of multiage groups diffuses the exclusivity that can be engendered by such uniformity.

Developmental diversity is *harnessed* in both overt and subtle ways. One child may help a younger classmate read directions, solve a problem, tie shoes, or run an errand within the school. Or the teacher may ask two children to work together on a collaborative activity, knowing that one is ready to incorporate the understandings modeled by the other. In addition, a child may be allowed to sit quietly, observing another. When children watch and listen to each other, they can learn everything from classroom routines, to how to trade ones for tens in math, how to play computer games, or how to use quotation marks. Perhaps a child will ask another simply to play a game. In these instances the teacher functions more as a guide or an observer, sometimes choosing not to intervene in a natural process and sometimes encouraging positive interactions.

A multiage class is characterized by children's constant interaction with each other, with the materials in the classroom, and with the available adults. Children talk with one another and take advantage of the abundance of concrete materials—teddy bear counters, blocks, Cuisenaire rods, pattern blocks. In their variety, these materials reflect the different needs of different developmental stages. Children can use them informally and in learning guided by adults. Many kinds of learning take place and in many modes, from constructing with blocks to writing a story or completing a page of addition practice. All are valued.

Then, too, this is not a classroom where a "second-grade" curriculum and a "first-grade curriculum" go on simultaneously. All children may work on the same topic but in different ways or at their own individual speed. Learning to read, for example, progresses on an identifiable continuum. Children are measured against themselves in determining their growth toward a goal along that continuum.

Some who have written on the topic of multiage classrooms insist on the label "nongraded" or "ungraded," because they have observed classrooms in which grade-level references are still used. In moving toward a multiage classroom, it is sometimes difficult to eliminate grade-level labels completely, but it is a desirable goal, particularly in avoiding the stigma of failure when a child needs an extra year before moving ahead. Whenever possible, therefore, I will describe children not by grade, but by age or by interests and achievement.

WHAT A MULTIAGE CLASS IS NOT

Some class configurations are called "multiage," but they do not fit our definition. A multiage classroom is not two grades put together for convenience, perhaps to accommodate a population bulge, and probably for only a year or two. Neither is it a "combined" class in which separate curricula continue, an unreasonable task for teachers and one that undermines the class as a community. It is a permanent class grouping of planned diversity.

WHY MULTIAGE?

I have asked other multiage teachers to tell me what they like and what they value most about teaching a group of children within a wider-than-usual developmental range. Most often they mention the following:

1. Multiage classrooms provide continuity for young children and their teachers, since they remain together for more than one year.

2. The teacher can observe children over a broad developmental range and see each child within that context.

3. The teacher can respond to the uniqueness of the individual learner at that student's own developmental level. It is easier to look at each child as an individual in this setting than in one that imposes grade-level expectations.

4. Class members become a "family" because they spend a longer time together. Since the class is made up of a natural mix of ages, with the teacher's help it can take on some of the aspects of a family, supporting one another's growth and development, which in turn supports the teacher's goal of building a sense of community.

5. A third to a half of the children return each fall, resulting in a smoother start to the year. Many children are already familiar with classroom

routines, the teacher and children already have a relationship, and the teacher knows their strengths, academic and otherwise.

6. Modeling by older students acquaints new members of the class with everything from classroom routines to acceptable behavior to the use of skills already learned, such as reading. Younger children see older peers reading and writing in functional ways.

7. Peer tutoring occurs often and naturally, just as it might outside of school. Children help each other, and the teacher can also structure such tutoring easily.

8. The teacher has more flexibility in setting up groupings for teaching, since they are rarely defined by grade level. The teacher can form both heterogeneous and homogeneous groups depending on purpose and need.

9. Children with special needs stand out less when everyone works at a different level and with a variety of materials.

10. Children have many opportunities for collaborative and cooperative efforts.

BUT WHAT ABOUT RESEARCH?

What about research? A valid question! Reports summarizing a number of research studies on multiage classrooms are available. The following are especially relevant: Margaret Gayfer (1991), *The Multi-Grade Classroom: Myth and Reality, A Canadian Study;* Bruce Miller (1990), "A Review of the Quantitative Research on Multigrade Instruction," in *Research in Rural Education* (reissued in *Multiage Classrooms: The Ungrading of America's Schools,* published by The Society for Developmental Education in 1993); and a review of sixty-four studies by Robert Anderson and Barbara Nelson Pavan (1993) in *Nongradedness: Helping It to Happen.*

The Canadian study includes a review of research literature and also questionnaires to teachers and administrators across Canada. Its summary of research states: "Do children get as good an education in a multi-grade classroom as they do in a single-grade one? The answer is 'yes.' The data bear out the findings of research about the many positive aspects of teaching and learning in a multi-grade class." In fact, it is more than "as good" in the realm of psychosocial development, where "researchers generally agree that students in multi-grade classes tended to be higher or better than those in single-grade classes in the following affective areas: study habits, social interaction, self-motivation, co-operation, and attitudes toward school." Studies of academic achievement showed that children from multigrade classes perform just as well or better on achievement tests than those from a single-grade setting.

Likewise, Miller reports that "the data clearly support the multigrade classroom as a viable and equally effective organizational alternative to single-grade instruction" and that "when it comes to student affect, the case for multigrade organization appears much stronger, with multigrade students out-performing single-grade students in over 75 percent of the measures used. One wonders, then, why we do not have more schools organized into multigrade classrooms."

Finally the extensive reports in Anderson and Pavan's book on nongradedness should be considered. In most cases nongradedness can be seen as congruent with multiage teaching. Original proponents of nongradedness eliminated grade-level labels but continued to educate children of the same age together. More recently, according to these authors, it has become apparent that multiage groupings best support the success of nongradedness. Their summary of research is therefore relevant: Standardized tests were used to compare academic achievement in fifty-seven of the sixty-four studies reviewed. Of these studies, 58 percent favored nongraded settings, 33 percent found nongraded settings to be as successful as graded classrooms, and only 9 percent favored graded classrooms. Forty-two of the sixty-four studies also contained a mental health component. These also strongly supported nongraded settings, with 52 percent showing nongraded settings as better, 43 percent as similar, and only 5 percent of the studies in favor of graded classes.

Anderson and Pavan also included seventeen longitudinal studies, of which 69 percent favored nongraded settings, suggesting that the advantages of such educational settings increase with the time spent in them.

A further quote from Anderson and Pavan bears contemplation: "The nongraded concept was developed to deal with the fact that individuals are different and different treatments are needed to maximize each individual potential. Schools that operate under this tenet probably would not be concentrating on high student performance on standardized tests. The finding that pupils in nongraded schools did as well as, or better than, pupils in graded schools is therefore rather remarkable. Overwhelmingly, nongraded groups perform as well as and possibly better than graded groups on achievement tests designed for the graded schools!"

Research on tracking, peer tutoring, and cooperative learning also supports multiage grouping. Multiage classes emphasize heterogeneity, as opposed to ability-level grouping or tracking, a practice that has been shown to perpetuate academic and social inequalities. They also lend themselves naturally to both cooperative groups and peer tutoring.

Anderson and Pavan surveyed studies of cross-age tutoring and found that not only do both tutee and tutor improve academically but the embarrassment of receiving help is less of a problem in multiage classrooms, where different ages regularly work together.

Cooperative learning is not a new idea. In 1913, John Dewey described children working together developing a "spirit of social cooperation and community." Current thinking about cooperative learning is summarized in *Multiage Classrooms: The Ungrading of America's Schools* (1993): "After nearly two decades of research and dozens of studies . . . America's leading researchers agree that cooperative methods can—and usually do—have a positive effect on student achievement." Opportunities to apply strategies of heterogeneous cooperative groups to practical problem solving abound in multiage classrooms.

There is another kind of research into multiage classrooms: qualitative and descriptive. In 1990 Charles Rathbone at the University of Vermont searched for answers to the question, What are teaching and learning like in multiage classrooms? Rathbone spent a semester as a participant-observer in my multiage class and a summer working with four teacher writers as they reflected on their multiage experience. His report, written for the Ford Foundation, has been transformed for teachers into the book *Multiage Portraits: Teaching and Learning in Mixed-age Classrooms* (Rathbone et al. 1993). In addition to describing one multiage model, Rathbone was able to suggest commonalties among multiage classrooms. Included in his list of eleven characteristics are the following: the teacher "has a perspective centered in child responsive learning"; "is both teacher and learner"; "plans for spontaneous moments"; and "uses open-ended activity times intentionally."

Teachers know more about multiage teaching than they think they do, because they have already experienced developmental diversity among their students. Every single classroom is multilevel. Every day, teachers meet with students whose language ability, interests, learning styles, and talents vary widely. All teachers have this in common. Moving into a multiage setting simply stretches them to accommodate a wider range of diversity.

There is more, however, to teaching in a multiage classroom. Teaching in such a setting embraces a specific view of children's learning and employs teaching practices incorporating that philosophy. The philosophy and practice emerge from what we believe intuitively and what we have learned about children, their learning, and their development.

CHAPTER TWO

■

BELIEFS THAT GUIDE
MULTIAGE TEACHING

I LOOKED at the heap of furniture and other materials piled in the middle of the new room. Tables and blocks from my kindergarten classroom mingled with cubbies and a book rack built by parents who were helping us set up our multiage classroom. A new rug was rolled up on one side of the room. On the counter, boxes of games and math manipulatives, some new, some old, stood in tipsy piles. Together, a group of parents and teachers were about to create something new, a classroom in which five-, six-, seven-, and eight-year-olds would learn together. It was August 1972, and although I was excited about the new classroom, I was only partly aware of how my beliefs about children and learning would serve as a source of energy in tackling the new and demanding job.

When the opportunity to join this new multiage team was offered to me in January, I talked it over with my family. It was not the best time for me to launch out into such a venture, one that I knew would be time-consuming. My own children were twelve, sixteen, and eighteen, and I often spent afternoons and evenings at basketball games, track meets, and other school events (their school, not mine). I had been teaching in Shelburne only a year, and we had lived in Vermont less than three years. Yet my husband knew, and I knew, that I had been offered a very special opportunity. He and the children supported me in my decision to say, "Yes, I'll do it."

Philosophically, the new program meant an opportunity to try out a teaching style to which I was strongly committed. We were attempting to provide a learning environment that was responsive to each individual, one that allowed children to make choices as part of their learning, and one in which they could interact with and observe children of different ages at work. We wanted to provide a classroom environment rich in opportunities to learn through doing, creating, experimenting, and exploring.

I had been introduced to the ideas of Jean Piaget not long before, and many of these ideas about how children develop the concepts of number and conservation fit what I'd observed in my own children. Hands-on learning made great sense to me.

There were grants available for innovative school programs at that time, and our school district, along with that of a neighboring town, had received a three-year grant from the New England Program in Teacher Education (no longer in existence). This provided a director, staff training, and some money for materials, which we spent largely on manipulatives.

Our model was the integrated day in some of the British infant schools of that time, made prominent by the writings of Joseph Featherstone (1971) and others. Our director, Marion Stroud, was from England and had experience in those schools. She was also founder of Prospect School in Bennington, Vermont, which was based on that same model.

It was the era of the "open classroom." Many parents were founding small private schools in an attempt to follow this same British model, but ours was intended to provide an alternative within a public school. Parents would have the option of choosing a multiage classroom for their children if they so desired.

A year of planning preceded any change within the school and involved teachers, school board members, administrators, and community members. During the spring of that year, those of us committed to teaching in the new classrooms made visits to schools with similar programs already in place, which included a four-day workshop at Prospect School. We always met with Marion Stroud after these visits to discuss what we had seen. What, in the classroom day we had observed, did we want to incorporate into our new program? We spent much of that summer in staff training, and several parents were actively involved in the school visits and training sessions with us. In subsequent years, I've come to appreciate how important that parental involvement was. It continues to be an important source of support.

Along with the excitement, there was the challenge! Once school was under way we discovered that teaching the children to make responsible choices was demanding because they were accustomed to a different school routine. Our mornings were given over to allowing children to choose their activities—projects, games, dramatic play, and art—from materials available in the room. They had to learn to complete and clean up their projects and to collaborate effectively. These activities were always followed by a class discussion to help them focus on the learning involved. The afternoons were more traditionally academic, but, here, too, children frequently chose which activities to undertake first.

Teachers moving into multiage classrooms today structure time a little differently. The day is less "wide-open," and whole language and interdisciplinary themes provide a more obvious underlying structure. Concrete experience with manipulative materials, however, an approach recognized as a necessity in learning math concepts, is similar to what we encouraged then. The philosophy underlying our classroom practice was not so different from that underlying today's multiage classes

What led me to become involved in the original multiage program were my own beliefs about how children learn and what constitutes a humane environment for learning, one that is responsive to the developmental needs of young children. Teachers who have had the opportunity to teach in a multiage classroom often share similar convictions. These underlying beliefs drive the work that must be done to teach in this way. It is probably easier for me to state them succinctly now. Some were pretty amorphous in those early years and some have emerged from the experience itself. Like many of my colleagues, I am more dedicated than ever to these convictions after having tried to act on them for so many years.

They are, for the most part, beliefs that are now shared by teachers in holistic, child-centered classrooms. The goals in multiage teaching and child-centered teaching are closely interwoven. For me, they are best achieved within the diversity provided by teaching two or three grade levels together. I can no longer imagine working contentedly with a single-age class.

While research about child learning and development supports the beliefs I list here, the beliefs also represent a philosophy and a value system: they are held not only in the head but in the heart. Many teachers in multiage classrooms are convinced that this kind of learning is best for children. What are these beliefs? They include:

A belief in child-centered learning. An understanding of child development is basic to creating a productive learning environment. The emphasis thus is on providing conditions that will foster natural learning rather than simply imparting knowledge. Essential to this process is the understanding of each individual child within this developmental context. In a child-centered classroom, attention is focused less on decisions made by children than on decisions made with and for children.

A belief that active, concrete learning experiences are essential for young children. Research supports the need for active learning in early childhood using many kinds of concrete materials. This is the bedrock upon which decisions about learning experiences are based, and it is a major factor in planning learning materials, classroom layout, schedules, and thematic activities.

A belief in the whole child. Children bring to school everything they are. The ability and the motivation to learn depend on what is happening in other areas of their lives. Children have difficulty focusing if they are concerned about unresolved issues at home or on the playground. Physical health and well-being have a profound effect on learning, as does a child's social network or lack of one. Recognizing the needs of the whole child in the learning milieu requires an awareness of these issues.

A belief in the importance of community. Providing a supportive, caring classroom community is an important school function both for children's learning and for their social development. Such a community recognizes the needs of the whole child and provides a supportive network for each individual. It recognizes, too, the need to educate children not only in the three "R's" but also in the skills of living together, respecting others, and solving problems that arise.

A belief that many kinds of learning are essential. Schools need to meet the needs of learners with varied strengths and weaknesses. This belief is supported by the theory of multiple intelligences (Gardner 1983, 1993) with its implications for classroom practice, as well as by the recognition that children have different learning styles. It accommodates children with special needs and it recognizes that the academic model alone is insufficient in a society that requires a variety of skills.

A belief that human interaction, including conversation, supports rather than detracts from learning. A multiage classroom can appear noisy to an unprepared observer. Because multiage teachers believe that children learn from and with each other, as well as from adults, there are few absolutely quiet moments. They understand that children learn together and that this learning must be processed verbally for understanding and mastery. Teacher guidance may be needed to ensure that children's conversation is supporting their learning and not distracting them from it.

A belief that continuity in the school setting is of value to young children. In multiage classrooms the teacher and the children have a relationship that continues over more than one year. This means that teachers also have long-term relationships with families, and that children experience immersion in a stable "family" group over time in school. For some children, this may be a partial antidote to the discontinuities in family life that accompany separation and divorce.

A multiage classroom also encourages continuities in curriculum. As children work together over time, they can see and discuss connections between last year's projects and this year's topics. Making connections of this sort allows them to build a broad base for a deeper, more complex understanding of the world.

A belief that the traditional role of schools in society remains important. This includes providing for the development of literacy in language and mathematics and nurturing children's acquisition of a growing body of information about the world. The traditional role of schools hasn't changed, although the schools have taken on added responsibilities. What has changed is what we know about how to achieve those traditional learning goals.

A belief that children's progress should be assessed by looking at their own growth rather than by comparing them with others in their age group. The purposes of assessment are to aid teachers in planning instruction and to report their child's progress to parents. Children's own reading, writing, projects, and presentations provide ample material for assessment. Collections of a child's work and descriptions of other projects and activities can be used in parent-teacher meetings, and will give parents far more information about their child than letter grades. Parents will probably want to know in general terms how their child's progress compares, but it is a lack of individual progress, not where a child stands in relation to others, that should be of greatest concern.

A belief that the learner can be trusted. Not every aspect of a child's learning needs to be directed, supervised, and observed by the teacher. Young learners will progress if they are given a rich environment structured for learning and reasonable guidance. This means that children can be given choices and allowed to make decisions about their own learning, a process that supports growth in self-confidence.

A belief that the teacher is also a learner. Just as when children learn from one another they are all "teachers," adults are learners. The teacher needs to constantly reflect on what is happening in the classroom in order to enhance skills and understand each child's need.

A belief that a wider-than-usual range of ages best supports these convictions. Developmental diversity supports developmental learning. A mix of ages provides a natural movement away from "grade-level" thinking, which raises only limited expectations for children and assures failure for those whose pace and style of learning are different.

HOW THEORY INFORMS BELIEF

I can still remember reading about the Swiss psychologist Jean Piaget's experiments with the conservation of liquid: children before a certain age were convinced that there was more liquid in a tall, thin glass than a short, squat one, simply because the liquid came up higher on the tall glass. It was one of those "aha" experiences for me as I recalled trying to convince my own children that they each had the same amount of juice when glasses of different diameter were used. I read material on Piaget voraciously, and what I read informed my beliefs about how children learn.

Some of those ideas have become an integral part of my thinking, supported and modified through the years by my experience with children and by further reading and study. When working with children, I tend to apply automatically my understanding of a developmental sequence that at least partly comes from Piaget. While it is important not to be rigid about ages and stages, it helps to have that sequence in mind. If I recognize that primary-age children may have difficulty with an abstract concept, it encourages me to provide concrete and representational experiences to support their understanding. I may even need to modify my goals and develop more appropriate expectations.

I recently visited a classroom of five- and six-year-olds who were studying mountains. Although it is valuable to talk about the geological history of mountains, the unbelievable ancient forces that produced them, and the soil and rocks of which mountains are made, it is even more important that children paint mountains, read stories about mountains, and perhaps even climb a mountain. These activities make new concepts real by enabling children to connect them with their own experience. This illustrates another important Piagetian idea.

Piaget used the terms "assimilation" and "accommodation" to explore the process of how we integrate new information into what we already know and then modify our previously held ideas on the basis of new experience. We don't simply replace one idea with another. We see if we can make them jibe to decide whether or not they can fit together. If not, then we change our thinking to accommodate them, which increases our knowledge base. Piaget emphasizes the important role of discontinuity in the growth of knowledge. Recent research on how the brain works also suggests the importance of connecting new information with what we already know. (We will return to this in Chapter 7, "Classroom Talk.") Above all, Piaget's theories about how young children think led me to fill my classroom with materials children could touch, handle, use for construction, and combine in a variety of creative endeavors.

Much more has been added to my thinking since Piaget first began to influence my work with children and my beliefs about learning. I have struggled to understand the thought of Lev Vygotsky, a contemporary of Piaget's writing in Russia in the 1930s. Vygotsky emphasized the social nature of learning. Two of his ideas seem particularly relevant. Vygotsky observed young children talking to themselves as they played and found that they used this monologue to plan and to reflect on their activity. This, he suggested, becomes internal speech, or cognition. Thought arises from an internalization of dialogue—"speech for oneself originates through differentiation from speech for others"—which emphasizes the role of language in thought and suggests the importance of talk in learning.

More familiar is Vygotsky's theory of the "zone of proximal development," an idea that arose from his observation that children were able to accomplish tasks with the support of others that they could not do on their own. He defined this "zone" as the distance between a child's "actual developmental level as determined by independent problem solving" and the higher level of "potential development as determined through problem solving under adult guidance or in collaboration with more capable peers." This is the edge of understanding where new learning occurs. Where better than in a multiage classroom is this "collaboration with more capable peers" possible? Children are constantly observing and working with someone only slightly ahead in development, well within that zone of proximal development. Exposure to the thinking of older peers also provides children with opportunities to make the accommodations in their thinking that Piaget writes about.

Recognizing and accommodating "individual differences" had been a stated goal, I think, in every school in which I have taught, but somehow it was often "just" words. Nothing substantive was being done to understand the differences in the way children learned. In 1987, while I was on sabbatical visiting multiage classrooms, Charles Rathbone handed me a copy of Howard Gardner's *Frames of Mind* (1983), in which he introduces the theory of "multiple intelligences." To me, it is one of the most helpful attempts to define an important aspect of individual/intellectual difference, and I use it both in setting up classroom space and materials and in trying to make a range of activities available. (This is discussed in more detail in Chapter 5.)

Although intuitively I felt that young children need to talk rather than remain silent in school, during much of my teaching I lacked an adequate theoretical base for this conviction, as well as guidance in how to support various types of productive conversation. Recently, I found what I was looking for in *When Students Have Time to Talk* (1991) by Curt Dudley-Marling and Dennis Searle. These Canadian educators clarify the oral language development of children in primary classrooms and the relationship between language and learning. Talk, they write, is important in making what we learn our own. It is through talk that we integrate new experience with what we already know, Piaget's process of "assimilation and accommodation." "When they have time to talk students learn to use language as a tool for thought, for working with others to clarify and communicate ideas, for becoming independent problem solvers . . . we can offer dialogue as a model of effective thinking and invite them into the process so they can assimilate effective thinking strategies" (Vygotsky's concept of thought as inner dialogue).

While theory informs our beliefs, developments in the practice of education suggest ways to build on what we know about child development. In recent years there has been much practical growth in curriculum that supports child-centered classrooms. All that is written about whole language and thematic education provides us with structures on which to base an active, child-centered program. Science and math workshops, such as *Mathematics Their Way* (1976) by Mary Baratta-Lorton, have helped teachers move toward more hands-on learning. More tools are available today for acting on our beliefs.

The National Association for the Education of Young Children (1988) has developed a position statement, "Developmentally Appropriate Practice in the Primary Grades," pulling together beliefs, developmental theory, and classroom teaching and learning practices. A further NAEYC statement (1991) focuses on curriculum and assessment.

We all need to take time to examine the beliefs we hold about children and education. Whether we recognize it or not, they influence the way we set up our classrooms and all the decisions we make about curriculum, methods, and learning materials. Our beliefs enter the classroom with us every morning.

PART TWO

---■---

PREPARATION

CHAPTER THREE

■

STRUCTURING SPACE:
JASON'S ROOM

J A S O N is still thinking about the boy in the book *Dragonling* and about dragon valley as he leaves the rug and gets out his reading and writing folder. It was a good story that Mrs. B. had been reading. He opens his folder and sees the castle book he's been working on. Oh yeah, he wants to start on the drawbridge today. He chooses a desk that stands alone against the wall. Usually he likes to sit at a table with other kids, but today, he plans to work by himself; he has a lot to figure out.

He puts the folder on the desk to claim his place and moves quickly around the room gathering what he needs: a pencil and crayons, some tape and scissors. Looking over these supplies as he places them on the desk, Jason has another thought. He takes the scissors and returns with two short lengths of string.

Jason has been working on his castle book for two weeks. We met him in Chapter 1 as a seven-year-old, a strong reader helping his friend Mark construct a sign. Here, we observe him a year earlier, at six.

His book is made up of intricate castle pictures, the walls drawn one stone at a time. He is now involved in the time-consuming process of giving each picture a three-dimensional quality, his own idea. Today he wants to create a drawbridge that will open and close.

Despite my requirement that each page have words as well as pictures, there is barely a sentence on each. A year later, however, he will produce a remarkable book on Jackie Robinson that had far more sentences than pictures.

Watching Jason move around the room, select a place to work, and gather his materials, it may not be immediately apparent that the arrangement of classroom space has made these tasks easier for him. A variety of work environments are available: on the floor or at a table, alone or with a partner. Things that are used together are stored together, and low, open shelves make them readily accessible.

When I was preparing to teach in a multiage classroom for the first time, I attended workshops, made classroom visits, and had conversations with more experienced teachers. One thing I found most helpful was sharing ideas about setting up the physical space of the classroom. Although I am not sure whether this occurred at a workshop at the Prospect School in Bennington, Vermont, or with our program director, Marion Stroud, I can remember sitting with a large sheet of newsprint in front of me sketching in fixed classroom features and then roughly dividing the paper into quarters. This was intended to help me think through the variety of activities I could expect to take place in the room. In which section of the room would I want to structure space for messy activities . . . noisy ones . . . a quiet corner? Every August since, I begin my preparation for setting up the classroom in this way.

Children learn best when space and materials lend themselves to projects that are developmentally appropriate and interesting, when the environment is responsive to their needs. Our beliefs about children and learning guide our decisions about classroom space. We need to support children in planning and organizing their own projects in order to support many kinds of learning.

Multiage classrooms are informal, in both their arrangement and the style of teaching that takes place within them. This informality is a direct result of beliefs about the importance of developmental theory, active learning, conversation, and community. Because informality is not chaos, however, considerable attention must be given to the underlying structures, such as the space through which children move and work. In multiage classrooms, there is often a need to provide a wider variety of materials than in other child-centered classrooms. The writing area, for example, should have room for several different kinds of paper, some with picture space and some without. The arrangement of furniture needs to be flexible so children can collaborate in a variety of ways—now in a homogeneous group, later in a group comprised of older and younger children working together. Books, games, and math manipulatives need to be visible and readily available to the children.

Along with our beliefs about child development and how children learn, there are many practical matters to consider in planning classroom layout.

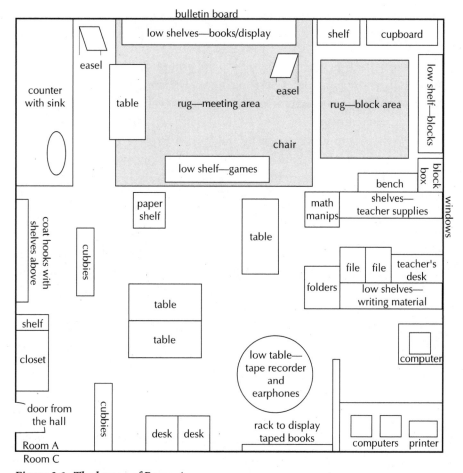

Figure 3.1 The layout of Room A.

Before the children arrive in the fall is the ideal time to consider traffic flow, work space, and storage of materials. Although you may decide to make changes in the room arrangement during the year, many decisions are best made in advance so that the year gets off to a smooth start. Appendix C includes floor plans from multiage classrooms in different school settings that will suggest additional possibilities for new and older buildings.

In 1994 my former multiage teammates moved into a new space, but I will be describing the one I know best, Room A, a traditional room with four walls.

I have not always used the same floor arrangement, but there have been certain constants. First there are the "givens," the fixed structures, that even an empty room presents.

THE FIXED STRUCTURES

Traffic In and Out

A basic question is where the door is and where children will store their coats, lunch boxes, and other personal items. Is there a coatroom? This information enables us to predict what the traffic flow will be when children enter the room each morning.

My school's multiage program includes an Explore Time during which children may move about and choose materials in any one of four rooms. In setting out their floor plan, the teachers in these rooms must also consider how to accommodate this traffic flow in and out.

Water

If there is water in the room, where is it located? Many art activities and messy projects are best planned for this quadrant of the room. Can you find storage space for paint nearby? Place painting easels nearby?

If you plan to do some cooking and have equipment, these items should also be stored near the sink. One year my team received a small grant with which we bought toaster ovens, hot plates, and pans. Hopefully, this area has been left uncarpeted for easier cleanup.

Built-in Storage

In my room, there is a counter near the sink with built-in storage beneath it. Any built-in shelves, closets, or storage areas should be considered at this time: what can best be stored there? Generally, I keep materials the children will have regular access to on open shelves. For materials behind closed doors, which I monitor more closely, they check with me first.

Adjoining Rooms

Which walls adjoin other classrooms? The block area in my room is one of the noisier spots, so I avoid placing it next to a wall adjoining another classroom. When a large tower falls, at least the sound is somewhat muted. Cleanup in this area can also be noisy. Since the room is uncarpeted, a small rug helps muffle the sound.

If your classroom is not totally self-contained, but is open to other rooms, you may need to consider special planning for shared space or equipment. A block area is a workable shared space.

Electric Outlets

Where are the electric outlets? Computers and listening areas with tape recorders need easy access to outlets. A new computer network in my school requires that computers be placed on a specific wall near the connecting box. For this reason the computer area, like the block and paint storage area, is one of the spaces I define early in my planning.

Bulletin Boards and Chalkboards

Where are bulletin boards and chalkboards or, in a more modern classroom, whiteboards? A large, old-fashioned blackboard stretches across the south wall of my room. In the early days of the school, that blackboard marked the front of the room, and the rows of desks faced it. But I use the blackboard infrequently, so I pay little attention to it in planning the room layout.

The bulletin board is more important. It takes up most of the wall at the north end of the room. I try to let displays of student work dominate the walls, so this is a key space. The bulletin board most often holds student-developed displays relating to the theme we are currently studying. I arrange shelves below it to provide a place for other thematic material and for books related to the theme. A large rug for group meetings is located nearby, since it is usually most convenient to be able to have the class meet in this area. A calendar, schedule, announcements, and a few rules are posted at one end of the bulletin board, information we may need when we meet together.

An easel added to this area functions like a small chalkboard to record brainstorming, discussion, and planning for the group; to show examples of work to be done; and to list instructions for a project or assignment. The bulletin board/rug area is thus the nerve center of the room. The children agree. When Charles Rathbone was observing in Room A, he asked the children, "Is there a place in the room where you could take a picture that would stand for multiage?" This is the area they chose.

Floor Plan

Some of the fixed structures have begun to dictate what the floor plan will be. In my case, the group meeting area has been determined by the location of the large bulletin board. At this point I make a rough sketch of the room, dividing it into four quadrants with light pencil marks (this may help in separating noisy and quiet or messy and neat activities). On this sketch I place all the fixed items I have listed: doors, coatroom, water, counters, built-in shelves and cupboards, closets, chalkboards, bulletin boards, electric outlets, carpeting if it covers only part of the room, or rugs if I know where they will go. I also indicate walls that adjoin other classrooms and halls and sketch in areas I have already determined, such as a computer area, a listening corner, and a space for painting.

Windows

I also indicate where the windows are. In Vermont, we are heavily dependent on artificial light during most of the school year, but if you have good natural light you may want to think about locating some of the children's desks and tables to take advantage of it.

My classroom faces east. On especially clear winter mornings the sun pours in during the early hours—always into someone's eyes as we sit together in our circle. We reluctantly pull the shades, only to raise them again as soon as possible. Sun is welcome to us here in the north, but this always makes me think of my fourth-grade teacher. When we asked her if we might pull the shades to get the hot sun off our backs and the glare off our papers, she would declare, "A little bit of Colorado sun won't hurt you!" In the west and the south, sun pouring in the windows can get hot in the afternoon. It may be better to locate desks and tables a bit away from the windows. Consider what it will be like to read and work in those spaces. The light is like all the fixed structures in the room.

ARRANGING THE FURNITURE

Now I begin to think of what needs to be added to that original space: desks and tables, movable shelves for storage, and learning centers.

I have some personal preferences. First, I like to break up the space in the room, reducing the temptation for exuberant children to run from one end to the other and creating some well-defined spaces for special activities. Some storage shelves become room dividers. In the Room A floor plan (see Figure 3.1) they partially "wall off" the computer area, separating it from the listening area with its tape recorders on one side and from my desk on the other side.

These dividers are low enough to control traffic while leaving the entire room visible to me. I usually place higher shelves along the outside walls, because I like to be able to stand in one spot and see most of what is happening. I want the children to be able to make choices on their own, but I also want to be aware of their activities.

Parent volunteers have made long, low shelves for the school's multiage classrooms. Some of them—the book shelves under the bulletin board, for example—are placed along a wall where built-in shelves might be found in other classrooms. Others are placed at angles to the wall or left freestanding, like the bookcase between the rug and work tables.

Work Spaces
The next important decision is how and where to position the desks or tables that constitute the student work space. This can only be decided after a number of other factors have been taken into account.

Figure 3.2 The work space in Room A.

Because so much work in a multiage classroom is collaborative, and because conversation is a useful part of this process, children need to be seated where they can work together, often facing each other or sitting side by side. If you have only student desks, you might try placing them in clusters of four, with perhaps a few desks in pairs. My students work mostly at tables because that's what the classroom is equipped with. But a few desks can also be useful. Placed either in pairs or singly, they create quiet corners on the edge of the room. Some children will occasionally choose to work at a desk alone, as Jason did in working on his castle book. Some may need to be asked to work by themselves from time to time.

In Room A children usually choose where they will work each day. Although I have occasionally found it necessary to assign seats, flexibility is important because the same children will not always need to work together.

It is best to spread out these work spaces rather than clumping them together in one part of the room. This helps to balance the need for conversation and quiet. Also, when children who need to talk together are spread out, instead of concentrated in one part of the room, there is less need to raise voices to higher and higher levels in order to be heard.

In my classroom children may also choose to work on the rug, using a lapboard. A friend across the hall has mini-desks or floor desks for children to use. The round table in the Room A listening area is low so that children can sit on the floor when working at this table. I made it from plywood, left over when we built our house, and screw-on coffee table legs. It is actually made of two half circles, which can be separated into two tables when necessary.

If children don't have individual desks, where do they store papers and library books? Where is their personal storage space? Individual "cubbies" are the solution and those in Room A were made by parent volunteers years ago. They also serve as room dividers, one creating a coatroom. Some schools have individual lockers.

Centers or Special Areas

If you plan to have formal learning centers in your classroom, now is the time to locate those that haven't yet found a place. In my planning, a listening area, a block/construction area, a computer area, and an area for painting are already in place.

Do you plan to have a classroom library or a quiet reading corner? I had a cosy reading corner for many years, with a floor mattress and pillows. Then, over the years, the books just seemed to spread out all over the room. Needs change and space stays the same. I liked having books in a number of different places, so one year when I needed more space for computers I got rid of the mattress and pillows. Some classrooms have a special reading loft where children can curl up with a book.

A large collection of paperback books is usually stored on the low shelves under the bulletin board. Many other books, including armfuls borrowed from our school library and books relating to a current theme, are kept in colorful plastic baskets nearby. Science and reference books have their own special space, as do biographies and poetry.

I create a tiny "office" for myself along one wall using a desk, shelves, and some file cabinets. Although I rarely use it during the school day, it is my space for collecting what I need for present and future activities. Some teachers have found it possible to dispense with this space, but I always seem to find it useful.

Some classrooms also contain items that reflect the teacher's special talents or interests—a piano, a costume corner, a puppet theater, a workbench with tools, a sandbox. Although one classroom may not include all of these at the same time, some can be temporary additions during the year. When teachers work together in a team, the various classrooms can feature special areas that all the children share, like the block area in Room A.

STORAGE OF MATERIALS

When children are allowed to choose from many hands-on and creative activities, there is usually lots of "stuff" involved. Appendix A lists materials I have gathered together for a multiage primary-grade classroom. Fitting it all into the classroom space can be a challenge.

As I have already mentioned, books are everywhere in Room A—on shelves, in thematic displays, and in brightly colored plastic baskets. In the listening area, each book and its related audiotape is stored in a Ziplock plastic bag.

In my room I have no formal science, math, or writing centers, but I try, whenever possible, to store related materials together. They may be used near the storage area or taken to desks or tables in other parts of the room.

Small plastic baskets or boxes can hold the most frequently used tools, such as pencils, erasers, scissors, thick and thin markers, and crayons. It is also useful to place these supplies in two separate locations so that children needn't crowd together in one place if, for example, we all start to write at once. The containers are color coded: all the red ones are kept on one side of the room, the blue ones on the other. This enables the children to maintain both storage areas at cleanup time. Less frequently demanded tools, such as string, a paper punch, masking tape, clear tape, rulers, and glue, are stored in a single location.

Paper is kept in two locations as well, construction and drawing paper in one area, writing paper near the box where student writing is stored. A date stamp and material for book covers are close at hand.

Near my desk, in plastic dishpans, individual math folders and reading-writing folders are filed. These contain children's current assignments, writing, and personal wordbooks. A nearby basket contains reading logs. I organize student work so that it is easily accessible after the children leave for the day.

In addition to the blocks, other construction materials—Legos, Geoblocks—are stored in plastic tubs near the block area. Sometimes we have a "Lego week" or a "block week," or combine materials in creative ways.

Math manipulatives are gathered together on a nearby shelf so they can be used in building activities. Some of these materials are stored in plastic boxes with lids, others in plastic dishpans. Multilink blocks are wonderful free-construction materials, as are Geoblocks and Cuisenaire rods, with their inherent mathematical structure. The children love to have the teddy bear counters inhabit their block houses or ride in their space ships. Many materials are likewise multipurpose.

Games and puzzles occupy shelves near the rug, where they are most often used, and again there is overlap. Many games are math-related. Those the children enjoy choosing on their own during Explore Time stay near the rug; those for which special instruction may be needed are stored elsewhere and taken out for a specific purpose during math time.

A cupboard in one corner stores most science supplies, but others, such as pets and plants, may be placed in various locations around the room. Some science materials, like magnets, batteries, and bulbs, might be set out in a plastic dishpan or basket for a while, then packed up and put away to make room for other materials.

. . . .

Some materials may change places during the year, but consistency in most areas helps children pick up and care for the room themselves.

THE CLASSROOM AS A TEXTBOOK

In *Teaching and Learning Through Multiple Intelligences* (1992), Linda and Bruce Campbell and Dee Dickinson speak of the classroom as a textbook. Renate and Geoffrey Caine use the term "peripheral learning" in *Making Connections: Teaching and the Human Brain* (1991): the learner is always monitoring the entire environment. The learning process is naturally one of making connections between information from our senses and other knowledge. Modern brain research supports Piaget's theory of accommodation. We surround children with visually appealing materials that support this learning process.

How do we create a rich peripheral environment, a classroom that is itself a tool for learning? A couple of things come to mind. One has to do with the aesthetic nature of the classroom and the values it reflects. The second questions how the total environment can contribute to curriculum—to learning to read or acquire knowledge about a theme.

Children's art displayed on the walls speaks of the importance of their ideas and what they produce. Everyone's work is included because everyone is valued and their work is valued. If, in addition, the art is displayed in an attractive arrangement, it will make an aesthetically pleasing statement.

Children begin very early to make aesthetic decisions: What colors do they like? what shapes and textures? what tastes? We can give them aesthetic models and, through the environment, raise their awareness of how they make aesthetic decisions. When Jason chooses a cover for his castle book, I can ask why he chose that color from the assortment available. When I mount children's art for a display, I can consult the children about the colors I choose. When studying Mexico, we can talk about the texture and the design of a Mexican rug on display, and its unique color combinations.

The walls of the classroom also feature a great deal of print—large charts of poetry and songs as well as writing by the children—so that we read from the walls themselves. The value we place on literacy is inescapable.

I love to have the walls reflect our themes, too, so that the year's curriculum gradually accumulates around us. A huge painting of undersea life that indicates the ocean zones may be seen in a corner of the room. A collage of Vermont animals hangs nearby, even as the children busy themselves with a new theme—drawing bones, veins, and arteries on large, cutout body outlines.

Last year's themes stay with us, like so many of last year's children. A large Chinese dragon remained on display high above the bulletin board for

Figure 3.3 Paintings, poetry, and writing that reflect our themes are posted on the wall.

a second year, as did a mural showing the sequence of life on earth. We were able to reflect on past experiences as we moved into new themes and new knowledge, the continuity nurturing connections between past experience and present learning.

The room as a whole, and its contents, also reflects the value we place on many kinds of learning. Peggy Dorta tells me that she always considers Howard Gardner's multiple intelligence theory when she sets up her classroom. She designs different areas of the room around the seven "intelligences" Gardner enumerates: linguistic, logical-mathematical, spatial, musical, bodily-kinesthetic, interpersonal, and intrapersonal. Books, writing, and a listening corner provide aspects of linguistic experience. A construction area combines spatial activities, bodily-kinesthetic activities, and interpersonal cooperation. The addition of math manipulatives, such as Cuisenaire rods, allows children to combine math with spatial experiences. Musical instruments can be available. Cooperative activities of all kinds encourage interpersonal development, and quiet areas to read or work alone encourage the reflection necessary to intrapersonal or inner growth.

According to Gardner's theory, we all come to know the world in these varied ways, but some of us show decided strengths and weaknesses. In a plan such as Peggy's, every child is considered. There is a place for everyone.

Perhaps the most important overall principle for structuring classroom space is this one: children should feel that it is their own room. Is it easy for them to use? Does it look like a living and learning space for children, full of inviting colors and displays? Will it engage their interests, their curiosity, their thought? Does it welcome them as they walk in each morning?

CHAPTER FOUR

STRUCTURING TIME:
STACIE'S DAY

S T A C I E jumps down the last step and off the school bus. Going inside through the big doors she climbs the stairs, a vivid turquoise and cherry-red backpack across one shoulder. She turns left into Room A, drops her pack on a table, and hauls out her lunch box, which she places on a blue shelf. She then drops the backpack in a large basket under the coat hooks and hangs up her jacket. She's glad spring has come. No more boots and snowpants.

"Good morning, Stacie." Mrs. B. is mixing paint at the sink. Stacie stops to tell her about a fox she and her dad saw yesterday. Mrs. B. likes stuff like that. Then she crosses the rug to turn over her name on the attendance board so the tag says, "I'm here, Stacie." She glances around the room. Two boys are looking at a Nintendo catalog. Her bus is early, so she goes over to the block area to check out a house two of her friends made yesterday. It looks like a floor plan, with furniture made from bits of cardboard. She moves some of the little teddy bear counters around. The teddies live in this house. Soon Emma joins her; it's Emma's house. They rearrange one of the rooms and make a sign that says "Furnachur Store." They talk about Emma's upcoming birthday party, her eighth. Stacie will be seven for quite a while longer.

A bell rings and the children gather together in a circle on the big rug. It's Emma's week to take attendance, so she gets the "slip" and writes down the names of children who are absent. She asks how many children want to order a hot lunch and how many want milk. Stacie raises her hand for milk.

Mark has had a birthday and he has something to share with everyone: a volcano kit. Mrs. B. gets a newspaper for him to spread things out on. Stacie watches as he mixes his "chemicals." She holds her breath when lava pours out of the miniature volcano. Some kids want to make more volcanos at Explore Time and Mrs. B. asks them what they think they will need for this project.

Then sharing is over. It's time for math.

"Stacie and Ron, I'd like you to teach Betsy the subtraction trading game," says Mrs. B. "I've set out the basket of Base Ten Blocks. If you have time later, there's a practice page in your math folders."

Stacie and Ron get the blocks: there are tiny wooden cubes (ones), wooden rods that are ten cubes long (tens), and flat pieces with one hundred square cubes outlined on the surface (hundreds).

Stacie learned the game last week. She knows that you start with a hundred squares and when you roll the dice you take away the number you get. She and Ron will show Betsy how to trade the hundred for ten rods, and then probably a ten for ones, before you can take anything away. She knows that when Betsy has learned the game, too, Mrs. B. will meet with all three of them to teach them something new about subtraction. As they play, she looks around. Some children are sitting at tables with their math folders and papers. Patty's mom has come in to help and joins Mike at the computer. Mrs. B. is settled on the rug with a group of younger kids doing something with pennies and dimes.

After math, Stacie goes to gym. When she comes back it is Explore Time and she knows she can get out her snack if she wants, and that there will be a nice long time to work on the project she started several days ago. She and three others are making a backdrop for the play. She gets a box of pastel chalk and goes out to the hall, where a long strip of brown paper is taped to the wall. Houses have been sketched lightly with pencil. It shows a street scene with trees, flowers, and a street lamp, a backdrop for the play *Mary Poppins*. Next week the class will start rehearsals.

Stacie remembers the play they did last year. She still has a cardboard dragon she made for *Everyone Knows What a Dragon Looks Like*. She knows that next week most of the day will be taken up with work on the play. Selecting a piece of blue chalk she starts coloring around the windows of her house.

Stacie has finished the window trim and colored the bottom half of her house bright pink when Explore Time is over. She took some time out to help Kent draw a tree, and now the two of them gather up the scattered chalk pieces.

During the discussion after Explore Time, everyone quickly tells how they used their time. Emma and Beth explain about how their block house has turned into a shopping center. They point to all the signs. Then the volcano group shows the class how they mix vinegar and baking soda together. There is another eruption and the lunch bell rings.

After lunch and recess, Mrs. B. reads a chapter of *Mary Poppins Comes Back*. The play is not about this book, but it's fun to hear some more Mary Poppins stories.

When story time is over Stacie gets a book out of her cubby. She's glad Mrs. B. is meeting with some other kids to read today. She and Cindy and Mark are reading a book called *A Toad for Tuesday*. They picked it out yesterday when Mrs. B. showed them three books they might like. Stacie hurries. She and Emma like to read under the easel where it is kind of private, not the paint easel of course, the other one. Emma is reading *Aldo Applesauce*.

Pretty soon Mrs. B. suggests that everyone find a stopping place in about five minutes. Stacie finishes the page and gets her writing folder. She really wants to work on a story she has started. It's about a trip she took to the ocean with her dad. They saw a seal and went fishing and there was a storm—lots to tell. She remembered a lot of these things in a talk with Mrs. B. two days ago, and made a story web. Now she wants to finish the story and make some pictures. Maybe next week she'll read it to the class. So today she writes only a sentence in her reading log, notes the date, and gets on with her story.

This day ends with a singalong. Every Thursday the four multiage classes in Stacie's school get together in Room C for a singalong.

The routines of Stacie's day have become very comfortable for her. She knows what to expect. There is teacher direction, but she can also plan some of her own time. She has opportunities to be with friends, to learn from others, and to help others.

Stacie's Day

MORNING:

8:10	Children begin to arrive.
8:20	We meet in a circle on the rug for attendance, lunch count, and announcements. Each day a few children share experiences from home and family.
8:35–9:15	Math (cleanup at 9:10)
9:15–9:55	Music, gym, art, or library
10:00–10:45	Explore Time (cleanup about 10:40)
10:45–11:15	We meet to share and discuss the activities children were involved in during Explore Time. Members of the class con-

tribute information about topics, make suggestions about changes or improvements to projects, and plan for the next day.

11:20–12:15   Lunch and recess

12:20–2:20   Language arts and theme
Read-aloud story
Quiet reading
Writing and other language activities or thematic work
Sharing of work on some days

2:30   Buses leave

Time provides another dimension for structuring the informality of a child-centered classroom effectively. Stacie's day illustrates two concerns in determining the appropriate use of time: First, the formal curricular goals of an elementary school influence what must be included each day and each week. Stacie is working on subtraction of two-digit numbers; and she is reading, writing, and recording her work in words and pictures. Routines revolve around activities necessary for acquiring literacy, understanding number and problem solving, and the content that makes up the rest of the curriculum. Second, but of equal importance in planning the school day, are our knowledge and our beliefs about child development and learning. How do our beliefs affect what we do about structuring time, and what are some of the specific considerations involved in developing daily and weekly schedules? How can different alternatives affect children's learning and behavior?

These questions will be the subject of this chapter. In addition, we want to look at whether multiage classes have unique time requirements. The variety of projects and open-ended assignments necessary to meet the needs of different ages demand plenty of time. Time is needed for children to interact, to help one another, and to watch and observe others as models.

Appendix B contains the weekly schedules of several other multiage teachers, which present further options.

MAKING UP THE SCHEDULE

Work on the schedule, like preparing the room, precedes the children's arrival in September. Some of this work is done by the individual teacher and some by a team; some is a function of school scheduling. The school schedule

. . . .

determines the fixed time structure just as the features of the classroom determine the space.

The length of the school day, arrival and departure times, lunch break, and any all-school recesses establish the basic framework. Next are the schedules for any classes such as music, art, physical education, and library.

Special education schedules may also come into play at this time if children are pulled out for special help, and particularly if work with special needs students occurs in the classroom. The tutor should be coming in at appropriate times during the school day, during the language block, for example, to work on reading. Sometimes this scheduling is done after classroom schedules are in place, sometimes concurrently.

ROUTINES THAT RESPOND TO CHILDREN'S NEEDS

My friend Peggy Dorta likes to make a distinction between routines and schedules. A schedule, she says, is rigid and defines a specific timetable: Room A must be at lunch or children must board the school buses at a fixed time. Routines, on the other hand, are expected but flexible sequences of activities: noon recess is usually followed by a story, then quiet reading, followed by writing or other language activities. Time is a little more loosely organized here. The story may take fifteen minutes or twenty, occasionally more.

Children respond well to expected routines that provide security. However, rigidity in the flow of the day can be frustrating to everyone. Rigid timetables make it difficult to respond spontaneously to individuals, children's interests, and unexpected events. When Mark arrived with his volcano kit, it was important to give him time to share it and, during Explore Time, to allow other children to follow up on his demonstration. Their gathering of books about volcanos and study of volcanos could follow. There is enough flexibility in the daily routine to allow this to happen if interest remains high. Reading and writing are a struggle for Mark, so his success in spearheading this activity is significant.

PLANNING TIME IN FLEXIBLE CHUNKS

Making volcanos was a hands-on project. We know that young children learn best when they interact with concrete materials and with people. But this kind of learning takes time. To allow it to happen we must avoid the fragmentation that so often characterizes the school day when it is divided into arbitrary "periods" for different subjects. We need large blocks of unhurried time. Molly McClaskey, a fellow writer on multiage topics, calls this the "chunking" of time.

Stacie's schedule includes two such chunks: Explore Time, the morning choice time, and an afternoon language arts block. Both provide a good deal of flexibility. If a child finishes an art project, a construction, or a game during Explore Time, she can move on to another activity. Many children, however, maintain their interest in a single task. Contrary to the idea that they have short attention spans, children can sustain themselves for long periods when they are involved in projects that are meaningful to them.

It is important to provide time when children can focus on a task without interruption. The children's lives outside of school often do not. There is the rush to get breakfast and catch the school bus, while other family members rush off to work. After school there may be a baby-sitter, lessons, errands, and especially television. From "Sesame Street" to commercial television, with its constant interruptions, they learn to concentrate in short segments, with quick cuts to something new. Problem solving requires a different approach.

Recently, I watched my husband spend an entire morning removing a large branch from a dead tree near our house. The branch had to come down before the tree could be safely cut. But the branch became caught on another tree. Patiently, he tried one trick and one tool after another until he got it on the ground. Whether it is a mechanical problem or a problem involving people, we have to be willing to take time, and children need to experience that kind of unhurried time.

The language arts block, Stacie's other chunk of time, usually takes up most of the afternoon. It, too, has a great deal of built-in flexibility: Stacie could choose to spend most of her time today working on her story. In *Full Circle: A New Look at Multiage Education* (1994), Penelle Chase and Jane Doan describe a similar chunk of time in their classroom routine. They call this "Communications Workshop." I like that name! "Workshop" aptly describes the productive atmosphere in the room during these large blocks of flexible time.

The language block in Room A has been designed to incorporate a whole language approach to literacy and, as part of that philosophy, to absorb integrated themes. It is always used for a variety of reading and writing activities. On some days, however, those activities are entirely theme related, and children apply their reading and writing skills to the process of gaining new knowledge and to developing projects that embody that knowledge in concrete ways.

In their theme study of the United States, the children pored over books about Arizona, Florida, or whatever state they had chosen, and then wrote and illustrated travel brochures and picture postcards, designed T-shirts, and made colorful posters that conveyed the information they had discovered.

Whether this block of time is used to work on a theme or to pursue other experiences with written language, it allows for a combination of individual, small group, or whole class activities. The whole class can plan an activity, discuss a topic, or share some of their work with one another, and small groups can meet together while other students work alone or with a partner.

Groups of children reading at the same level or needing to learn the same phonetic skill may be called together for reading instruction. Or heterogeneous groups of children can collaborate. Jason, age seven, and Chuck, six, researched the state of Texas. Jason did most of the reading, but they both discussed the book's illustrations and planned their posters together.

These longer blocks of time provide opportunities for children's choices as well as for teacher-directed activities. Children develop more positive feelings about learning—and about school—when they take part in decisions related to their own learning, when they can choose activities that interest them. The children studying the states decided which state they wanted to research and which projects they would undertake. After Mark's volcano demonstration, some children decided to make volcanos during Explore Time; others could choose to use part of their language time reading about volcanos.

The greatest success in reading and writing often occurs when students have a personal interest in the topic. Stacie's story topic, her trip with her dad, was self-chosen and personal, so she was eager to work on it. Her parents were divorced, and writing about time spent with her father was particularly important to her.

Stacie was also learning to set priorities by choosing which written language activity to focus on first. She decided to work on her story instead of a cursive poetry book, an ongoing assignment, or a word search that I had also tucked in her folder, and she spent less time on her reading log than she did on other days. Stacie decided to use Explore Time, on the other hand, to pursue her interest in drawing. Explore Time reserves significant amounts of time for a variety of kinds of learning in less conventional modes. Spatial activities like block construction, for example, are available to eight-year-olds as well as to five-year-olds, since the need for a variety of learning modes does not end at age six.

This expansive chunk of time also supports interaction among the children. They talk about what they are doing, they watch one another, and they tutor each other informally, as Stacie did when she helped Kent draw a tree. Friendships, like that of Stacie and Emma, are cemented, strengthening children's self-esteem and contributing to a sense of community.

Developing the skills of self-directed learning, applying learned skills to self-chosen activities, and building social skills are important achievements. They are worthy of a significant block of time reasonably early in the school day.

Following Explore Time we gather for a class discussion. I can shorten the discussion and stretch Explore Time when children are deeply involved in a project. They may even continue working until we go to lunch, with no discussion at all, which happened during the final days of scenery preparation for our production of *Mary Poppins.*

There is no midmorning recess in Stacie's class. The multiage teaching team eliminated this in order to allow a long Explore Time. Children who have been sitting all morning need a recess to let off steam, but not if they have been able to move about, explore materials, and socialize.

I have discussed the use of large blocks of time in some detail because they are a dramatic departure from the organization of the conventional school day. A language arts block is certainly a departure from a schedule in which reading, writing, and spelling periods are all separately delineated, but it is familiar to those of us implementing whole language programs. Integrating theme studies into time otherwise spent for language activities contrasts sharply with a succession of discrete periods for science, social studies, and health. Perhaps most unusual is the inclusion of a long daily Explore Time for primary children, one that is neither a break nor an indoor recess but a time for learning.

A SPECIAL MATH TIME

Along with making large blocks of time available to children every day, we also need to plan for shorter periods with a special focus. I have found it essential to schedule a daily math period, for example. When I first started teaching multiage classes, the children's choice time took up most of the morning, while the afternoon included both language arts and math. Children frequently decided which activities they would do first and almost everything was individualized. We worked this way for a long time, but I have come to realize that individualized work can only be part of the picture. Learning also comes from the exchange among different ages and different individuals as they work together, and we need, therefore, a time when everyone is focused.

I also find it harder to integrate math into our thematic activities than language. Graphing and measurement frequently find their way into themes, but numeration and computation seem to be neglected. A separate dependable math time needs to be part of the routine. In Room A, math is most often planned for the morning, either before Explore Time or just before lunch. When it is first thing, as it was for Stacie, parent volunteers find it a good time to come in, and I have enjoyed having their help.

CLASS MEETINGS

Our daily routine also includes times for the class to come together as a community. As children share aspects of their own lives or their opinions on a topic, they come to know each other better. These are ideal moments to encourage a respect for differences and to support a sense of mutual responsibility. Stacie's day included a morning meeting for announcements and sharing, a discussion after Explore Time, and a read-aloud story.

There are other occasions that call for class meetings besides those that are regularly scheduled. When we are planning thematic activities, we may find an early afternoon meeting, before we leave the rug after storytime, to be a good idea. Once or twice a week we close the afternoon with a gathering at which children can share stories they have written. We also meet to share projects, watch related films, or interview a visitor. If a problem develops on the playground, children may request a problem-solving session, and we fit in some extra community time after lunch.

We move from a whole class meeting to individual and small group work, then back together. We come together for planning and sharing on a regular basis and then disperse. The regularity of our coming together and scattering is the rhythm of breathing in and out through the school day.

TRANSITIONS

In planning the daily schedule, I try to strive for comfortable transitions. Frequent interruptions make it harder for children to become involved in a task, but the transition from a read-aloud story to quiet reading and then to writing is easy and natural. Block planning makes for fewer major transitions each day, because children don't all move from reading to writing at the same time.

Some things, like a special class or lunch, will inevitably bring about a more abrupt break in the routine. The transition back to class is easier if the children know what is expected and can proceed on their own. When Stacie returned to Room A after gym, she was able to start her chosen Explore Time activity immediately. While she gathered materials for working on the play backdrop, other children moved right to the blocks or the computer, or sat down at a table with their snack. Sometimes I designate the time after noon recess for quiet reading instead of storytime, because children can get started immediately as they come in from the playground, without having to wait for the others. During a Vermont winter, some children need far more time than others to get out of their winter clothes. Casual conversation on the rug can precede the story, or I can accommodate the season by changing the schedule. Anything that will transform a major upheaval into a smoother transition is helpful.

The transition from one activity to another often involves a change of pace. The intensity of project work needs to be followed by quiet reading, storytime, or class sharing. Even though young children learn best when they can move around and interact, curling up for a story or sitting in a circle for discussion provide a welcome change. Few children are able to maintain the same level of activity continuously, so this helps create an easy, natural rhythm to the day.

ESTABLISH PREDICTABLE ROUTINES EARLY

Sometimes we need to turn our normal routines upside down. One year, an artist-in-residence assisted the multiage team with a theme on Native Americans. This young woman helped the children shape clay pots, create sand paintings, share their own family legends, and participate in a Native American ceremony. We had to restructure our day to enable her to work on these projects with all four classrooms.

Another time, working with a dancer necessitated scheduling some of her sessions solely around the availability of the gym. Other parts of our day had to give way or be rescheduled.

It seems strange, but we achieve this kind of flexibility by starting the year with a clear, dependable framework. Once that is in place, time becomes more malleable. The variety, fun, and learning that flexible scheduling allows are a direct result of children's initial experience *within* a structure. Children are more comfortable departing from a known schedule than not knowing how the day will unfold.

Stacie did not have to wait for me to tell her what to do next. Comfortable routines, routines that made sense to her, were well established. But she could adapt if necessary.

BACK in January Stacie spent most of one day on a panda project. During math she and Jason measured and cut large pieces of brown paper to be used for stuffed animals. When Explore Time started Stacie headed for the rug to look through a large box of books about endangered species.

"Have you seen those two books about pandas?" she asked Emma.

"I think Cindy has them."

Stacie found Cindy and arranged to share the books. They both needed a good panda picture to use as a model for the large paper stuffed animals they planned to make. As they worked together, the resulting pandas reflected their very different developmental stage. Stacie was able to copy a panda sitting with curled legs, chewing on a piece of bamboo. Cindy represented her panda teddy bear style, with legs and arms outstretched. They collaborated happily, undisturbed by this difference.

While they drew pandas, Suzie was looking at pictures of polar bears. Polly was mixing paint to try to find the right gray for her wolf. Mrs B. was helping Chuck staple the edges of a giant paper sea turtle. Other children were making clay animals or working on dioramas. Most of the children were devoting their Explore Time to thematic studies.

Instead of discussion, the class watched a film on extinct animals and the causes of extinction. Stacie thought about her panda report. She remembered reading that pandas might become extinct because people are moving into the forests where they live. Now the food they need is hard to find.

In the afternoon Stacie, Emma, and Alex volunteered to make a world map for the bulletin board. Mrs. B. put a map on the overhead projector and they outlined the projected image on a large piece of paper. Stacie found the continent where pandas live and figured out about where China would be. Then she finished copying her report. Each child in the class would now be able to find the area where their animal lives and put a picture there. The usual time frames of the day were changed to accommodate this intensely focused work on a theme.

When children can make these switches smoothly and comfortably, they can integrate and use skills in interesting new ways and we can stretch time if necessary to provide for longer theme projects. We need to be able to depend on the children's flexibility as well as our own.

When routines have been established children always have something to go back to with confidence. Her panda report complete, Stacie easily picked up on work she had started earlier. She turned to a collection of poetry, copy work in cursive, and then wrote about her new kitten. The transition was easy because she already knew how to use her time. Stacie was also comfortable with these changes because this was her second year in the same classroom. She remembers, for example, how work on a play changed the schedule last year. The continuity of multiage classrooms makes it easier for children to adapt to changes in routine.

Figure 4.1 A drawing made during our theme study of endangered animals.

TEAM DECISIONS

If you work with a team, and not all multiage teachers do, you will need to plan together the times your classes share. Some teams may schedule their entire day together, all doing math and quiet reading at the same time, for example. My team schedules Explore Time together, and children can choose activities in any one of the four classrooms during this time. We plan a weekly singalong, when the four-classroom extended family gathers. We also plan some themes together, such as the endangered species study. Different projects were offered in each of the four rooms: paper stuffed animals, dioramas, clay animals, and the preparation of an endangered species quilt.

Planning a theme together takes time. Team meeting times must be scheduled. The more a team does in concert the more time that team needs to meet together. Schools with team structures provide for this in various ways. One way is to schedule special classes so that each class within a team goes to music, art, gym, or library at the same time.

Teams need time not only to plan but also to talk about children and to fulfill other school requirements, such as reporting from committees and preparing for parent nights. Plenty of after-school time as well as lunchtime meetings will probably be needed, but there should always be regularly scheduled team meeting times during the day. Once a week is a minimum.

Now the question arises, should multiage teams regroup children for some of their academic work, forming large instructional groups working at a similar level? (Grouping for academic work will be addressed more fully in Chapters 8 through 10.) If your team regroups students for ability level in reading or math, this naturally affects scheduling. What are the pros and cons of this form of organization?

The claim is often made that teacher planning and preparation are easier in ability-level groups because the children have similar needs. Most research, however, does not support ability grouping, unless the instruction is carefully geared to each individual child's needs. In and of itself, grouping by ability does not enhance academic progress, while for those in lower-level groups it can have a negative impact on self-image.

In my experience, most multiage teachers prefer to take responsibility for their students' skills development. They have become accustomed to individualizing work, both in terms of level and learning style, and find more disadvantages than advantages in this sort of regrouping. If a student of mine is assigned to another teacher for reading instruction, I am deprived of the experience and information I need to guide related learning.

In addition, when instruction is given individually and in small groups, the teacher receives immediate feedback about each child's understanding. This does not happen in large groups. The child, too, can receive immediate feedback, or the teacher can initiate a different approach. The teacher could, for example, substitute a different math manipulative or game, select an easier book, or initiate a dramatic activity to help the child understand a story. The time together may be less if you are meeting with several small groups instead of one large one, but the quality of that time is greater because more interaction with the individual child is possible. Small groups also provide flexibility. You need not meet with the same children each time.

Reporting to parents also becomes more complicated if you regroup— should both teachers meet with parents when conferences are scheduled? Such regrouping also leads to less flexibility in scheduling: It is more difficult to schedule those large blocks of uninterrupted time. It changes the nature of the class community and leads to a decreased sense of family. In many ways it seems to work against some of the very advantages we are trying to gain through multiage grouping. I prefer to take responsibility for the academic progress of my own students, in all their variety.

EACH DAY LOOKS DIFFERENT

We have seen some of the changes that take place through the year in a multi-age classroom. Once you have established a clear time structure and expectations, you are free to become more flexible. What a visitor sees in January will probably be quite different from what that same person might have seen back in October. Once the year is well under way each day may look different; visitors need to realize how difficult it is to know a program after only one visit.

My own experience as a visitor illustrates how often an outsider can miss the total picture. A number of years ago, after spending the day in a classroom, I asked the teacher to tell me about the reading program. It was my impression that not much reading instruction was going on. I'd visited a class of six- to eight-year-olds the day after their field trip to an environmental center to study the harvest season. They had spent a good deal of time working on murals to record what they had learned. During math time they had made corn bread, with all the measuring any cooking project entails. Each child had chosen a key word from the field trip experience, put it in a sentence, and shared it with the group. There had even been an impressive book sharing time after quiet reading, when some children talked about the characters in the stories they were reading. I'd seen a lot of theme work but only a tiny piece of a reading program, one day's worth out of a whole year.

The days of the week may also be different. The block of time given to language arts will look different from day to day: sometimes it will be taken up mostly with individual work, while other days it may include class time for mini-lessons or sharing writing, or the whole block may be taken over for a theme. Any single day provides an incomplete picture of what the total program offers.

As you review your planned routines, what is the atmosphere you want to create for the classroom community as you open and close each day? Do you want a businesslike start to the day? Do you want a relaxed, friendly beginning? These goals are probably not incompatible. How do the children arrive? Do they come in all at once from playground or bus, or gradually, a few at a time?

Children in my class come in over ten or fifteen minutes, directly from school buses as they roll in. After about ten minutes of informal socializing we meet in a circle on the rug for lunch count, announcements, and sharing. We start with a meeting because our school has lunch choices and orders need to be sent to the office early.

Another option, especially when children arrive gradually, is to begin with Explore Time. Children immediately become involved in their individually chosen learning activities, and the social contact provides a nice bridge between home and school. This has not worked out in recent years in our school because our schedule of special classes would interrupt the Explore Time block too soon, but many multiage teachers like to begin this way.

I once visited a class in which children picked up quiet reading immediately on arrival. They had already had time for socializing and greeting their friends on the playground. But children who arrive by bus from scattered neighborhoods and come immediately to the classroom, as ours do, need an opportunity to greet friends at the start of the school day. Allowing for these social needs helps children focus on school jobs with less distraction later.

The end of the day is important, too. It can be a time to consolidate what we have done and plan for tomorrow. Reading a story aloud can be a quiet, relaxed way to end the day. Sometimes each child in the class circle might simply share something from the day. One two-class team I visited gathered everyone in a big circle, held hands, sang a song, and then passed around a hand squeeze before departing, a simple community ritual.

The way each part of the day is used delivers a message to children. This may be a message about the importance of learning, about the importance of community, about their own importance as people. When their needs are considered in framing the school day, we acknowledge that they are indeed very special.

PART THREE

LEARNING
WITH CHILDREN

CHAPTER FIVE

—■—

SELF-DIRECTION: EXPLORE TIME
AND OTHER OPTIONS

CHILDREN come in gradually, returning from the library, and stash books in their cubbies. Some search their cubby or open their lunch box to find a snack. Then they head for games, blocks, or the tape recorder. They bring out paper and markers and find a work space at one of the tables. They curl up with a book or get out story writing. No one is in the computer corner yet, but then, there is a no-food rule there.

Patty puts her apple down on the table and begins to lay out newspapers. She chooses a brush from a plastic tub on the counter beside the sink and opens two yogurt tubs filled with paint, one black and one white. She's going to paint her chickadee today.

Last week everyone was doing research on something they wanted to know more about. Patty started a project on "Birds in Winter." Later she sketched a chickadee, a nuthatch, and a cardinal and put them on a poster. She did the research during a language arts time. Then during Explore Time she looked at her sketches and modeled the same birds out of plasticine. I thought she might like to have those three-dimensional models in a more permanent form, so I helped her mix some bread dough sculpting material. We talked about creating a model tree out of a branch she had brought in; she plans to glue her birds in the tree. Now that they are dry, she can add some color. She dips her brush in the paint.

"Could I use some black paint, too?" Betsy stands with a brush poised. "I need to put dots on my dice." Her project is "Dice Games," and she holds a pair of giant cardboard dice.

· ·

Ron joins the other two. He has a spaceship to finish. "I need a little black and a little white to mix." He finds an empty yogurt cup on the counter and sets to work mixing gray paint.

One of the basic tenets of a multiage philosophy (see Chapter 2) is a "belief that the learner can be trusted." Acting on that trust allows children a certain kind of growth: the experience of making decisions for oneself and taking responsibility for those decisions. Taking responsibility can be as simple as finishing what you have started and cleaning up your own materials. In a collaborative venture children have to find ways to make decisions together, and that is another kind of responsibility. Sharing one's project with the class carries responsibility a step further: you must explain what you did and why.

The process of decision making and of taking responsibility for decisions is one kind of learning that takes place when children are encouraged to make choices. Another is growth in the ability to solve problems encountered during work on self-chosen projects, both alone and in groups. Jason (see Chapter 3) was problem solving as he tried to figure out how to make a three-dimensional working drawbridge on one page of his castle book.

When children make choices at school, they engage in the process of "learning how to learn," a lifelong skill that involves self-motivation and knowing how to set priorities. Patty is determined to extend her study of birds through the models she is making, so she has given that first priority for today's Explore Time. Self-confidence, too, grows from the experience of solving your own problems and directing your own learning. Let's take a closer look.

A CLOSER LOOK

What follows is a detailed look at what each child is doing during part of a forty-minute Explore Time. It might be interesting to look for evidence of the beliefs cited in Chapter 2. Keep in mind that there are four multiage rooms in our school. As I have noted, children are free to choose activities in Room A, B, C, or D. On this particular day, there are almost thirty children in Room A, more than the normal class size.

"HAVE you done puzzle six, the turtle?"

"Let's see. Yep. Need help?"

"No, not yet, but it's hard. Did it take you a long time?"

"I don't remember." Mac stops to watch Joel work on the Tangram puzzle. He's not sure he remembers how he did this one.

Walking into Room A, a visitor first encounters six children gathered around a large table. It is strewn with colorful Tangram pieces and laminated puzzle sheets of pictures that can be created using these geometric shapes. Four boys and two girls, seven and eight years old, work with this ancient Chinese puzzle. The plastic dishpan in which these materials are stored sits in the center of the table, which is actually two rectangular tables that have been pushed together to form a large square. A number of Tangram sets, each in a separate small Ziplock plastic bag, remain in the dishpan.

To the right, near the wall, is a low table, a green circle in the middle of a small rug surrounded on two sides by racks of books and tapes. Two six-year-old girls sit on the floor listening to a taped book, *Little Rabbit's Loose Tooth*. They are sharing the book between them and following along with the tape. Their earphones blot out other conversation. For the moment, their whole focus is the story.

At the same table, Cindy and Stacie are writing a story together. "The starchild is sad. Let's say she's sad because her Daddy went away."

"Wait, I'm still writing about the war. 'He goes to the other side of the sky, but he sends a letter home.'"

"Yeah. And then, and then, while he's gone she grows up and she falls in love and ..."

The girls talk a little more. Then Stacie, who seems to be the scribe, writes on the paper in front of them. She is a year older than Cindy. Judging by their stack of paper, this could be a small novel in the making.

"Raaay!" Cheering breaks out in the corner behind the listening area. On the other side of the divider, a cluster of children stare over the shoulders of a child at a computer. Wendy, age eight, is using a spelling game. As letters fly across the top of the screen she needs to choose those that are missing in the word below and shoot a missile to catch each letter she needs. The fast-paced game has lots of appeal, but she also has to think about whether she is looking for a vowel or a consonant and remember known words. Ben can't resist suggesting a letter.

"Try a *b!* Try a *b!*" he shouts.

"Will you stop telling me the answer. I want to do it myself!" Wendy asserts herself. She wants to be independent today. On other occasions this game can be a cooperative venture for two or three children.

At another computer, Polly and Suzie, six and seven, are playing a concentration game. They have to match tunes, a tricky challenge, and since they don't have earphones they need to listen carefully. They manage despite Wendy's cheering section nearby.

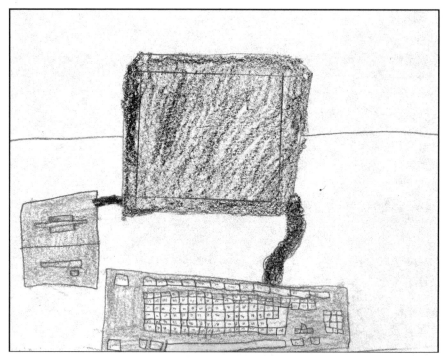

Figure 5.1 Computers are part of our classroom.

Two children are working alone in the center of the room. Kent, who is six, is at a desk by himself drawing dinosaurs. Patty is finishing her bird project at a table near the sink. She has finished painting the chickadee and looks around to find some red paint for the cardinal. The other painters have finished and moved on.

"Hey wait. I got a great idea. You need one of those things that sticks through paper and bends."

"Good idea . . . Mrs. B., have you got some paper fasteners?" Jerry, age eight, has just created a grasping claw out of rolls of paper. Up to now he has assembled it with tape. As they talk over some of the problems he has encountered, Jason, two years younger, suggests paper fasteners. A battery-operated "robot arm" in the classroom may have suggested this project to the boys.

"We'll test this with some Unifix cubes. Do you think we can pick them up?" asks Jerry.

In the back corner opposite the computers rises a mountain of blocks, surrounded by plastic dinosaur models. Mike and Alex are putting the last touches on their model volcano, started two days ago. A flashlight hidden inside the mountain lights up the red cellophane inserted in the top.

"Hey we need some lava." Ron, who has finished painting his spaceship, darts across the room. He gathers scissors and red paper from the "scrap box."

I have encouraged this project by helping the boys find library books about volcanos and by locating a flashlight and red cellophane. It is a welcome change from building the tallest possible structures, which they enjoy knocking over.

On the big rug, where our class group meets, Betsy and her friend Catherine, from Room C, are playing "Tricky Fingers," a visual/fine-motor game. Anna, six, is watching these two seven-year-olds. I expect that tomorrow she will ask me to play the game with her. Today she is learning the rules by watching.

I note that two eight-year-old girls and a younger boy from Room A are missing. Since everyone here seems to be busy and involved, I step into the other rooms myself for a quick look around. I'd like to see how these three are using their time. The six-year-old boy is painting at an easel across the hall and I find the girls playing the piano in Room C. Liz Farman, my colleague, makes the piano available to children certain days of the week, and she is there to listen in or help them learn a tune. I'm happy to see these two so focused. They sometimes drift and need to be nudged to get involved with available materials.

THE OTHER TWENTY-FIVE MINUTES

That's fifteen minutes of Explore Time. What about rest? Some of these children will maintain their involvement with one task throughout the forty minutes. The children working with Tangrams will probably stay with this today. I just put the materials out last week as a new challenge. They seem highly motivated to try to solve each puzzle in the folder.

Patty is tenacious. She won't move from her project until it is complete.

The writers, too, are pretty involved, although they may go on to illustrations and bookbinding.

Mike and Alex will continue with the blocks if all goes well. Mike is easily discouraged and sometimes gives up when faced with a problem. Disruption in his family, as his parents separate, makes it harder for him to concentrate, but this is his second year in Room A, so he doesn't have to face so much change at school. Alex, on the other hand, is a fairly persistent problem solver. Both he and Ron are inclined to ask for help rather than abandon a project. They are good models for Mike, and provide support for him.

Other activities are shorter term, so children may put away what they are doing and move on to something else. Kent may drift off from his drawing and watch someone. If he decides to watch Jerry and Jason test their paper claw, I hope they will be open to his involvement. He has difficulty socializing and often works alone, so I make a mental note to keep an eye on him.

When Explore Time is over today we will have a fairly easy cleanup. Some days, when there is lots of cutting and pasting or major paint projects, cleanup seems a massive job, but everyone helps and it always gets done.

DISCUSSION

On this day when we gather on the rug following Explore Time, I give the children two questions: Did you learn to do something new today? Did someone help you or did you help someone? We take a quick trip around the circle; those children who wish to may reflect on the questions. This is not an everyday process, but once in a while it helps the children focus on some of the purposes of Explore Time. It is their responsibility to use the time well.

"Now who has something to show or share?" Patty's birds, the spaceship, and the dice have all come to the rug. Hands wave. Jerry demonstrates the paper claw with mild success. The volcano builders explain their project, and the flashlight is turned on with the room lights off so we can admire the effect. Some of the Tangram group want to show their individual record sheets, supplied to them in the folder of puzzles. They have checked off each puzzle they were able to solve.

This community time gives the children a chance to appreciate the work of others and to get ideas for new projects. They make a few suggestions to Jerry about problems with his paper claw, but it is clear to him that everybody thinks it is a neat project. He may try a few new ideas tomorrow. He's known in Room A for his unique 3-D paper constructions.

The discussion gives me a window on how children are using their time, especially on days when I may be busy with a small group for part of the time. Along with my observations of the children during Explore Time, the group discussion gives me clues about special interests and talents. I have discovered Patty's extraordinary interest in nature, for example, through her projects and sharing.

When Kent shows us his dinosaur picture (see Figure 5.2), I enter in to direct the conversation a bit more. Since he is often alone, I wonder if I can arouse interest in an activity others might share with him. So I bring out our basket of drawing books and show them a dragon. I mention the dinosaur drawing book in the library and ask if anyone would like to look for it later, during quiet reading. Jason and Kent both raise their hands. I suggest they search for the book together, and it is time for lunch.

Figure 5.2 Kent's dinosaur picture.

OTHER DAYS, OTHER CHOICES

Part of my job is to see that the room is provisioned for a variety of activities. The availability of many kinds of materials is essential for a successful Explore Time. Some materials are always out on shelves. Others will be brought out for a few weeks or some part of the year. Here is a list of activities that might be happening on other days, although it is impossible to be comprehensive, given the creativity of young minds. (Appendix A will suggest more.)

    modeling with plasticine or clay
    cut-and-paste paper projects
    weaving with paper or with yarn
    braiding and finger knitting with yarn
    construction involving pulleys and string
    building with Legos, Geoblocks, or Cuisenaire rods
    designing with pattern blocks
    painting at the easel or with watercolors
    reading
    making booklets about chosen topics
    puppet plays
    chess

using computers for writing, games, or graphics
taking opinion surveys and producing graphs
experimenting with batteries and bulbs
planting seeds or cuttings
exploring with magnifying glasses or microscope
exploring with magnets
using science experiment books
having fun with drawing books, riddle books
theme related projects, including bulletin boards
observing a visiting pet
researching a special topic
working on math papers
playing with the marble maze
games and crafts of all kinds

Now let's go back for a moment and look at the various activities in an attempt to characterize this time and determine what qualities are being encouraged in the learner.

MULTIAGE GROUPINGS

Many of the children are working in multiage groupings. On their own, children have not necessarily gravitated to single-age groups. The boys in the block area and the children at the Tangram table are multiage groups. Of the two girls writing together, the older one has taken over as scribe, a good example of the leadership roles available to older children in a multiage class.

In *The Case for Mixed-Age Grouping in Early Education* (1990), Lilian Katz, Demetra Evangelou, and Jeanette Allison Hartman review research on the social effects of mixed-age groups. They find that, along with increased opportunities for practicing leadership, the older children also exhibit more prosocial behavior, such as helping and sharing with younger peers.

A variety of activities are offered during Explore Time, some more appropriate for some ages, some for others. Most six-year-olds, for example, are not likely to try the computer game Wendy is using. They will watch this year or participate with a group, and it will be there for them another year.

CHOICE

In each case, it is the children who have chosen, created, and learned. They have a sense of ownership—of the project and of the learning that take place.

When my husband and I built our house, we each had some specific thoughts in mind about design and about what we wanted to include. The "good-morning stairs" are his design and the hearth on which our woodstove rests has bricks laid in the curve that I envisioned. Each of us has made a mark on the finished product and retained a sense of ownership throughout the process.

Whenever we have a part in decisions affecting our lives, we feel that measure of control and ownership. None of us like having critical decisions made for us without being consulted. When this happens we are less enthusiastic about participating. We all, for example, like to have a say about where we will go on this year's vacation trip. In the same way, children who participate in decisions about their learning—the materials they will use, the topics they will research, the projects that will result—feel more motivated and enthusiastic about their time in school.

In *Nongradedness: Helping It to Happen* (1993), Robert Anderson and Barbara Pavan report on research related to interest and its influence on learning. Individuals who have a personal interest in the task at hand have been shown to attend better, persist longer, and acquire more knowledge—and qualitatively different knowledge—than those without that personal interest.

According to Douglas Barnes in *From Communication to Curriculum* (1992), when we use knowledge for our own purposes, then we truly "incorporate it into our view of the world." Thus, our trust in the child as learner plays out in more successful learning.

HANDS-ON LEARNING

As we look at the record of this day, most of the work involves concrete materials and, in many cases, a product that can be handled, viewed, and discussed. From the piano to the Tangrams and the volcano, children are learning in the way what we know about development suggests is best for them. Many had something concrete to show at the end of Explore Time: evidence of new knowledge (birds in winter), something created (drawing, story, 3-D paper work, volcano), problems solved (Tangrams).

MANY KINDS OF LEARNING

Patty and Jerry are a lot alike. Both have great success with projects involving spatial relations and three-dimensional representation. But if they are persistent problem solvers when it comes to creating clay birds or paper claws, they are both having a slow time learning to read. Even though they struggle with written language, they can experience success and be admired for their Explore Time projects.

Like most children, they come to school with unique strengths and weaknesses in their abilities and their approach to learning. We want to help children develop their strengths and experience success. We also need to address areas of weakness. Strengths can often be harnessed to help the learning process in other areas as, for example, when Jerry writes a story about his inventions. I find Howard Gardner's (1983, 1993) theory of multiple intelligence one of the most fascinating and useful efforts to make sense of these differences.

How many of Gardner's intelligences are represented in the Explore Time snapshot? Language pervades the scene—lots of talk—but also the pretty typical school activities of reading and writing: two children are listening to a story, two others are writing, and a cluster of children are observing Wendy's spelling game at the computer.

Math is represented in the geometry of Tangrams. On other days activities might involve measuring or graphing. Many manipulative materials, while not in use on this day, have strong mathematic and spatial possibilities. Cuisenaire rods, Geoblocks, and pattern blocks are examples of attractive materials that represent inherent mathematical structures. Children learn from these structures even as they construct and design freely.

Some real teaching advantages accrue from children's creative exploration of these materials during Explore Time. When I choose to use the Cuisenaire rods or pattern blocks in a designated way for math instruction, for example, children find it easier to follow directions because they are already so familiar with the materials and have unconsciously absorbed their structures—such as the size relationship between different Cuisenaire rods. In this way math is integrated into the school day.

Many Explore Time activities involve spatial relations, like the Tangram puzzles on this particular day, and construction with blocks and paper. Spatial skills are rarely called on during traditional school time, but they may be highly represented during Explore Time in the games, structures, and drawings children produce.

How about the other areas of intelligence? On this day children are using the piano and playing a musical computer game.

Fine motor skills are in constant use. In most cases children are learning through physical activity, demonstrating use of a bodily-kinesthetic mode as well as mental activity.

Inner-psychological, or intrapersonal, work is going on wherever creativity and imagination are evident: in the volcano, Patty's birds, Jerry's paper project, drawing, writing. As projects are completed and children's sense of self-direction and organization grow, they also experience enhanced self-esteem.

Interpersonal growth is represented in the socialized nature of many activities, in the collaboration and interaction that accompany them, and in one child helping another.

Our Explore Time came to mind when I read Anderson and Pavan's (1993) description of the "Flow Activities Room" (FAR) in the Key Elementary School in Indianapolis. The Key School staff has designed an exciting program that is intended to apply Gardner's theory of multiple intelligences in an elementary school setting. All students spend three forty-five minute periods each week in the "Flow Activities Room," where an assortment of games, art materials, and construction supplies are available. The teacher in charge of FAR keeps a record of the activities each child pursues and links each activity to a particular intelligence. Examples given are: Othello/spatial, Scrabble/linguistic, Twister/bodily-kinesthetic. In observing our own children during Explore Time we need to note the special interests and talents they exhibit when they choose how to spend their own time.

Schools, too, need to expand their definition of "significant learning" in order to support all children. This includes children for whom special education intervention is needed in learning to read, spell, or compute; some of these children will be the scientists, the builders, the musicians, and the artists of the future.

OPPORTUNITIES TO DEVELOP SOCIAL SKILLS

Our belief in the importance of the whole child means a commitment to the social or interpersonal process. We look for a variety of ways to support growth in social skills, and Explore Time offers rich opportunities. Most of the children in our Explore Time snapshot are working with at least one other child. In the Tangram group and in the block volcano project, a collaborative, problem-solving process is taking place.

"HEY, you guys. We need some lava. Here's the stuff to make it."

"Where do you think we need some more?—No, not there. It's going to run right into that dinosaur."

"He better get out of the way! Run, run!"

"I think we oughta measure this volcano."

"Yeah, what do we need—a yardstick. I'll get it."

"How about one of those tape measuring things to go around?"

Later: "It won't go around."

Figure 5.3 Making friends while working on an Explore Time project.

"Here, I'll hold this place with my finger. You move the tape."

"Thirty-six plus . . . somebody get a calculator."

"I'll write it down now. Just a sec. I need paper."

These boys are focused on their task, cooperatively solving their problem together. Together they find the right tool, a measuring tape, figure out what to do when it won't go all the way around their volcano, and help each other, first with a calculator and then with a pencil and paper for recording. Business leaders often want employees who can work in groups to solve problems, and formal cooperative groups are frequently organized in school to develop this skill. Here it evolves spontaneously.

Friendships evolve during Explore Time, too. School has always been a place for children to make friends, although usually this is not thought of as a function of schools. Today children have fewer free-play opportunities after school than used to be the case. They may go to a baby-sitter or have lessons, Scouts, or organized sports. Children in cities may not be able to visit friends after school conveniently, and children from suburban and rural areas may come from widely separated neighborhoods. Opportunities to make and maintain friendships often present themselves mostly at school. One place this happens is on the playground, but this does not provide the best social situation for some children because there may be conflict and bullying. The more aggressive children often dominate. Yet making friends and establishing a support system for one's life are social skills needed constantly in adulthood. Children need them too, and Explore Time provides many opportunities.

CONTINUITY

There is continuity here that may be invisible on a one-day visit: social continuity and continuity of curriculum.

The support Mike finds in friends at school has grown gradually over more than a year in the same classroom and with the same teacher. His aggressively defensive behavior when he first swaggered into Room A put him at a social disadvantage. He could not depend on his world at home, since his mother was usually not there when he arrived home from school and his father had moved out, so he didn't expect to depend on the school world either. It took time for the children, who were at first afraid of him, to discover that he could be an innovative, enthusiastic playground companion. They first discovered this during the more controlled experience of Explore Time. Mike reveled in the blocks, constructing towers and adding pulleys and string on which the teddy bears sailed from upper levels to the floor below. His troubles didn't end, between his need to dominate or, alternatively, to give up on a task, but he gradually began to find friends he could depend on. That helped us both.

There is another, entirely different kind of continuity here as well. Some projects reflect curriculum that involved many of the children a year ago. The dinosaurs posed around the volcano reflect last year's study of "prehistoric life."

Children have opportunities to make connections with prior knowledge from home or school, integrating the new with the known. When Patty shows her birds to the group, Jason recalls another bird, a beautiful dead waxwing brought in a year ago. Someone else remembers a collection of bird nests we examined a few months earlier.

The volcanos, too, are an example of curriculum continuity, since the two volcano stories occurred two years in succession. The children recalled Mark's volcano after the block one had been constructed, and we reviewed the "recipe" for making the volcanos erupt.

LANGUAGE DEVELOPMENT

Part of the scaffolding when we learn from each other, the support given children working within Vygotsky's "zone of proximal development," is constructed from language. The boys discuss how to find the circumference of their volcano, Stacie and Cindy talk about what to put in their story, children at the computer or in the Tangram group consult with each other, and Jerry and Jason solve a problem related to their invention.

The early school years are crucial for developing the ability to use written language, but these are important years for expanding competence in oral communication as well. There is probably no language skill more needed in the world outside of school, and in industry, than the ability to communicate through spoken language. In *When Students Have Time to Talk* (1991), Curt Dudley-Marling and Dennis Searle expand on the benefits of classroom talk and on what defines a rich, supportive language environment. That rich language environment includes an authentic use of language, opportunities to experiment with language and try out vocabulary without risk of correction, and challenges to our use of language, as in trying to explain a new experience to someone. The informality of Explore Time conversation and the discussion that follows support these experiences.

Listening, too, is a part of the Explore Time scene. Polly and Suzie listen closely to the music on the computer to match tunes, and two other girls are listening to a taped story. Anna listens to find out how a game is played. Even the individuals working alone are listening, and move in and out of the talk.

Explore Time also gives me an opportunity to listen to the children talk and to converse informally, in contrast to the usual kind of talk during an instructional sequence. I can evaluate language and at the same time support its varied functions. (More about this in Chapter 9.)

APPLICATION OF LEARNED SKILLS AND KNOWLEDGE

When the boys building the volcano explain the process of its construction to the rest of us, and when they take time to read about volcanos or write about their project, they are using their learned language skills for a project that is their own. When they measure, they apply a math skill. Here they can find an immediate need for those skills learned elsewhere during the school day and, in practicing them, acquire greater proficiency.

Late one spring, a group of girls volunteered to clean out a large box of mixed blocks. It was a job for which I'd been asking help. This box, an old wooden toy chest, contained our blocks of odd shapes—arches, cylinders, wood turnings, triangular pieces—but a number of other items had fallen into the box throughout the year.

Kate, Emma, and Polly attacked the project with surprising enthusiasm, and when I checked their progress later I found the box empty and everything sorted into groups. The girls were busy counting, adding, and recording.

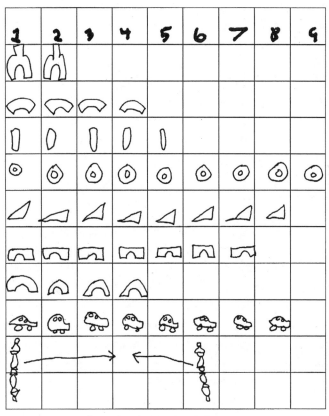

Figure 5.4 Graphing the objects that belong in the box of mixed blocks.

They had taped two large pieces of inch graph paper together and, as information came in from the other two, Kate was busy constructing a graph to show everything that belonged in the box and how many of each item we had. They planned to post this near the box to guide future cleanup. Using graphing skills they had learned in another context, they had transformed the housekeeping chore into a great learning experience I could not have imagined in all my careful planning, and they were having fun in the process.

An adult who enters the room as an untrained observer, some parents, for example, will need help in discovering these skills in action. What may look like play is totally different from the "indoor recess" it might seem to resemble. Since play is a means by which children learn specifically, we look for the developing skills of independent learning: choosing, finishing, and setting priorities; demonstrating particular interests or talents; collaborative problem solving; social and language growth; and the application and practice of new skills and knowledge.

KID WATCHING

Explore Time provides the teacher with the best opportunity of the day for observing children. Sometimes I find myself deeply involved with an individual or a group working on a particular project—the supervision of a mural, for example, or the large class totem pole we constructed one year. I might be playing Mancala with Anna, mixing bread-dough clay with Patty, or finding materials for a science experiment Mark has found pictured in a book. It is also possible to sit down with a group working with clay and participate or just listen to the conversation. It is a time to further develop a relationship with one child or several.

This opportunity to sit back and watch or participate feels like a luxury for a teacher who is not used to this kind of time in the day, but it is not really a luxury. Knowing the children better can support and enhance everything else we do.

Sometimes we need to be more active in the process of observing. I occasionally roam about with a clipboard, as I did to record the scene I describe here. On the clipboard is a class list and I make quick notes beside each name, usually recording the activity each individual child has chosen and anyone they are working with. It is valuable to extrapolate information about the type of intelligence represented, language development, or skills and knowledge applied. (Some of this can best be derived from the record after the children have gone home.) It is amazing how much of this kind of information a teacher carries in her head.

At times, however, we also need to be able to back up what we know about students with records and samples of their work. In recent years our report card has included a section on Explore Time, added at a parent's suggestion! We note the child's ability to choose, complete, and cooperate in the context of Explore Time, and the kinds of activities the child most often pursues.

TEACHER MANAGEMENT OF EXPLORE TIME

Now to some practical matters: How much teacher direction and intervention are needed and appropriate during Explore Time? How much planning is necessary in developing this part of the school day?

Teacher involvement is needed to help children mature in their ability to make decisions and use their time well. My questions during the discussion following Explore Time were intended to help the children see it as a learning time and reflect on their projects in that light. Another day, instead of asking

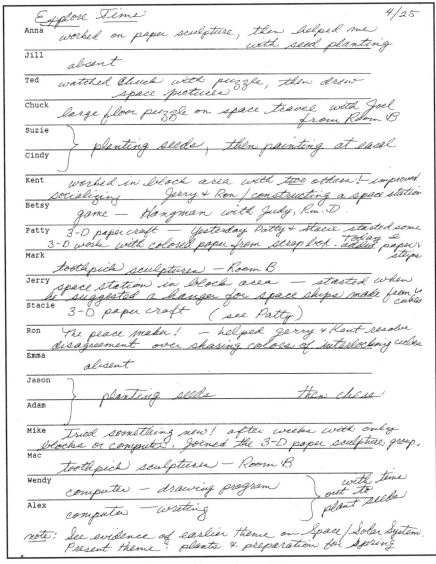

Figure 5.5 Quick notes record what each child is working on.

whether they had learned to do something new, I might have asked, "What did you learn today?" or "Who tried a new game or some new materials?" One purpose of the discussion is to help the children develop that responsibility for their own learning. Another is to help them extend what they have done into greater depth or new areas.

One year, after some spontaneous competition around the size of block towers, we decided to keep a large chart near the block area to record certain data about major constructions. The chart named the building and the team of workers involved. Then it recorded height, width, and circumference. Recording and measuring became a regular part of work in the block area. Alex (who suggested a measuring tape for measuring around the volcano) remembered that experience. The chart itself had been my suggestion during discussion, and the details were worked out within the group.

Through ideas and questions from their peers during discussion, children may discover that they could do more with a project or that they could search for more information. It's a little bit like a writing conference. Open-ended questions from an adult can influence class discussion in these directions. "Is there something more you would like to know about birds in winter?" "What other materials might Jerry have used to construct a claw that would open and close?"

When children see what their classmates have made and what they have done with their materials, they are often inspired to try something they have not done before. If Alex demonstrates how to measure the circumference of the volcano, other children will acquire a new understanding of how to measure. When one child gets out origami books and paper, there is usually a flurry of origami for a while. I see that measuring tapes and origami books are available, but it is often the older children who introduce these materials to our newer class members.

Sometimes, as an outgrowth of the discussion, we plan for the next day. I ask a group of children what they are thinking of doing next on a project they have started, indicating perhaps that it is not quite finished, or we talk about materials they will need for ongoing work.

Planning also takes place during our short meeting at the beginning of each day. At that time I may tell the children about some new materials I will make available during Explore Time.

I have also written about "nudging" children to get them involved with materials, about "encouraging" a project. This is part of my job during Explore Time, planning, and discussion. I encouraged the volcano project by helping the boys find books and pictures, and by locating a flashlight and red cellophane. These things helped them sustain the project and move into more depth. Another example is helping Patty prepare permanent sculpting material for her birds, increasing the quality of what she produced.

Once in a while some children need more than nudging. These wanderers never seem to settle down to work, never seem to have anything to show during discussion. They may float from room to room. As a team we take responsibility for such children until they can be responsible for themselves. I may ask a child to play a game with me, have a conversation, or even assign a task. It doesn't happen very often.

Our team has a few simple rules for Explore Time:

1. Find an activity that interests you.
2. Finish projects you start.
3. Clean up your own mess.
4. Put away what you have used.

If an individual child is having trouble with any of these, it is important for an adult to step in, especially if this is causing a problem for others. Most children learn to use the time well.

Other children who may need special guidance are those who choose the same activity day after day and those who never venture outside Room A to explore what our other multiage rooms have to offer. This year a fifth rule was added to the list above: Try new activities.

The loner is another child to look out for in the process of "kid watching." Kent was an example. In our Explore Time snapshot, Kent was drawing dinosaurs alone, not particularly unusual, since he was rarely seen interacting with others during Explore Time. He also complained about problems on the playground, so he obviously needed help in finding friends and socializing. I tried to discover an interest he might have in common with another child, in this case drawing dinosaurs with Jason, and I set up a situation where they might make a trip to the library together.

Another one of the teacher's roles in relation to Explore Time has to do with arranging and provisioning the room, providing an environment that is inviting and supports different kinds of learning and varied interests (see Chapter 3). Over a number of years I have acquired a large assortment of manipulatives, games, and books. Each year as I think about what materials need to be replaced and what new materials we need, I also give some thought to the different developmental levels represented by the class. I may decide we are short of easy, predictable reading material for beginners or easy board games, or I might discover a math manipulative to enhance problem solving with the more advanced math students.

As we have seen, most of these materials are stored on open shelves where children can easily find them. Some, however, I save to bring out as "new" during the year. That and the changing themes provide for variety and newness in Explore Time choices. When I bring out materials that are new or have been put away, I ask everyone to spend some time with them over a two-week period. We post a checklist. I want everyone to be exposed to all the materials available and to know how to use them. This is another kind of teacher intervention in the choice process, but it should happen fairly infrequently or we undercut our primary goal of learning though self-direction.

When the children were studying sea life, I brought in a computer program that focused on whales, which included many interesting graphics. Children could move the whales about, remove the skin and muscle to see the skeleton, and observe the spouting patterns of different kinds of whales. I expected everyone to explore this program, the older children with partners and the younger ones with either an older tutor or a parent volunteer. I posted a checklist to see that everyone had a turn and directed someone to this program every day.

When the Tangrams came out, we worked with them briefly as a group so I could explain the materials and encourage children to try them. The puzzles are kept in four folders, numbered to indicate four levels of difficulty. Children were initially asked to try sets I and II. The children described in this chapter were working with the puzzles in set III. They all decided to use the individual record sheets I had tucked into each folder, and they had completed and checked off each puzzle in level II. In fact, some of these children worked on level II last year and found their record sheets in the folder. Later the Tangrams will be available on open shelves for the rest of the year.

Periodically, I also introduce new board games to the group during discussion, or we review the rules for older games. Sometimes I ask, "Who knows the rules for this game?" Then I ask children who are interested in the game to look at the show of hands and find someone who might teach them. Even a brief introduction makes it more likely that those games are used. Once again the older children are often the ones to introduce materials to the younger ones. Acting as a tutor, knowing something you can teach another, is a positive experience.

Themes inevitably make their way into Explore Time. Sometimes everyone is expected to participate for a while in thematic projects. In Chapter 4 Stacie was participating in a study of endangered species during Explore Time. This theme was undertaken by the entire multiage team and children signed up for a craft of their choice from among those offered in our four classrooms. They were then called, a few at a time, to work on that project during Explore Time.

When we were studying Mexico I displayed artifacts from that country around the room, as well as many books and pictures. We were surrounded, as much as I could manage, by pieces of Mexican culture. The children kept the labeled sketches they made from these sources in a folder. I set aside time each afternoon for this work. However, some children became so involved they worked on their sketching during Explore Time as well. A similar thing happened during a study of early American life when we again had many artifacts displayed around the room. Surroundings and ongoing studies influence student choices.

During a theme on prehistoric life, children were called to the hall, a few at a time, to paint their contribution to a mural. While studying Native Americans, a few children at a time helped construct a totem pole the class had planned together. Although each student was required to contribute to the mural and totem pole, they determined individually what their contributions would be.

Cleanup is an important time to encourage both individual and group responsibility for the space we share all day. There are several things I do to help cleanup go smoothly. One is to assign jobs. Even though students are expected to clean up what they have used, sometimes they forget. Sometimes there is so much coming and going during a project that some children move on while materials are still in use, so in actual practice we sometimes need to clean up after each other. So we list areas of the room to be checked at the end of cleanup time by various teams. All children have a turn at each job. These jobs are changed weekly and include the more usual classroom tasks such as sharpening pencils and watering plants. These, too, are done at the end of Explore Time in Room A.

Another way to facilitate cleanup is an early warning for children with bigger than usual cleanup jobs, such as in the block area. If these children start five minutes early they are not in the middle of a noisy block pickup when everyone else is finished and meeting on the rug. Block projects often last several days, but the area is always cleared once a week so it can be vacuumed.

Here then is a summary of the teacher's role in helping children grow in this process of self-direction:

nudging	planning with the group
encouraging	provisioning the room
introducing ideas and materials	asking questions
guiding discussion and sharing	thematic work
assigning (occasionally)	kid watching

WHEN EXPLORE TIME IS NEW FOR CHILDREN

Careful planning is needed in introducing Explore Time to a group for the first time. Children often need training to become responsible in how they use what they regard as "free time." They need help to see this as a learning time and to value it as part of the educational program.

One thing a teacher can do is start with fewer choices. In this way you are more likely to guarantee success than if you start with wide-open choices, even if that is your eventual goal. Begin by putting out a few materials on tables, and talk about how they might be used. See how the children do with three or four choices. Begin with twenty or thirty minutes. Establish cleanup procedures before you begin, and always build in time to share and talk about what everyone has accomplished.

The same choices should be available for a day or two. Then move on to something else while children are still interested in these materials. They can come back to them again as part of a larger array to choose from.

In addition to fewer choices initially and a shorter time, Explore Time can be offered less frequently at first, twice a week, for example, until the children become accustomed to managing their time. I would like to think a reasonable goal might be forty minutes daily, or at least three times a week, followed by ten or fifteen minutes of discussion.

CHOICE THROUGHOUT THE SCHOOL DAY

Explore Time is a period given over to learning self-direction, but there are many other ways in which choice can be a part of the school program.

When children decide what they will write about, the ownership they feel in that piece of writing will be a motivating factor. They will approach it in a different way than an assigned topic. At times, some children might want to gather facts about a topic while others are producing a piece of fiction, a letter, or poetry. The writing program should include self-selected topics and genres. Children may even be able to choose whether to begin a language arts period with story writing, handwriting practice, or spelling.

So too with reading: some part of the program needs to give children a chance to self-select what they will read. In my schedule, that time is usually quiet reading. If I ask children to read a specific story or to work with me, there will be other days when they can pursue their own choices.

Sometimes I offer readers a limited choice. At other times it is wide open. Beginning readers may be offered a basket of books from which to choose, or a choice between two or three books. Kent loves animals, so on some days he needs to be able to sit and pull books off the science shelf during quiet reading, poring over the pictures. If I am working in a literature group with more capable readers, I may have that group choose a book from among several I introduce to them. These same children will have times during the year when they may read their individual choices.

Even in math there can often be a choice of which manipulative to use along with a practice page. A variety of counters can be available to beginners: teddy bears, chips, buttons, pebbles, shells, cubes. Children can also be encouraged to choose between similar games, two games that provide addition practice, for example, or trading games using chips or place-value blocks, once they have been introduced to both. For practicing math facts, the choice might even be whether to use a game or a page of problems. Either one can achieve the same goal.

By building self-direction and choice into the school day we encourage motivation and success, and enhance self-image. Every time a child is treated with trust, his or her self-concept is strengthened. For the teacher, Explore Time is an exercise in trusting the learner. For the child Explore Time is:

- learning to make decisions
- becoming responsible for those decisions
- being motivated by a sense of ownership
- feeling oneself a trusted person
- learning how to learn
- supporting the learning of others

CHAPTER SIX

■

THIS FASCINATING WORLD:
INTEGRATED THEMES IN
THE CLASSROOM

"THIS story is about how my mother and I went out to see the penguins. She works at the museum. We went on Saturday with her friend. They put tags on the baby penguins when their parents were away from the nests."

I am at the Macandrew Bay Primary School on the Otago Peninsula near Dunedin, in southern New Zealand, and I am talking to a student, age seven, about a report she has written. I had always thought of penguins on ice and snow, but since I have been here I, too, have visited the yellow-eyed penguin colony. The children in this class, mostly eight- and nine-year-olds, are studying local sea birds.

Robin Murray, their teacher, tells me that although few teachers she knows teach through the use of integrated themes, she is committed to this philosophy. She shows me some of her favorite books on the subject and her own planning for the sea bird theme. She is incredibly organized. I feel fortunate to have made contact with her through the friend of a friend.

It is March, and only about five weeks into the school year. Although a thematically organized classroom is new to some of these children, all seem comfortable with the process. A number of children were Robin's students last year, they know her routines, and I'm sure they have helped others make the transition.

Just now, most of the children are involved in art work related to the theme. Yesterday, a parent, the mother of the seven-year-old who reported on the penguins, brought in two mounted birds from the Otago Museum, a penguin and a shag (what I would have called a cormorant). The children sketched these birds with pastels on large sheets of paper. Now many are completing these drawings. Others are working on different projects using a variety of books about sea birds. I move around the room to see what they are doing, and the children chat with me comfortably. I ask about a drawing showing eggs, young birds, and birds in flight with arrows in a circular pattern.

"This shows the life cycle of a royal albatross. See—first the eggs on the ground, then the baby birds. When they grow up they live way out over the ocean. They come back to nest every two years. I have to put in words now."

"Could you help me edit my letter?" Another child is at my elbow. I look over the letter this girl has written to the Department of Conservation. She is reacting to a report in the newspaper about a tourist guide who ignored warning signs and took tourists down on the beach close to the endangered yellow-eyed penguins. She writes, "I reckon you should have taken away his license because if he gets away with it other people will think they can get away with it too."

Robin is working with a group of children on the rug, explaining another art project: they will use chalk, crayon, and dye to create a sea bird scene having a stained glass effect.

When she organizes a theme, Robin asks the children to choose projects from a list of about fifteen suggestions, including "Your choice. Check with me first." The projects are grouped in three categories: one focusing on reading, one on writing, and a third emphasizing the arts. Children are expected to do something in each category. Other projects include poetry, stories, factual reports, tourist brochures, food webs, maps, drama, and other art work.

Most teachers are now familiar with the concept of "theme" as an approach to teaching the content material we have labeled science and social studies. A second word, "integrated," is also important. With an integrated theme, content—such as sea birds—spills over into the entire school day and becomes integrated into almost everything children do. They learn skills as well as facts. Robin Murray showed me a planning sheet for her sea bird theme in which she outlined specific work in the following areas of curriculum: reading, written language, oral language, presentation/communication, art, social studies, science, health, and math.

When we as adults use information in our lives outside of school, science and social studies overlap. For example, a flood occurs. Human lives are affected as people are evacuated and need food and shelter. The use of the land, the way people have lived along a river, may be related to the causes of the flood. This is the material of social studies, but the causes and effects of flooding also involve science. So does the effect of the flood on plant and animal life in the area.

· ·

Figure 6.1 Drawing is one skill we develop in our study projects.

In the same way, information can be blended in natural ways in a school setting. A study of Mexico can involve climate as well as culture, and the two are intimately related. A theme on animal life might be seen as a science study, but it can include the impact people have on animal habitats and how animals contribute to human life.

Language and math skills are not isolated in real life either, and motivation for using reading and math is usually related to goals. While studying North American mammals, children in my class pored over books and pictures of wild animals; read to find answers to questions we, as a class, had posed; recorded those answers in writing; shared orally information and pictures they had gathered in booklets; and even collected certain statistics about their animals relating to size, weight, population, and the number of young in a litter. Skills are developed as well as applied through their use with interesting content. When we studied prehistoric life, prehistoric animals provided some wonderful opportunities for measurement. It is exciting to see how long a brachiosauras really was or how big a mammoth's footprint would have been.

Some theme projects require other kinds of skills—making an Indian pot, Japanese paper folding (origami), modeling dinosaurs, creating three-dimensional insects out of found material, dramatizing a story, painting a sea life mural.

Important skills, beyond the traditional "three R's," are developed through thematic study: observing, asking questions, searching for answers, thinking critically, organizing material, problem solving, working together, evaluating, developing computer skills, presenting information—orally, pictorially, graphically, in writing, with models.

THEMES IN A MULTIAGE CLASSROOM

Themes are ideally suited to a multiage classroom. When a variety of projects are going on at the same time, there is something for everyone. Children can work alone, with a partner, or in heterogeneous groups based on their interests.

A project usually has two parts: first, the investigation of a topic—research and information gathering; then, consolidation and demonstration through an activity that shares the information with others, both orally and visually. The projects—reports, models, drawings, poetry, charts—will naturally be completed by each child according to individual ability and developmental level.

How do we gear the information to such a range of ages? Children are capable of more than we sometimes give them credit for. Six-year-olds frequently surprise me, so I hold to the idea that when presenting information to the whole class, "shoot high." Don't neglect what the oldest children need.

Materials, such as books and periodicals, should present information in many ways—in pictures as well as print. Books on a variety of reading levels need to be available, along with other resources such as films and filmstrips. I found a computer program on deserts that related to our study of Mexico, and one on whales when we were investigating sea life. One eight-year-old girl developed her own list of endangered species using a word-processing program.

Sometimes working with a partner or in a group will offer support to younger children in gathering information or completing an assignment. Both the helper and the helped learn more through this process: there is no better way to learn about a topic than to teach it.

"oooh, Mrs. B. come see the whales spouting." Anna tugs on my hand. She and Emma have been working their way through a computer presentation on whales, Emma reading and both girls taking turns following the directions.

Emma looks up eagerly as we arrive. "Did you know that each kind of whale has a different spout? Watch the screen." We all exclaim as the tiny whales on the screen spout sporadically. Indeed, each spout is different, and we soon have a whole congregation "ooing" and "aahing" around the computer.

During a food and nutrition study, I brought in a large variety of plant foods, including onions, broccoli, celery, strawberries, and some spices. The children were assigned the task of sorting these items according to the "food" part of the plant—root, stem, leaf, and so forth. The sorting was done by groups on large paper grids, a perfect task to stimulate discussion and take advantage of a range of ages and experience. Later, children were to record the information on small charts in words or pictures.

"WE CAN'T figure out the onion," Stacie tells me as I settle down on the floor beside one group.

"Yeah," agrees Ron. "I think it's a root because it is underground, but she thinks it looks more like a stem."

Cindy adds yet another viewpoint. "You know what it reminds me of . . . sorta? Those bulbs we planted last spring in front of the school."

In the end, this was one we all had to look up, including me (nice for the children to discover that adults don't have all the answers).

For the food and nutrition study, children were assigned to heterogeneous groups, but they can also be encouraged to group informally, especially for projects and activities like word finds and crossword puzzles. The younger children learn puzzle-solving skills as they help and are helped by more experienced classmates.

One year I had some interesting worksheets on the solar system. If these fill-in-the-blanks activities are not your constant repertoire, they can be used and enjoyed along with other activities. The younger children very much wanted to have these worksheets so once again we set up partners, with some children choosing to help a younger classmate and others preferring to work alone.

On the other hand, when the children were studying China, I gave only the eight-year-olds a map on which they were to locate major cities, rivers, surrounding countries, and the Great Wall.

A DEVELOPMENTAL MODEL

A number of years ago a visitor to Room A asked, "Is this the art room?" I was quite mystified at the time, but I guess there was a good deal of children's art on the walls and many concrete projects in process around the room. Art, of course, is one path by which we can discover and impart what we know. In *Art: Another Language for Learning* (1984), Elaine Pear Cohen and Ruth Straus Gainer say: "Art . . . is not a diversion from the business of learning. Studies of children's development indicate that art activities provide direction, clarification, and reinforcement of new concepts. They are sought out with relish and diligence by curious youngsters."

The study of themes, and the projects that grow out of these studies, provides us, as teachers, with another way to make real our beliefs about children and learning. Active learning, with many concrete projects appropriate to young children, is always a major part of thematic work.

In fact, many of the advantages that accrue from Explore Time can be observed during thematic work: the application of skills, a variety of concrete experiences, the social development inherent in teamwork and in learning from one another. There is a buzz of conversation as children gather information and work on projects. Whole class projects, such as murals, large maps, and bulletin boards, may be included, all involving a group planning process.

Other activities offer opportunities to approach learning through varied intelligences. A study of Native Americans may include reading, telling, and writing stories based on Indian legends. It can include work on crafts, such as making pottery, creating costumes, and weaving—spatial and kinesthetic experiences. It can include music and dance, both traditional and invented. Indian games and sports provide another source of bodily-kinesthetic activity. The geometric patterns of Indian designs and dance rhythms bring mathematics into play. Looking at the problems of Native Americans, historically and today, challenges children's understanding of other people's lives and feelings.

Themes and projects also further learning and memory in other ways. In *Making Connections: Teaching and the Human Brain* (1991), Renate and Geoffrey Caine advocate the thematic approach and interdisciplinary learning as "methodologies for brain-based schooling." These approaches, they say, establish and support patterns and connections that are significant because the brain learns through patterns. Learners connect new information with what they already know and with what they experience directly. By providing children with real experiences that are physical, sensory, creative, and practical, we give them "hooks" on which to hang new ideas. Thematic study helps connect knowledge with experience and new ideas with what children already know, in Piaget's terms, "assimilating" and "accommodating" new information.

Themes also take advantage of the intrinsic motivation that makes most young children willing learners. When topics are geared to children's interests and allow an element of choice, children are eager to participate.

TOPIC CHOICE AND CURRICULUM

In *Multiage Portraits* (Rathbone et al. 1993), Molly McClaskey describes a theme study that is initiated when a child brings a cow skull to school. The children measure and weigh the skull. "When this was completed the room was buzzing with conversation about bones and skulls others had at home. Ian's skull launched a larger research study for the whole class." When Molly arrived home that afternoon she started planning for a theme inspired by the children's excitement about the day's events, and before their study was completed, they had investigated topics from joints to archeology.

All themes don't begin with this kind of child input, but it is wise to leave room for such happenings. Topics for thematic study usually come from three sources: one, as in Molly's bone study, is the interests demonstrated by individual children or the class as a whole. Another is teacher-identified curriculum needs or subjects known to be of interest to children generally. A third is the school-mandated curriculum. All of these can be valid, and over a year's time, themes will usually come from a variety of sources. Often the mandated curriculum has been thoughtfully developed for a particular school by a teacher committee, which gives careful consideration to developmental issues, and it will not be so demanding that there is no time to include anything else. On the other hand, if the children's interests were the only source, we might study dinosaurs every year and neglect topics seemingly less vital to them, but which they would find fascinating if presented in lively, developmentally appropriate ways.

While one might think that studies of plants or nutrition, likely to be part of a science curriculum, would be dull for children, this is not necessarily so. Most children love to plant seeds and cuttings, to watch plants grow, to look at sprouting seeds through a microscope, and to experiment with withholding light and water. They also enjoy pressing leaves and using their various shapes in their drawings and designs.

Children in my class have had fun trying their hand at drawing still lifes of fruits and vegetables, sprouting legumes and grains, making musical instruments from these same seeds, and tasting different varieties of apples and cheese. Cooking, of course, is always a popular activity. The point is that this subject matter can be made concrete, lively, and interesting.

One question teachers moving into multiage teaching often raise is how to use mandated science and social studies curricula that are tied to grade level. What do we do with a curriculum designating that first graders will study animals and magnets, second graders, plants and weather, and third graders, rocks and electricity? Working with separate topics for different ages would defeat the purpose of multiage organization.

One solution is to develop curriculum cycles that repeat every second or third year. Here is one my team developed for a first- through third-grade grouping:

Year One: Animals native to Vermont
                Prehistoric life
                The human body
                Shelburne, Vermont, USA
                Colonial life, life in early Vermont

Year Two: Insects
                Plants
                Food and nutrition
                North American neighbors
                Native Americans

Year Three: Ocean life
                The solar system, space
                Ecology, conservation
                Other regions of the world
                Peace and friendship

In addition, some other subjects, notably physical science topics such as light, sound, and electricity, are deliberately integrated into Explore Time. Every winter, for example, I pull out batteries, bulbs, and small electric motors. Usually several discussions focus on these objects.

We have found this to be a demanding curriculum cycle, however, and it hasn't left much room for other themes that develop more spontaneously. When a Japanese visitor was available to come to our school for three weeks and share aspects of Japanese culture with our children, we dropped another topic from the year's cycle in order to take advantage of this valuable resource.

Our curriculum cycle seems always to be in the process of review and adaptation, since there are more possible topics than time allows. Perhaps we will reduce the number of planned themes per year. Teaching the skills of learning—of knowing how to search for information and discover knowledge on your own—is our most important goal. "Learning how to learn" is what we desire for the children.

How many themes should you plan for the year and how long should they be? Certainly there is no set rule. The length of time the children spend on each theme will affect how many themes will fit into a school year. It is satisfying to have several themes each year that represent work in depth and take six to eight weeks. Planning for four or five themes over a year is probably workable, allowing some flexibility in length and some opportunity to pursue a few other subjects more briefly.

SCHEDULING THEMES

A regularly scheduled time every day may be set aside for theme work, or you may integrate this work into existing time blocks. I have done both. When thirty or forty minutes are scheduled for science/social studies, this period can be used for introducing information, for research, for discussion and sharing, and for working on theme-related projects. I have called this "theme time." As the theme progresses and children's enthusiasm mounts, the work may spill over into other parts of the day: research into reading-writing time, information sharing into discussion, graphing or measuring into math, and related stories into read-aloud time.

An alternative to a regular "theme time" is to use blocks of time that have been scheduled for more than one purpose: the language block, which can sometimes be used entirely for reading, writing, and literature, and at other times direct those same skills toward a theme; discussion, which can sometimes be used for presenting, talking about, and sharing thematic information. As we saw in Stacie's day, I have often set aside most of the afternoon for such a multipurpose period. The only way we can possibly fit everything into a school day, week, or year is to accomplish several goals at once.

SPECIAL THEMES

IT WAS snack time. I passed out small baskets borrowed from students and friends. Inside each, wrapped in a napkin, was a piece of corn bread, some dried apple slices, and a small bit of maple sugar. Earlier we had read from hornbooks and made our own quill pens and copybooks. We were playing out an "old-fashioned school." The children in the room, six- through eight-year-olds, were not members of my usual class. They were children from all over the school who had signed up for my workshop on early schools.

During the year of our state's bicentennial, the school celebrated with a schoolwide theme—a three-week study of life in early Vermont. My school workshop was one of many, including, among others, basket making, stenciling, candle making, maple sugaring, toy making, and music and dance. Classroom teachers were responsible for developing background information for their own class. Then all school staff and a few volunteers offered a variety of workshops. Children signed up for their first, second, and third choices before a master schedule was developed. Two sessions for the first workshop were scheduled one week, two sessions for the second the next week, all at the same time, resulting in a grand game of "musical classrooms." During the final week, displays were set up in the halls and the public invited to visit the school. A storyteller and folk singers presented programs for all students.

Other schools have experimented with schoolwide themes and found them, as we did, ideal experiences for drawing the entire school together. They can also provide a good public relations vehicle, which is a nice spin-off. The public may be invited to visit the school to view student-prepared exhibits or some type of presentation. Newspaper publicity and newsletters to parents can emphasize not only the projects and exhibits but the learning they demonstrate. The public can thus be educated about developmentally appropriate education for young children. Such overall themes are a great deal of work for all the staff, and require hours of planning and scheduling. For this reason, many schools find once a year too often for schoolwide themes.

Another year we developed a simpler plan for an all-school theme on the environment. Our team's study of endangered species was part of that theme. This time, there were no schoolwide workshops. Children stayed within their own teams. However, an environmental play was brought in for the entire school to enjoy. Again the halls were filled with exhibits. Each team presented a different topic—forests, oceans, endangered species, birds—and the public was invited to tour the school.

Another kind of study that is popular with some teachers is a year-long theme. This provides the opportunity for the class to work in depth, to explore several related topics, and to work without time limits on research and projects. Year-long themes offer more possibilities if the topics are holistic and inclusive.

An example I found interesting one year was the theme of "change." I started the year by having the children look at how their own lives had changed by bringing in baby pictures and creating personal time lines. They made graphs comparing their length at birth and their present height. A new baby came to the classroom for a visit.

Then we explored how the lives of children in general had changed over a longer time period. Students interviewed their parents and wrote letters to older relatives, such as grandparents or great grandparents:

DEAR Grandma and Grandpa,

Can you tell me what life was like for you when you were my age? In school we are studying about changes in the lives of children. We have interviewed our parents to find out about life when they were our age. Here are some things we wonder about:

What was your favorite toy?
What kinds of games did you play with your friends?

	favorite toys	favorite games	favorite stories	favorite foods	other
me _____					
parents					
grand-parents					
great grand-parents					

Figure 6.2 A chart to compare the kids' interests with those of their parents and grandparents.

What were cars like?
Did you have TV?
What did candy cost?
How was your life at home different from ours?
How was your life at school different?

Please write a letter back about some of these things. Thank you for helping us. Our teacher is a grandmother, so maybe we will interview her too.
Love,
Alex

Responses to these letters were overwhelming. As letters came in from these older relatives, we read them aloud, continuing for more than a month. The letters were family treasures and I'm sure most families saved them carefully. They told stories about early automobiles, iceboxes, five-cent ice cream bars, toys, favorite games, and fathers going off to war during World War II. We made a chart that compared child life today with that of parents and grand-parents (see Figure 6.2).

Later in the year we pushed further back in time and looked at life in Early America. We talked about how towns had changed. We made another time line.

The theme of "change" also lent itself to a study of seasonal change and plant growth during the spring. Had there been time, prehistory and the development of life on earth would have fit in beautifully. Choosing something wide in scope, a universal thread that ties together related material, is the best way to succeed with a year-long theme.

PREPARATION AND PLANNING

Themes may be scheduled and planned by teams or by individual teachers. If teachers plan themes together, they can divide various aspects of the theme and supervision of different projects among team members.

When my multiage team first set up our curriculum cycle, we had no plans to work on these themes at the same time. Later we tried planning one or two themes together annually, all four class groups sharing special events. One year we planned every theme together, but this required so much team planning time that we returned to sharing only some themes.

Working together on themes is great fun. We will never let our teammate, Jane Perry, forget the year she proposed that each class make a six-foot-high totem pole. The work continued for weeks. It seemed unending, but the children were proud of the results, and we had totem poles representing Rooms A, B, C, and D for more than a year. I drove the team crazy one year by planning a series of "prehistoric snacks," including everything from a "paleozoic pasta salad" to fossil bones made from a peanut-butter-honey-powdered-milk dough. This at least provided great hilarity at team meetings. If you are not working as part of a team, you may find it fun to plan a theme with another class from time to time.

Teacher Planning
When preparing for a theme study don't feel that you have to have every detail in place from the beginning. Planning with the children is a part of each theme: this is one way they learn the skills of organizing, questioning, and researching. Often, too, they have wonderful questions that can help direct the study and they suggest good ideas for projects. The process of developing a theme together stimulates their creativity and excitement. This experience of ownership in the process is so important to the students

that, while I plan thoroughly, I also try to remain flexible and open to change, a challenging balance. What follows are my suggestions for teacher preplanning.

1. Start by brainstorming on paper. What do you know about the topic? What do you need to know? List questions. You will think of more questions as you go along, even if you have used the theme before. Jot down your initial ideas for activities, projects, special events. You will need to keep brainstorming as you go through the next steps.

2. Gather materials. If you are lucky your school librarian or resource center person will help. Gather stacks of books, pictures, models, maps, films and videos. These are for you to look at first. It is not yet time to put them out in the classroom.

If you live in a community where museum kits are available, plan ahead to reserve these valuable resources. They often offer the opportunity to handle and view historical artifacts or those from another culture. Our school library has developed a few kits of its own, such as a box of materials used in an early American school: a quill pen, slate, reader, copybook, and hornbook.

Don't forget community resources. Is there someone who could be invited to talk to or be interviewed by the children? Consider field trips at this time too, if not much sooner. We often have to schedule popular trips months in advance, locking in at least this part of the theme schedule.

3. From the materials you have gathered, choose a few to read and study yourself. These might be children's nonfiction books or teacher resources. You don't have to learn it all, because you will also learn along with the children. What you need now is enough background to evaluate the questions you have raised already and to set some goals.

4. List a few basic concepts and attitudes that you want the children to gain from the study. These are your goals. The children may later develop some of their own.

For an environmental theme called "Earth Our Garden," one of my conceptual goals was for students to develop an understanding of the interdependence of life on earth, and our ultimate dependence on earth, soil, and plants. An attitudinal goal was to have children demonstrate concern about the use of the earth's resources and interest in what they could do to conserve them, such as recycling.

5. List sources of information to use with the whole class. You will have many materials that individual children can pore over or work with, but earmark some resources for use with the entire group (these could be stories, pictures, and audiovisual materials).

6. List possible individual and group projects through which the children might show, in concrete ways, that they have acquired the knowledge and attitudes you have defined as goals.

Here is a partial list of project types: charts in which information is gathered and recorded, graphs, maps, written material in which new information is presented or incorporated (reports, stories, poetry), murals, sketchbooks, paintings, posters, three-dimensional models of all kinds. Such models may be animals, plants, foods, toys, and objects from another culture or historical period. They may make use of cardboard, paper, clay, drinking straws, paper plates, yarn, fabric. Other possibilities are drama and puppet shows by a small group or as a class project. Elementary teachers know that this kind of list is endless.

In planning projects, other goals can come together with those of developing concepts and attitudes. You may wish children to learn how to use a certain art medium: papier-mâché, clay, watercolors. You may wish to emphasize a process needed to develop quality work. One example would be having children sketch plans for a poster or their contribution to a mural in advance, working from objects or pictures they examine carefully. This is like a "first draft" and helps ensure that the finished poster or mural is one in which they can take pride. At the same time, they learn and practice a process for doing quality work.

7. Think about a culminating activity that will be a vital group experience and give a feeling of closure and accomplishment. A trip is often a fine culmination. Alternatively, a field trip can serve as a kickoff for a theme or as a means of gathering information. A play or presentation to another group might be your culminating activity. Individual projects can also be combined into a bulletin board, display, or class booklet. One year we served international snacks after a study of other countries.

Planning with Children

OCEAN. I write the word in the center of a large piece of newsprint. "What do we already know about the ocean?"

"It's salt water."

"Deep."

"Whales live in the ocean. Some might be almost extinct." Wendy, Cindy, and Ron start us off with a few facts about oceans.

"Sharks" . . . "Octopus" . . . "Squids" . . . "Electric eels." Kent, Jason, Mike, and Jerry kick off a long list of ocean creatures about which we know something and want to know more.

"Sometimes it gets polluted," Patty reminds us.

"We eat fish from the ocean," Wendy chimes in.

"I saw on TV about an ocean sailing race." Someone is bound to get to boats eventually. Living on a big lake as we do in Shelburne, several families have boats. Alex's family has a sailboat.

I write as fast as I can, filling the paper with ocean-related words and ideas.

Sometimes, if our brainstorming seems to yield a good deal of prior information, I transfer these words to three-by-five-inch cards, and we spend another discussion time grouping them. "Ocean animals," "How people use the ocean," "Facts about the ocean," "Boats," could all be categories arising from the above discussion. This helps us organize the topic and together we discover the parts involved within the whole. Already we begin to notice patterns—patterns that will help us learn and remember. This process also helps the group generate questions we might want to answer as we proceed through the study. This kind of discussion can provide a model for a lifelong process of searching out knowledge about all sorts of things.

If the children are doing individual research, make some decisions together about what basic information is needed. For a study of North American mammals, I put together small booklets: My Research Booklet about _____ (name of mammal). In it were pages for information about animal homes and habitat, food, enemies, defense, tracks, "other interesting information," and drawings of the animal and its habitat. The emphasis on habitat was my contribution. All other ideas came from questions the children had.

> What is its habitat? (circle)
>
>   forest   wetland
>   field   lake
>   pond   other
>   river
>
> What kind of home does it have?
>
> Who are its enemies?
>
> How does it defend itself?
>
> What does your animal look like? (drawing)
>
> What does it eat?
>
> How does it get food?
>
> Tracks: (drawing)
>
> Other interesting information:
>
> Picture of home and habitat:

Once a theme is under way, children will bring related things to class—shells from the sea, artifacts from another culture, books—each of which can be examined and appreciated. Bringing things to class is a function of their involvement with the theme. They are making it their own. This process of developing a theme together, watching the inherent connections grow through our mutual planning and questioning, is fundamental to learning how to learn. And gathering information through theme studies and expressing what we learn through projects jointly developed by teacher and students is so much more interesting for us all than working from a single textbook or a prepackaged study. I'm convinced also that the fun, the stimulation, and the excitement enhance the learning.

■

CHAPTER SEVEN

CLASSROOM TALK:
LANGUAGE AND LEARNING

"I THINK her mom and dad died, but she has this doll they made for her."

"And her grandma and grandpa."

"What about her grandma and grandpa?"

"They died, too."

We are trying to decide why the little girl in Tomie de Paola's book *The Legend of the Bluebonnet* is called "She-Who-Is-Alone." Ron finds the page that explains. He reads, "It seemed long ago that they had died from the famine."

"What's famine?"

Gathered with me on one corner of the rug in Room A are four six- and seven-year-olds. Around us children work alone or in partners, at tables or sprawled on the floor. There is some partner reading going on, some writing, and two children are having a writing conference at the other end of the rug. The room is not silent. Our small group book conference is just one of many kinds of classroom talk. A multiage classroom is most often buzzing with conversation. We encourage collaboration, and different ages are learning together. What are some other forms this conversation takes, and why is it important?

Classroom talk takes a variety of forms, among them small group formats, whole class meetings, informal chat. Small groups can be organized by the teacher—as in the book discussion above or when I ask Stacie and Ron to teach Betsy a math game. They can be formed by students themselves—to create a block volcano during Explore Time or to work together on a project. They can be informal or have an assigned task, such as measuring the classroom. Some groups—book discussions, math instruction, a phonics workshop—may be led by the teacher, or the students may take charge themselves, as in the case of cooperative groups. There may be groups of two, partners with a special focus, such as a math task or a writing conference. In multiage classes such small groups are based on interest or need and cut across age barriers.

The whole class meeting, in contrast, provides time together for the entire classroom community, as well as guided discussions on a particular topic and other instructional activities. Talk is a vital part of building community. Each of us has a story to tell. Our stories—arising from our thoughts, beliefs, and experiences—represent who we are. Children, too, present and define themselves by telling their stories.

When Betsy tells about her family's trip to Nashville, Tennessee, to visit the Grand Old Opry, she defines a life experience different from that of Patty, who has returned from a camping trip in the Adirondacks.

"MY AUNT'S barn burned last night," announced Wendy one morning, just as we were beginning to settle on the rug.

"Oh no!" gasped Emma. "What happened to the sheep?"

"They got them out"

"We were just there," Emma tells the group. "We had a Brownie meeting at Wendy's house last week. Her aunt is right next door, and we went to look at the sheep. I'm glad they're safe!"

"I have something from the fire." Wendy pulls an asymmetrical blob of metal from behind her back. "My dad and I found it this morning. The fire was so hot these nails just melted together."

There is a general gasp and several children crawl forward to have a closer look. Wendy offers to pass her souvenir of the fire around the circle.

Like adults, children come to know each other through listening to such stories. Not knowing the others in the class can isolate some students and encourage cliques. Knowing each other better can result in trust, understanding, and collaboration.

One year, I noticed that the class sharing and discussions seemed harder to get started. Children's participation was more limited than usual, and a few children dominated the talk. Reflecting on the situation, I realized that a larger-than-usual number of new students had joined our multiage program. An expansion of the program, then an option in our school, had required the addition of another multiage classroom. Several children who would have been seven- and eight-year-olds in my class had been assigned to the new room to help the "new" teacher, actually an old friend from a first-grade classroom down the hall. This meant that I had several seven- and eight-year-olds who were new to the multiage experience. Ordinarily, the older children arrived in September knowing each other well from previous years, and only the younger ones would need help in becoming a part of the group. In this case several older children also had few friends in the class, and our routines, along with my expectations, were unfamiliar to them. As a result, they held back and did not participate, an unexpected confirmation of why we prefer the continuity of several years with one teacher.

During the year I have been working on this book, I have become part of several new groups. No longer in the classroom daily, I missed seeing my best friends, my former colleagues. So, in need of new social connections, I joined a women's group and agreed to serve on the board of our local parent-child center. Since I knew few people in either group, one of the first things I found myself doing was finding opportunities to talk to people, to get to know them better. Through talk I discovered common strands of interest and experience and made new friends. As a result, I felt more comfortable in each group, and ready to contribute and participate fully. Because children have less social experience than adults, the teacher needs to orchestrate these same kinds of interaction and sharing within the classroom. In this way, children find commonalties of interest and experience and become full members of the community. All this is made possible and encouraged by talk.

Informal chat is another form of classroom talk. It occurs around the edges of the school day as children arrive, during lunch and recess, and also during Explore Time and while working on projects. Once banned as inappropriate in school, informal chat now has a valued place in developmentally appropriate classrooms. It, too, contributes to the process of defining self and knowing others. The children in my class come from widely separate neighborhoods, so school represents a place for forming and maintaining friendships.

This informal chat includes the teacher as well. I have an opportunity to get to know the children individually while we have one-on-one conversations.

"I think Mike won't let me play because of my new glasses." Kent might never have been able to express this fear to me if he was expected to come into the room and sit quietly. Since our relationship is informal and personal, he is able to give me a hint of an issue I need to deal with, not only one-to-one but in conversation with the whole class.

When Stacie comes in from the bus, she not only tells me about the fox she and her dad saw but talks about the newcomer at her house. Her mother has just remarried and "Kevin" is trying hard to fit in, making an effort to play games with Stacie and her sister. She expresses tentativeness about the new relationship, which gives me a window on the stresses in her life just now.

At the beginning of their wonderfully clear book, *When Students Have Time to Talk* (1991), Curt Dudley-Marling and Dennis Searle answer the question, "Why is it important for students to have opportunities to talk?"

- Children need to try out their language, listen to the responses of others, both adults and children, and hear how others talk. This enables them to get the information about language they need in order to develop and grow.
- If they feel safe, they can stretch their language resources as they struggle to make sense of their world and to communicate and clarify their understanding with others.
- They can talk about their personal experiences and use their own background knowledge and experience to make connections with new knowledge, revising when necessary. Students' talk is a "major means by which learners explore the relationships between what they already know, and new observations or interpretations they meet."
- Teachers can listen to children to understand their language development and their thinking. When they discover a need for new experiences, they can plan activities to help children make connections between what they know and what is new to them.
- The children and the teacher come to know one another better as unique individuals. "In such an environment classrooms become places for people."

We have already looked at the role of talk in community building. The other benefits listed above refer to two further functions talk serves in the classroom: the first is that of learning language itself and its varied functions; the second is the immeasurable contribution talk makes to other kinds of learning.

LEARNING LANGUAGE

The image of silent children in our classrooms does not fit with what we know about language development. In the past we seem to have assumed that oral language learning is fully accomplished when children enter school and can be set aside while they work with written language. But improving our use of oral language, increasing vocabulary, and fine-tuning our language to a variety of functions and situations is a lifelong task. We not only learn new vocabulary and forms of syntax, but we must also learn to adapt these things to the audience and the situation in which we find ourselves. Children need to practice language in a variety of natural situations and with varying audiences. In a multiage class, developmental diversity provides an audience with an ideal mix of experience and language development. A child's encounter with language becomes very limited if only teacher-child interaction is allowed in school.

JASON has just read a story he wrote to the class. It's about the future, not the usual spaceship story, but reflections on life in the future.

"How'd you know to write about that?" asked Stacie.

"The idea just popped into my head . . . Well, actually a *3-2-1 Contact* issue came and got me thinking about the future. I decided I would take a few articles about the future and think about the future, and then I wrote about it."

"You know, they've already invented a skateboard based on magnetism. It just kind of floats over the ground." Jerry supports Jason's speculation about new forms of transportation in his story.

These three older children have just provided a model of a fairly sophisticated conversation, one that is quite focused. Jason especially serves as an unusually mature model of thinking and planning and of using language. Such modeling is a daily part of life in a multiage classroom.

Throughout the day a variety of circumstances that encourage talk present themselves. Talk in the block area differs from that involved in solving a math problem or planning a mural, just as collaboration in a research lab differs from a corporate presentation or conversation at a social gathering after work. As adults, we use talk in a variety of ways and develop a sense of the language appropriate for those different situations. Schools need to provide children with opportunities to learn these skills.

Because large groups offer fewer opportunities for each child to speak, small groups are a very important part of planning for oral language development.

"WHAT shall we put in the nursery?" I ask a group preparing a scene for our *Mary Poppins* play.

"Toys . . . a b-ball, trucks, s-s-stuffed animals," suggests Chuck.

Kent tells us, "I wanna paint a fish bowl . . . here on this wall."

Cindy contributes her idea, "Let's put a window in the middle."

Everyone has a say because everyone will paint something into the scene, including Chuck, who is somewhat less likely to speak in the whole class group.

Sometimes even more unique experiences can be provided. One year a group of Japanese college students visited our school. They were attending an English language program at a nearby college, and a parent involved with that program helped make the arrangements. Each visitor was greeted by two or three children and spent about an hour chatting and working on origami with them. Then we shared songs. The children were challenged to make themselves clear in new ways and, as "native speakers," they were the experts.

Dudley-Marling and Searle, however, emphasize that contrived tasks are not necessary. There are natural opportunities in the school day for a wide variety of language functions: "Reading, writing, math, science and social studies all have the potential to excite children's interest and stretch their linguistic abilities. But the potential of school learning to do this depends on how well it fulfills students' need and satisfies their natural curiosity."

Students talk more when they have some control of their own learning and when the topic or project genuinely interests them. In addition, in such circumstances their language becomes more varied and complex. In this regard, the authors quote the educator Courtney Cazden: "the greater the degree of affect or personal involvement in the topic of conversation, the greater the likelihood of structural complexity."

EMMA tells a visitor about her travel brochure, a project she has chosen for our USA theme:

"It's on Arizona. I chose it because I liked the desert pictures in this book. It's really different from Vermont. See the cactus on the cover? Saguaro! They're as big as trees. I'd sure like to see them sometime." She opens the brochure to show the visitor a page of Indian designs and a mountain picture. "There are mountains in Arizona, too. Now I'm trying to copy this picture of the Grand Canyon."

Open-ended tasks and questions will generate more talk and more varied language. A question with one right answer obviously limits the students' opportunity for exploration. Because Emma could choose the state she wanted to research and the project she wanted to do she feels a sense of ownership of her work. She is eager to talk about something in which she has been so personally involved.

If children are to talk about their work, they also need attentive listeners. The teacher who shows a personal interest in the speaker provides a model for other listeners. This attending to others can be encouraged in other ways. I talk to children, for example, about the need to see the speaker and attend visually. Group discussion should be set up so that children can see each other's faces, and this is why we most often sit in a circle. Ideas such as "active listening" and "wait time" are important but do not replace a genuine response to the speaker.

When the teacher identifies a student with actual deficiencies in language, what then? The above points continue to be very important, especially using language within the context of something vital and interesting to the individual child. Like the other children, these students need plenty of opportunities to try out new words and language structures, even those they may only partially understand. Whether or not to reword the child's language as you talk must be decided with special sensitivity, since the child can easily interpret this as criticism or correction.

Some activities encourage specific kinds of vocabulary. Science experiments lead to discussions of cause and effect. Storytelling may emphasize sequence and repeated language patterns. Block construction, on the other hand, encourages the use of words describing position and shape. Children in my class enjoy a castle-building game in which two partners begin with identical sets of blocks, both sets varying the same way in shape, size, and color. With a screen between them (we use a game board set on end), one child begins to build, describing each step. The other tries to follow instructions and finish with an identical structure. Both carry equal responsibility for giving clear instructions, listening carefully, and asking and answering questions when needed.

The child with special language needs should also be referred to a language pathologist. This specialist can formally evaluate and remediate or make recommendations.

THE ROLE OF TALK IN OTHER LEARNING

Beyond learning to use language effectively in communicating with others, language also has a distinct role in developing our thinking and our ability to reason. To understand this, it is worth revisiting Piaget and Vygotsky.

Learning is more complex than simply adding new pieces of information to stores we already have. Such pieces will not be accessible to us, nor will they be of use, until they fit in with what we already know and use. Modern brain research suggests that we remember through networks of information, by making connections. Piaget labeled our efforts to fit new events and knowledge into previous experience "assimilation." Its twin, the other necessary part of the process, he called "accommodation." In "accommodation" we modify what we already "know" in the light of new information and thus change how we interpret the world.

During a discussion of endangered species a difference of opinion emerged concerning wolves.

"THEY'RE cute."

"They live in families and take care of their pups. They should be protected and not let get extinct."

"I saw on TV a wolf pack chasing deer. They killed one and ate it."

"I saw that too. It was gross!"

In gathering information on the topic we heard Polly and Emma tell us what they had learned from a computer program on wolves. Then we brainstormed a bit about wolves in stories and movies, and on TV. A wide range of different images of wolves emerged, along with reasons for our differing opinions. We also encountered new information to integrate with what we already knew or believed about wolves. Some of the new information did not fit with the traditional image of the "big bad wolf."

Teachers can create opportunities for children to talk about their previous experience, about what they already "know," and thus encourage "assimilation and accommodation." In Chapter 6, I suggested that children brainstorm about what they know and what they would like to find out when they begin a new theme study. Prior knowledge also contributes to reading comprehension and it is useful for children to look over a story or an article and discuss what they already know before they begin to read. On this basis they predict what might unfold in the story or nonfiction book. When they finish reading, they can discuss their predictions and how they worked out in actuality, not so much to find an "error" as to think about the decisions the author made in writing the story or to accommodate new information. Talk provides a way to build a bridge between what we know and what is new to us.

Talk also can lead the way to more complex thinking. As children experience the process of interacting with others to clarify meaning, and as they are exposed to the thinking of others, they encounter a variety of new thought patterns. Dialogue becomes a model for thinking.

Vygotsky regarded thought as the internalization of dialogue. Developmentally early speech is social, but, he noticed, later children begin to talk to themselves during play to plan, recall, reexperience, and reinterpret events. Eventually such talk becomes internalized and is used in our own thinking and imagining. This, according to Vygotsky, becomes the "inner speech" of adults.

Talk, then, is both a means through which we communicate and acquire information in a social context, and a way to make meaning for ourselves as we internalize new knowledge. Talk—oral language—then, cannot be shunted to the fringes of the language arts in school.

The buzz of conversation, however, may be alien to our own school experience as children. Few teachers have actually been trained in handling the lively interaction of children learning together out loud. I have never gotten over the need to look over my shoulder from time to time when the noise and activity level seems high. Usually a look around the room assures me that most of what I see is appropriate and "on task," but some talk may also be irrelevant to the task at hand. This is a challenge, but to stop all conversation would be to overlook how necessary it is for children to talk as they grow in language and learning.

Peggy Dorta tells about hurrying toward the water table in her room when the group working there seemed unusually loud. She stopped herself a few feet away instead of plunging in to quiet them. "I'm so glad I did," she says. "There was all sorts of measuring going on. They were exchanging ideas. The learning level was great."

PUBLIC TALK

Many aspects of oral language play a part in multiage classrooms. Conversing, collaborating, responding, and listening are all a vital part of learning situations in the classroom. Talk also has some special public uses. Making class presentations and putting on plays are an important part of the education of young children.

When we studied prehistoric life, the children became "paleontologists." After doing their research, they were interviewed in our class circle by their classmates. The class developed a set of relevant questions that were included in the interviews. The questions related to the prehistoric animal about which each child had chosen to become an expert. I gave our experts a hard hat and a rock hammer as marks of their profession and videotaped the interviews.

The children enjoyed seeing themselves on television later, but such recordings can also serve to chronicle and assess progress in presenting work orally and learning within a theme. Here, children not only reported the specific information they had discovered in their research, but also conveyed their general understanding of prehistory and paleontology.

Drama is a special kind of presentation that children enjoy immensely. I often start with pantomime, which doesn't involve any speech at all, and then go on to improvised skits that include speaking. The pantomimes are simple circle games at first and then evolve to children acting out something the rest of us have to guess. We have organized sessions around topics such as seasons, weather, and machines: children demonstrate seasonal sports or become a blender, toaster, or lawn mower. It's great fun.

Improvisation is a way to introduce speech into skits. One year, after reading *Winnie the Pooh,* we discussed the animal personalities involved in the stories. Then I divided the children into small groups to create new scenes they felt were in character with these personalities. Some of these scenes became part of a play we produced called *The New Pooh.*

Drama can be anything from a simple puppet show developed by a few children during Explore Time to a full-blown production with invited guests (parents or another class).

I learned how to pull together a full-fledged play by watching my across-the-hall colleague and good friend, Marilyn Johnson. Every spring her class presented an annual traditional tale for parents, complete with scenery and costumes. The play provided an exciting experience of working together and a great end-of-the-year celebration. With her help, I finally got the courage to try.

One year my colleague Liz Farman and I produced *Peter Pan*. The large cast of Pirates, Indians, and Lost Children could easily involve two classes. Liz contributed her musical talent so we could include singing, and she even choreographed an Indian dance and one for Peter Pan and his shadow. I took charge of the scenery. (Drama is a wonderful opportunity to integrate the diverse skills and talents of teachers as well as children.)

Another play we presented with great success was *Mary Poppins*. During that production a troubled boy whose father had lost his job was transformed into a lively Burt, with a borrowed golf cap set at a jaunty angle on his head. Another child became Mr. Wigg, filled with "laughing gas" and pillows. A row of Victorian houses on brown paper graced the background. Toys and goldfish filled a nursery as we sang "A Spoonful of Sugar." Finally Mary Poppins "floated" out of the room under her umbrella while everyone sang "Let's Go Fly a Kite." The parents beamed.

When the play is over, excited children always ask, "What will we do next year?" Giving a play is a thrilling year's culmination. Giving a play is also one very specialized part of the entire picture of classroom talk. Through classroom talk we help children develop the tools for communicating and thinking that are important for functioning in society. Teachers must not silence voices in the classroom. Instead, we can learn to pay attention to the different kinds of talk that occur, support them, and use them to nourish other learning.

CHAPTER EIGHT

■

ACQUIRING THE TOOLS OF OUR CULTURE: A MULTIAGE PERSPECTIVE

T H E developmental task of young school-age children, according to the psychologist Erik Erikson, is to acquire the tools of their culture. This happens in many ways, in school and out.

PATTY pushes the zero end of the yardstick against the wall and lays it on the counter. "Keep it straight, right along the edge," Jason reminds her. "Now, Anna, you put your finger right here."

Six groups of children are scattered around the room, each with a yardstick, pencil, and clipboard. They are gathering information to create a scale map of the room.

One group has finished their measuring. Jerry is cutting pieces out of one-inch graph paper to represent the tables in Room A, one inch for each foot measured. "Ask Mrs. B. what color we decided to make the tables," he tells Chuck.

The groups are heterogeneous. Each child has a job: one is to oversee and approve all the measurements, and one to be sure that everyone has a turn. The third is in charge of equipment.

THE CLASSROOM is unusually quiet. Children are writing. I am writing, briefly at least. Over in one corner, Wendy and Emma are curled up comfortably on a rug. Wendy has been writing a dragon fantasy inspired by our read-aloud book, *Dragonling*. She reads her unfinished draft to Emma. "I can't figure out how to bring this kid back in time. Listen." Together they consider various possible turns the story might take.

In another corner Alex has just read his story to Kent. "I don't understand how the rocket ship took off. First you were outside the ship and couldn't get the door open. Then it was flying. How did you get inside?" Kent may not be reading or writing very much yet himself, but he has learned to frame questions that help Alex make his writing clear.

All around the room, other writers are at work. Cindy, putting finishing touches on her picture of a strip of sand and a wavy line of blue water, adds a tree under the smiling sun. She has written: "This is a See AND the SAND AND the SUN AND THIS IS THe HOWl WYD WhirlD."

Mac is drawing a man with an ax. His story: "this is mi dad cuteen dawn wood and me and mi sisturs haft to breeg tht wood ovur to piyuls and tha r hyuwj payuls of wood and i fawnd a pees of wood that lucs lice a gun."

Children five to eight years old are writing together, reading their work to one another, and helping each other make the writing clear for readers or listeners. They are learning, too, how to form letters, the rules for capitals and periods, and conventional spelling.

These classroom snapshots indicate some of the cultural tools children need to acquire. Primary among these are the language and math skills that have always been a major responsibility of elementary education: reading with enjoyment and critical understanding, writing accurately and understandably, and using numbers to count, compute, and solve problems.

Teachers in the elementary grades have always played an important role in guiding children in the acquisition of these tools. This has not changed, despite our advancing knowledge about child development, the movement toward more active, concrete learning, and the emphasis on the importance of social and emotional growth. Instead, these things have served to broaden our understanding of what is necessary for learning. Although new assignments—drug and alcohol education and computer literacy—have been added, teachers still have primary responsibility for guiding children in the acquisition of literacy, and it is a responsibility we take seriously.

Because a multiage classroom is a child-centered classroom, math and language arts are integrated with other activities: children make labels for their construction work and models. They measure their block towers. They use reading and writing to carry out research on space or oceans. While they learn and practice these skills in integrated work during Explore Time and in theme studies, they also learn them apart from these settings. I think this is equally important, especially in the early school years when children are just beginning to acquire these skills.

In addition to nonfiction writing on a theme, children should be allowed to write on topics of their own choice, to try their hand at different genres such as fiction and poetry, and to write about their own experiences, in their journals. They need to enjoy and respond to a variety of literature and to learn number and computation concepts.

In my own teaching I am always struggling to find a balance between direct instruction and the learning that comes from applying skills to the study of a particular topic—dinosaurs, ocean life, or another culture. My own solution is to concentrate on literature and writing for a time and then, in the midst of a theme, to encourage children to learn through applying those skills. And I am always more comfortable with a separate math time.

We will focus on language and math in the next two chapters. Those chapters will introduce pictures of some other classrooms as seen by the teachers in those classrooms, demonstrating a variety of options from which multiage teachers choose when building a program that best fits their situation. In this chapter we will look at general ways of adapting language and math teaching in multiage situations.

MAKING IT WORK: DIFFERENT AGES LEARNING TOGETHER

During the nineteenth century, before grade-level groupings were introduced into American schools, children of many ages learned together. In small rural schools teachers continued, for many more years, to coordinate the learning experiences of young children of different ages. Often the older children helped the younger ones. In 1936 Julia Weber Gordon wrote about such a school in *My Country School Diary* (1946): "Here I shall have an opportunity to live closely with a group of children and to learn to know them intimately. I shall have them long enough to watch them grow and develop their capacities . . . in as rich an environment as it is possible to make for them." How do teachers in modern multiage classes guide children in learning the traditional three R's?

It is in this arena that adaptations must be made. Although all teachers face a wide range of abilities, in multiage classes the stretch is even greater, with two grade levels or three. Yet multiage classes also have some real advantages. The modeling and interaction of diverse ages provides a supportive framework for learners. Working closely with a child who is beginning to read, a young nonreader shares a reading experience. The older child, just a step up the literacy ladder, provides an achievable model. The same is true for other skills. The models are there and they are using those skills in interesting and relevant contexts.

Individualized Learning
One of the most obvious results of having a wider diversity of ages in a classroom is the absolute need to individualize teaching where skills are concerned.

What is good practice in other classes is essential here. How does this affect how the day looks? One answer is that many, if not most, children can be doing something different from one another during a language arts or math time. In math, they could be working on activities ranging from counting games to building models for four-digit numbers to adding the prices of a list of toys from a catalog. During language arts children might simultaneously be reading different books, writing about a topic of their own choice, or practicing spelling and handwriting.

Even when the whole group works together, responses and follow-up vary from one child to another, depending on age and development. A discussion about counting money and making change might be followed by having older children write word problems using that same toy catalog, another group play a money board game, such as "Amusement Park," and still others play a trading game with pennies and dimes. From time to time small groups might meet in one corner or another, and some children might be working as partners, but in the background the individual tasks go on. Clearly, a multiage teacher needs to be able to tolerate all this diverse activity. It is possible to manage this kind of classroom if you trust that learners can progress without your constant presence.

Knowing the Children

Of course, individualizing work requires knowing the children well. In a multiage classroom one-third to one-half of the children are returning for a second year. In the fall I already know that Mike's parents now live separately and that there is a new baby in Anna's family. Jason's passion for baseball and Patty's skills with a pencil have been a part of my life for a year. I also know that Patty needs extra attention with reading, an area where she is easily discouraged. Knowing these children already gives me a head start in September.

In addition to welcoming these children back, I must get to know new class members, and so must the other children. I often start class meetings with a kind of group-interest inventory. I make a large class chart with the following sentences, or something similar, which each child completes during discussion the first week: "This summer I . . ." (swam a lot, rode my bike, watched TV); "I'm an expert at . . ." (soccer, roller skating, cannon balls off the diving board); "I'd like to learn about . . ." (nature, writing, carving). I record responses on the chart as the children talk about these questions. Individual-interest inventories can be used with older children, but starting with a group process renews friendships and builds community.

During the first week of school, I sometimes go home and try to write some of this down from memory—all the children's names and a special interest or something unique about each one. Don Graves suggests this exercise

Figure 8.1 Jason illustrates his passion for baseball.

in *Writing: Teachers and Children at Work* (1983) to help carry "unique . . . information about the children in memory." This kind of information helps me when children need guidance in choosing a book, selecting a writing topic, or planning for a project. I also find out what kind of books they enjoy.

I also need to learn about academic status, but I do not need to hear everyone read right away. I have a pretty good idea of the reading and math levels of the returning class members, so I concentrate initially on the new students. I watch how the six-year-olds handle books during quiet reading and find time to discover what each knows about words, letters, and sounds.

```
┌─────────────────────────────────────────────────────────────┐
│                                                               │
│          What kind of books do you like to read?             │
│         ──────────────────────────────────────────           │
│                                                               │
│                          Fiction                              │
│                          ───────                              │
│                                                               │
│    ☐  talking animal stories        ☐  science fiction       │
│    ☐  real animal stories           ☐  funny stories         │
│    ☐  stories about adventure       ☐  stories about real children │
│    ☐  mysteries                     ☐  other kinds of stories │
│    ☐  fantasy                          explain:_____  │
│                                                               │
│                                                               │
│                        Nonfiction                             │
│                        ──────────                             │
│                                                               │
│    ☐  biographies                   ☐  other nonfiction       │
│    ☐  science                          what kind? _____  │
│       what kind? _____                                  │
│                                                               │
└─────────────────────────────────────────────────────────────┘
```

Figure 8.2 Some questions that help me find out what kinds of books children enjoy.

A brief reading inventory with new readers gives me the information I need to plan for them. I make notes about reading level, miscues, cueing systems used, and habits of self-correction. The chapter on assessment in *Reading, Writing, and Caring* (Cochrane et al. 1984) has helped me develop a system for doing this. I use selected stories from an old set of basal readers. When children recognize their own errors and self-correct as they read, I breathe a sigh of relief. These children have their feet on a firm path, and I can see that they look for meaning, not just decoding words, in their reading.

I find time for these reading evaluations during quiet reading and some-times even at Explore Time, and I look at the children's writing as well. Then I'm ready to decide where to go and what the next appropriate steps are. Of the children who appeared at the beginning of the chapter, Cindy needs some work on lowercase letters, while Mac is ready for periods, and he also shows some understanding of long vowel sounds (he uses "pees" for "piece" and "lice" for "like"). He is willing to use descriptive words like "hyuwj," carefully sounded out for "huge," to make his writing richer. I will let him know that I value this.

During the first few weeks of math, I also inventory what children know and remember from last year. While the beginners make patterns with some of our math manipulatives—pattern blocks, shells, buttons, and Unifix cubes—the older children fill in hundreds charts. Then I ask them to show a variety of patterns on the charts ("count by fives and color all those numbers blue"). In Chapter 9 Justine O'Keefe describes how she initiates math in September with her multiage class. All the children work together on a math project, but her goals and observations vary with the age of the child.

Continuum vs. Curriculum

There are helpful ways for pinpointing where each child is in the learning process, deciding what is needed next, and keeping track of this progress. Foremost among these is a skills continuum. It may be in your head if you are an experienced teacher, or it may be on paper. It may be something your school or your team has developed. Many whole language materials provide examples. *Reading, Writing, and Caring* (Cochrane et al. 1984) includes a "Reading Development Continuum." The Impressions readers (published by Holt, Rinehart and Winston of Canada) include good unabridged children's literature and many predictable stories for beginners. In the back of the teacher's manuals are literacy checklists that could also be used in developing your own continuum. But be careful. Too much detail can make a continuum almost impossible to use. List major landmarks in describing children's reading behavior.

If your school has a grade-level curriculum in math, you can stack it up: first grade, then second, then third, and so on. But a continuum offers certain advantages over stacked curricula. In the first place, a continuum is a non-graded statement of continuous, seamless skill development. It is simply a statement of the usual sequence of growth. The word "usual" is important because, while sometimes skills necessarily build on those that come before, at other times children quite comfortably develop new skills out of sequence. Understanding the concept of tens and ones, for example, is necessary for understanding regouping or trading in addition and subtraction. At the same time, children can read and write many words before they know the sounds of all the letters.

A continuum eliminates the repetitive practice built into a curriculum, which assumes that children need considerable review each fall and results in much overlap from grade to grade. Review is quite unnecessary for many children. In actual fact, with an individualized program, children may be ready to move on to the next new skill at any time during the year, even though in the curriculum it would mean moving to the next "grade level." Review comes only when evaluation shows that a particular child has not mastered a certain area.

A continuum in math and language arts gets away completely from grade-level thinking and enables you to see how the child moves along a developmental path completely removed from age and grade. In evaluation and reporting, a written continuum allows the teacher to show parents their child's progress along a specific path, not in relation to other children or to what a second or third grader "should" be able do, but rather in relation to the child's own previous work. How has the child changed, what has the child learned, what new skills does the child demonstrate?

Grouping

Instruction and introduction to new material can take place in groups. These groups can be relatively homogeneous, that is, made up of children ready for the same new concept even if they are not the same age. The groups will be small enough so you have direct feedback from each child and can evaluate their understanding and readiness to move along. This individualized attention is not possible when skills instruction is directed at a whole class. It is easy to miss the child who has not "caught on."

"s-sat," calls Chuck.

"Fat, fat, fat cat," cries Jill, giggling and rolling on the floor. I write as fast as I can. Four beginners are helping me generate a list of *at* family words. Everyone else is busy with related language arts activities.

"Cab?" says Anna. I stop, my marker poised in midair, and say all four words together. "Sat, fat, cat, cab?" She shakes her head.

Small groups are ideal for introducing new concepts, but you can also individualize tasks when the entire class is working on the same thing. For a number of years my class had what was called Monday Journals, an idea I borrowed from another teacher (how often our best ideas are those a colleague has already tried successfully). Everyone wrote in these journals on Monday morning. At that time I had five- through eight-year-olds in my class. The five-year-olds might be drawing and labeling in their journals, using only a few letters and words at first. Older children might fill a page or more with their record of some special event. Some children needed an extra day to finish their journal entries. Still, we all wrote at once and frequently shared some of our entries. Children were developing the tools of writing as we wrote together but working at their own level of achievement.

I WATCHED Sue Graham, a teacher in New Zealand, present a lesson on prime numbers to a group of seven- and eight-year-olds gathered in front of her on a rug. I had been volunteering in the "junior block," with five- and six-year-olds, and was now visiting some of the other classes in the Kaikorai Primary School in Dunedin. After Sue had presented the concept to the whole group, she arranged for children to work, with varying amounts of help, in partners or in a small group.

Sue began by asking, "How many children do we have today? Figure it out." She left the group on their own for a moment, and went to get something out of a cupboard. The children milled about. Some suggested that they get into groups of two or three, some that they make a circle, which they were just beginning to do when she returned. As they discovered, there were twenty-nine children.

"I wonder if twenty-nine can be divided into groups? What could we try?" Someone suggested groups of one. "All right, everyone who is in a group of one sit down." They all sat. "Now stand up and make groups of two. When you are in a group of two sit down." They found, of course, that one student was left. On they went. They tried threes, fours, fives, sixes, and sevens before deciding that the number twenty-nine could not be divided into groups other than ones.

This was the end of the lesson, but only for the moment. After "morning tea" and playtime we revisited prime numbers. By this time Sue had revealed what such numbers are called and wondered out loud if there are other numbers like twenty-nine. She asked the children to search for prime numbers between one and twenty, suggesting that they would need counters of some sort and a paper and pencil for keeping a record of what they discovered. "How many think they will work with a partner?" A scattering of hands went up as a few children made eye contact or grabbed the hand of a friend. "How many by themselves?" A few more hands were raised. "How many would like to stay here on the mat and work with me?" Quite a number of hands now. "John, I want you to work with me, too." She looked around, "And Judy and Erin and James. Now the rest of you get what you need."

Open-ended Assignments

If tasks are sufficiently open-ended, individual work can occur in the context of whole group instruction. While reading *Charlotte's Web* aloud, an open-ended activity might be to brainstorm words Charlotte might weave in her web. An example of an open-ended math task would be to have the children work in groups to brainstorm everything they know about the number seven ($3 + 4 = 7$, seven cannot be divided equally, some of us are seven years old, $2 \times 7 = 14$, seven is a prime number, Snow White knew seven dwarves). Any age can make a contribution.

Letting the Children Help Each Other

Children do help each other in multiage settings, and letting this happen is more complicated than it first appears. First the teacher needs to tolerate a good deal of conversation. Then sometimes it is necessary to help children evaluate their conversations to decide whether they are helping or simply "telling" a younger child how to spell a word or answer a math problem. I have found that children need to talk about how to help one another, and that I am a constant model for this kind of helping. When Charles Rathbone was a participant-observer in my classroom in 1990, a discussion we had one day led me to try a meeting with the children that focused on how they could help each other with writing. We talked about where you could go for help, and we also talked about giving help. The children suggested questions you could ask about a story without telling a classmate what to write next. They suggested ways to help with spelling, such as sounding out the word with another child or finding it on a chart in the room. The next time the group was writing, Rathbone observed a dramatic increase in children helping children.

Sometimes a child will come to me and ask that the room be quieter. This input is helpful and it also becomes a topic for group discussion. We discover that some children need more quiet than others during writing or math time. We also establish acceptable noise levels for conversation. Some corners of the room can be designated as quiet areas, others allocated to writing conferences.

Diversity of Materials

A greater age diversity requires more materials, a wider range of books for reading, and a greater variety of math manipulatives.

RON'S mother, Carol, a parent volunteer, sits at a table with Jill and Anna. They choose a drawstring bag from my bucket of "counting bags" and open it up to find tiny shells. Carol gathers up a handful and the children start to count. They are working on counting from ten to twenty and will assemble some piles to represent the different numbers.

Chuck, Mark, Cindy, and Suzie are on the rug sticking Unifix cubes together. I've asked them to make a pile of tens, because we will be working together on two-digit numbers.

Emma and Stacie have the basket of Base Ten Blocks between them. As they work on a page of two-digit addition, they lay the tiny cubes and tens blocks beside their papers on the table.

Alex is using a hundred's grid and a handful of Unifix cubes. He stares at the pattern he has made by putting a red cube in every seventh square. Then he begins writing the seven times table in a small booklet.

A first-grade class might get along with interlocking cubes and a several kinds of counters, but Base Ten Blocks with fixed sets of tens and hundreds

1	2	3	4	5	6	7	8	9	10
11	12	13	14	15	16	17	18	19	20
21	22	23	24	25	26	27	28	29	30
31	32	33	34	35	36	37	38	39	40
41	42	43	44	45	46	47	48	49	50
51	52	53	54	55	56	57	58	59	60
61	62	63	64	65	66	67	68	69	70
71	72	73	74	75	76	77	78	79	80
81	82	83	84	85	86	87	88	89	90
91	92	93	94	95	96	97	98	99	100

Figure 8.3 Alex uses a hundred's grid to work on the seven times table.

are more serviceable for some of the work of seven- and eight-year-olds. They are great for trading games and also small enough to use along with a math sheet on a desk. A multiage class needs all of these materials.

Beginners in a Multiage Class
If you have five- or six-year-olds in your multiage class, they will have some special needs at the beginning of the year. Fives will be coming to a public school for the first time; they may be less independent and will certainly be unaware of many classroom routines. The advantage is that you will have only a few of these children and older students will be helping.

Six-year-olds may be moving from a kindergarten program into a class with seven- and eight-year-olds. Some or all will be emergent readers, and they will often need more of your time at the beginning of the year. In a class of six-, seven-, and eight-year-olds I have usually had from six to eight beginning readers (a lot easier than twenty or twenty-five). However, early in the year I depend on the ability of older children to work independently while I sit down with the beginners to help them get started.

ADAPTING NEW IDEAS FOR MULTIAGE CLASSROOMS

Often new instructional ideas and materials are introduced in the context of a single grade level. Again and again I have listened to conference presentations or read books introducing new teaching ideas that assumed these ideas were going to be applied in single-grade classroom. *Mathematics Their Way* (Baratta-Lorton 1976), whole language learning, and process writing are all examples of ideas I have had to adapt for a multiage classroom. I first learned about process writing at a workshop given by a first-grade teacher. Because I always had a three- or four-grade-level span, including both beginners and independent eight-year-olds, adapting new approaches could be a challenge.

My own introduction to whole language may serve as another example. At a workshop given by teachers of very young emergent readers, I discovered how enthusiastic these teachers were about what they were doing. Their excitement was contagious. They demonstrated wonderful whole class activities and did a great deal of work with charts and big books. They told us that these shared reading experiences were what defined whole language: children could participate as they were ready and phonics could be taught in the context of meaningful text. Their presentations emphasized these whole group sessions almost to the exclusion of other things. I wanted to make use of what I had learned because the philosophy behind the ideas was so congruent with my own, but I could not take exactly what they had demonstrated back to my classroom.

I tried. My seven- and eight-year-old capable readers, those with their noses in chapter books, enjoyed the chants and poems I introduced to the group. But when we started focusing on letters and sounds in this context, they didn't need it and they let me know. Then I tried working with part of the class while the others were reading quietly, but this was only moderately successful, because my group was, not surprisingly, loudly enthusiastic.

Time passed and I discovered a much broader definition of whole language. As I flip through an old notebook of mine, I find that I clarified my understanding by concluding that there are three important "wholes" in whole language.

First there is the wholeness of language itself, the fact that oral language and written language, as communicated and received, are both of one fabric. When you are using one you are increasing your skill with the other.

Second is the idea of learning about language through meaningful wholes—poetry, songs, chants, and stories—instead of through bits and pieces. The bits and pieces of letters and sounds must also be taught, but within these contexts.

The final "whole" involves the strategic approach to language learning. Phonics, or graphophonics, is one strategy or cueing system, but it is used along with clues involving syntax and meaning.

Now I would add one more "whole," a complex texture of methods—shared reading, silent reading, phonics, sight-word work—and materials—literature, nonfiction books, the child's own writing, books on tape, word puzzles—that are woven together by the teacher to support children as they learn to read. A single resource, such as a basal reader, is never enough.

What had appealed to me was the emphasis on meaning and the fun these teachers and children were having with language. When I realized this and discovered those "wholes," I found my way to a program that fit my situation. I came to the conclusion, rather smugly perhaps, that I'd been teaching whole language all along. Hadn't I always emphasized meaningful print, hung poems and charts about the room, and used the children's own dictated language? And recently my beginners were writing on their own, working with the sounds and letters they knew. We had been using songs on charts for our weekly four-class singalong. Now we recognized that this was also a whole language experience.

There were, however, many new ideas that I could use to enrich my program. I searched for delightfully predictable stories for beginners and emphasized literature even more with the older children. Writing became an ever more significant part of learning to read in Room A. And I found ways to work with small groups using shared reading techniques.

Whole language turned out to be perfect for a multiage classroom, where activities at many levels go on simultaneously and children learn from collaborating with one another.

Adaptation is one of the keys to multiage teaching. Look first for what you already have that fits the new model, philosophically if not exactly. Recognize those activities in your program that are working well, and do not reject them without careful consideration and solid replacements. Choose and adapt new ideas that make sense for your children and your setting.

> "Little Old Bee
> Little Old Bee
> Where have you been?
> In a pink apple tree . . ."

I am sitting on the rug at one end of Room A, my long legs stretched out in front of me, my back against a bookcase. Snug on either side of me are two six-year-olds, Chuck and Jill. We are reading aloud from *Good Morning Sunshine*. Quiet reading is not absolutely silent reading.

Mark and Kent are in another corner reading *Caps for Sale* to each other. Wendy is curled up under the easel with *Mr. Popper's Penguins*. Jerry is belly flopped on the rug paging through a book of dinosaurs, and Anna is in the listening area using a taped book and earphones.

In a few minutes I suggest that children find a stopping place and move on to other work in their reading and writing folders. Chuck and Jill tuck *Good Morning Sunshine* in their cubbies, and Jill joins Cindy at a table, where they put their heads together over a puzzle page related to recent small group instruction on "Magic e." Chuck puts his folder down next to Jason who is writing in his reading log. Sometimes Jason helps him find the right letter for a word he wants to write. Stacie finishes her log and begins to copy a poem from a card into a school-made "cursive practice book." Two children begin a writing conference at one end of the rug. Emma places a story in the editing box. Someone is working at the computer.

Whole language—in a multiage setting!

PART FOUR

■

OTHER VOICES
JOIN IN

CHAPTER NINE

■

PATHWAYS
IN MATHEMATICS

Justine O'Keefe, Peggy Dorta, and Anne Bingham

JUSTINE O'KEEFE: MAKING MATH MULTIAGE

I T ' S early September in my multiage classroom. About half of the children are just beginning those long whole days at school. Some have recently turned six, others will be seven in a few months. The rest are returning seven- and eight-year-olds new to their roles as older models and coaches to their younger peers. I want to begin a math study that will introduce the children to each other through cooperative groups, demonstrate the counting skills of the new students, and sharpen the operations and recording skills of those returning for a second year.

Several weeks before, after dinner one evening, I was wiping and putting away the dishes my spouse was washing. I put the empty cleaned salad dressing bottle in the recycle bin and its lid in a bag I kept for that purpose in the pantry. I had amassed quite a collection of jar and bottle lids, which I was saving for the math area at school. Now, I had a use for them. They would be part of a study of sorting, classifying, counting, and charting.

At school a few weeks later, as I was setting up the classroom, I began to pull math manipulatives out of the storage cupboard and arrange them on the two sets of shelves that define our math area. As I did so, I focused on materials appropriate to sorting and left the others in their hiding places under the counter for use at another time. Next to a large plastic tub labeled *Lids*, I placed another containing animal shapes in a variety of colors, three buckets of pattern blocks, Cuisenaire rods, a box of small ceramic shapes, and tubs of colorful dinosaurs, rabbits, and bears.

Placed on the shelves, too, were bins of inch cubes and Unifix cubes, along with hundreds boards with number tiles for activities children would choose on their own. Between the wall and one math shelf, I slid the tall, flat box of math mats. These are laminated 24-by-36-inch pieces of oaktag, each one labeled with an individual's name. They provide a space on which children can explore and build with the manipulatives, display completed work, and declare ownership.

Suspended from the ceiling were geometric models I had made, and taped to nearby walls, pattern block posters and a hundreds grid. I stood back to see if I had created a space that was inviting and that visually spoke to the beauty and grace of mathematics. I was satisfied that I had done my part. The rest would come from the children as they began to explore and create with the materials.

At the first sorting lesson the children and I were arranged in a ragged circle in our meeting area in front of the whiteboard. I had my math mat ready and a bucket of pattern blocks. Together we brainstormed a list of ways to sort them.

"PUT all the blue diamonds together," suggested newcomer Jeff. "Those are parallelograms," corrected veteran Elliot.

"Yeah, then put all the yellows together," offered Laura.

On my mat I sorted the blocks as the children had indicated. After a while I said, "What attribute are we sorting these by?"

"By their color," answered six-year-old Katie.

Dean raised his hand. "Well, by their shape too," he said. Thus we agreed that pattern blocks could be sorted by shape and color at the same time.

Next I asked if we could tell what kind of block we had the most of.

"The yellow pile's the biggest," stated Kate with assurance. There were nods of agreement among the younger children, but some of the older children shook their heads.

"Maybe it just seems like that because the hexagons are the biggest," suggested Ashley.

"Let's count 'em," Brad said.

"OK, let's do that," I said. "Let's make a chart at the same time."

On the whiteboard I drew seven columns. At the top of six of them I drew a different shape: hexagon, parallelogram, square, rhombus, and triangle. Then, in turn, volunteers counted each pile of shapes and recorded the number under the appropriate shape.

Katie counted hexagons, touching each piece and then moving it out of the way. Brad attempted to count the parallelograms, pointing randomly and losing count until Eli came to his aid. Dean began bravely to count the squares by fours and was assisted by his friends after he reached sixteen. When Laura counted the rhombi, I showed her how making groups of tens could help. And Ashley counted the triangles by twos.

Now we knew which block we had the most and the least of. We also knew that there were almost the same number of triangles as parallelograms and that there were many more triangles than squares. We agreed that we could change the column headings to say yellow, blue, orange, white, and green and the chart would still make sense. And Carl said the chart could also tell us how many blocks we had sorted all together. At the whiteboard he engaged in a lengthy computation of tens and ones to the utter amazement and confusion of most of his classmates.

"OK, now it's your turn," I said.

Children picked partners and found a spot on the floor for a math mat. I circled the room, dumping a pile of blocks on each mat. The partners went to work sorting and making a chart in their math books. I moved from group to group making suggestions, asking "how many more than or less than" questions, and holding rulers steady so small hands could draw reasonably straight lines. At the end of the period, we shared information from our charts and talked about other things we could sort.

Over the next few weeks, children sharpened their sorting skills and began to think of groups of things in terms of their various attributes. The heavy bin of buttons offered many attributes. Sometimes children sorted by holes: two-holed, four-holed, and one-holed ("Those are for special cuffs," I explained. "And why do *you* think there aren't any three-holed buttons?") When they sorted by size, the younger children gave free reign to their inventive use of language with categories for "teeny, eensy, humungus, smallish medium, and not so small" to complement their older partner's "small, medium, and large."

The children became adept at chart and graph making. And the older children totaled their charts using chip trading to help them with the double-digit addition required.

Through sorting, we brought math into the context of the real world. At group lessons, we sorted ourselves by hair and eye color, kind of shoes, patterns on shirts, number of siblings. We worked with the attribute blocks and began to look at the world in terms of categories: what or who fits into which group and why.

As a final activity we took a leaf walk around the school grounds collecting leaves in brown paper lunch bags. Upon our return, we sorted the leaves onto large pieces of construction paper and labeled the groups. Some children sorted by shape, but many sorted by color thanks to the abundance of maple leaves in Vermont. In addition to red, yellow, orange, and brown, close scrutiny of maple leaves revealed groups of pinkish, greenish-yellow, and peachy-red leaves. Size was also a popular attribute, while some leaf charts sported categories like no holes, small holes, big holes, and lots of holes.

After the charts came graphs on big pieces of squared paper. We also used our leaves for leaf rubbings, leaf prints, "scientific" leaf drawings done with the aid of magnifying glasses, and that old war horse of northern New England teachers, pressing leaves between two sheets of waxed paper. The children wrote about their leaf collections and what they had learned about why leaves turn color and what trees do in winter.

By the time all the leaves were on the ground and the unmistakable chill of late fall was in the air, we had turned our math focus elsewhere. But we revisited the skills the children developed and practiced during these early sorting activities throughout the year. Charting and graphing became tools that would be used in many settings, and I now had a clearer view of who needed more counting practice, who was ready for counting by tens and fives, and which of the older children had a rudimentary understanding of place value.

Just as important as the math, however, was the interpersonal work that had begun. Through cooperative groups, the children had come to know each other better and to appreciate the skills, knowledge, and understanding each brought to the task. As group leaders, the older students experimented with various methods for nudging their members to complete an assignment. They learned to be sparing with their criticism after a member left the group in tears, and realized the efficacy of praise in encouraging a peer to count yet another pile of buttons. The enthusiasm and the ready flow of creative ideas and language from the younger children brought respect from their more reserved older peers, while the accomplishments of the group engendered pride in all its members.

My goals in beginning with the sorting theme were broad and meant to encompass a wide range of learning and practice. I wanted the children to work together and to develop and sharpen their skills (in this case sorting, classifying, counting, charting, making, and interpreting graphs). I wanted activities everyone could engage in according to individual developmental levels, tasks that would engage the sophisticated learner in the addition of large numbers and the interpretation of data, while involving even the youngest child in the act of sorting real things into piles, attempting to count them, and writing down the number on a chart.

Further, I wanted the children to work directly with real-world objects. Buttons, jar lids, little plastic figures, and leaves are part of the daily lives of small children just as math is. When they stand back-to-back with a friend to see who is taller, divide a cookie in half to share with a sibling, or line up their tiny cars two by two on an imaginary road, they are practicing mathematics. An important part of our job as teachers is to help children make the link between these concrete mathematical experiences and the abstract symbols and language that represent them.

Thus, in the sorting exercises, children worked with manipulatives and then found ways to represent their findings symbolically. Long after the piles of buttons had been slid off the math mat and back into the bin, the information the children gathered from the activity was available on the chart with the wobbly lines and backward numbers.

Children need to be taught how creating a pattern or building a tower with manipulatives in three dimensions can be recorded with paper and pencil in two dimensions. Recreating the pattern block design using a template, drawing the layers of one's Cuisenaire rod tower, or writing equations from rolling dice all help children make that leap between what they are doing and how they can show it with symbols.

Conversely, more sophisticated learners should be encouraged to look at the three-digit regrouping problems they have just completed and think of real-life situations in which they could be applied. In what context might we be talking about numbers that large? Can they construct a word problem that uses similar numbers and makes sense?

The mathematics in which children naturally engage—those spontaneous acts of measurement, division, and counting in groups, for example—are the concrete math experiences we can use to foster an understanding of abstract operations and theory. Arithmetic alone is not mathematics. It is one part of the whole mandala of math, which also includes patterns, geometry, symmetry, spatial problem solving, wholes and their parts, numeration, measurement, and money.

All these varied and diverse aspects of mathematics—and their corresponding language—can be part of students' math experiences in school. Indeed, these aspects are not separate; they overlap. Our responsibility is to enable children to see their connectedness and then transfer what they have learned in one situation to another.

Throughout our time together, children will use the chart- and graph-making skills they have honed in those first weeks of school. They will chart the sizes, number of moons, and temperatures of the planets during our study of the solar system, and graph the relative lengths of whales during our oceanography theme. Later, perhaps even the following year (this is a multi-age classroom, after all) they will chart the sides and angles of the platonic solids they make and look for number patterns in the results.

This transfer of knowledge is not limited to mathematical experience. When I asked children to outline the important parts of their reading book plot along the horizontal points of a graph and the tension from calm to exciting along the vertical points, they had the necessary prior knowledge to complete the task. When they connected the dots on their graph, they had a visual picture of just how exciting they thought their book was. The plot information the graphs provided inspired many children to choose those books.

Mathematics is an integral part of our everyday lives. Children use it intuitively as a way to make sense of the world and their relation to it. Our responsibility as teachers of math is to expand on that intuitive sense and make their understanding explicit. Math is meaningful and we must not trivialize it with rote tasks that lack meaning.

Math is also beautiful. The patterns of shape and color found in nature can be used as models for children to create beauty of their own. An intricate pattern block design, the symmetry of a cut paper snowflake, and the patterns on a hundreds grid made by counting in groups all illustrate the order and grace of mathematics. The world of mathematics includes descriptive language; artistic renderings of pattern, shape, and color; thought-provoking problems; seemingly magical number play; and tools for ordering the universe. It is a rich and exciting world. So, go forth and multiply.

PEGGY DORTA: THE HOURGLASS

THE HOURGLASS sat in the math area on top of the shelf. Erin and Mark carefully pulled it down and turned it over to watch the sand sift through the narrow center to the bottom side.

"This would make a great math chat," declared Erin.

"Yeah. We could have the kids guess how long it takes for that white sand to fall to the other end when we turn it upside down," chimed in Mark.

"We'd have to have them write it down first and then see who got the closest guess," Erin continued. "Let's try it first ourselves. What's your guess Mark? I guess it takes counting up to a hundred."

"Naah, I bet half that, fifty."

What is it that these two "mathematicians" are planning? They are preparing to challenge their classmates with a lesson on estimation. They don't seem to see it as a teaching moment but merely as a way to set up a contest for the class. A real-life activity that prods the logical part of their brains to start functioning. Amazing!

How do we get children excited about setting up or solving mathematical situations? How do we approach math ourselves so that it isn't that "add-on" subject that just doesn't seem to fit within a theme? How do we avoid turning out math phobics?

The main question I have continued to ask myself (and keep trying to answer) is, "How can I get my students' attention, keep them engaged, and make some connections to real life, while keeping up with the curriculum guide that haunts me?"

I began thinking about how I teach reading and writing: We read, we write, we share good literature, I read aloud, we talk a lot about our reading and writing, we do projects, and we surround ourselves with words.

Ah . . . but do I teach math in the same fashion? Could I?

I've started talking with my eight- to ten-year-olds about math. We refer to this few minutes a day as our "math chat." We talk about math and about situations we've been in where math has helped us. We solve problems together, and we come up with challenges for other classes. We identify patterns, and we clarify, wonder about, and work through mathematical equations. We use what we know to accomplish something, like cutting a birthday cake into twenty-eight equal pieces or figuring out how many chopsticks we will need if we all eat at a Chinese restaurant.

Often I'll begin a math chat with a question: "How many ways can we count to one hundred?" "Why would I want to add seven fifty times when I can do it more simply like this: 7×50?" "What does the word *math* mean to you?"

From here the conversation takes us away. It's my job to follow and to lead, to find opportunities for future activities, and to focus the discussion. It's my job to listen carefully and find openings for commonsense math to take hold.

"Math is the lazy person's pursuit," says Rachel MacAnellan, Vermont's "math lady," at her courses and workshops. She explains math as a shortcut. If you want to get out of a lot of hard work, she says, learn to do math. Putting kids in enough situations where they use the long way to solve a problem while I take a shortcut gets them on board very quickly.

"Why don't you draw ten pizzas and see how many slices we'll get if each has eight. I'll use multiplication" ($10 \times 8 = 80$).

"How might you figure out how many pinecones are in those bags? You can count them all. I think I'll find a good way to estimate."

Presenting math concepts and skills to a multiage group can be an extra challenge. I am constantly searching for activities and projects that can be taught "individually all at once" to such a multilevel group. That is, I introduce one format or presentation to the whole crew, and then each child can continue work on it at his or her own level.

An example is the math "crossword" puzzle. A few years ago I found a challenging puzzle in the *Arithmetic Teacher* magazine. I tried it with my multiage group and they loved it. It was highly motivating for the students, while offering me a fantastic opportunity to assess the children's math sense and

1	2	3	4	5	6	7	8	9	10
11	12	13	14	15	16	17	18	19	20
21	22	23	24	25	26	27	28	29	30
31	32	33	34	35	36	37	38	39	40
41	42	43	44	45	46	47	48	49	50
51	52	53	54	55	56	57	58	59	60
61	62	63	64	65	66	67	68	69	70
71	72	73	74	75	76	77	78	79	80
81	82	83	84	85	86	87	88	89	90
91	92	93	94	95	96	97	98	99	100

1. 3 quarters and $.01
2. $6 \times 9 =$
3. XXIV
4. 28 divided by 2 =
5. What is one third of 48?
6. What number is between 43 and 48 that the digits add up to 9?
7. 14, 24, ____, 44, 54
8. What is the palindrome after 33?
9. 3 quarters
10. 30 divided by 2 =
11. 100 minus 36 =
12. $20 + 20 - 7 + 14 =$ ____. Switch the digits and what number do you get?

Figure 9.1 Tracey's math "crossword" puzzle.

observe them applying math concepts. So I extended the activity. We do the first puzzle together as a class, modeling how it works and practicing appropriate strategies. Then I challenge the children to make one of their own for their classmates to tackle. We brainstorm a list of math vocabulary and terms what we all know, and I suggest that they try to use as many as possible in their puzzles. For the next few days (or even weeks) I work with small groups and individuals on their puzzles. We do this activity three or four times a year, often to review what they know or to offer enrichment to some groups.

A Greeting
by Gordon, Molly, June, and Jesse

1	2	3	4	5	6	7	8	9	10
11	12	13	14	15	16	17	18	19	20
21	22	23	24	25	26	27	28	29	30
31	32	33	34	35	36	37	38	39	40
41	42	43	44	45	46	47	48	49	50
51	52	53	54	55	56	57	58	59	60
61	62	63	64	65	66	67	68	69	70
71	72	73	74	75	76	77	78	79	80
81	82	83	84	85	86	87	88	89	90
91	92	93	94	95	96	97	98	99	100

1. 20 - 7 =
2. 1 quarter - 2 pennies =
3. A palindrome between 23 and 43
4. 4 tens and 3 ones
5. LIII
6. 10 + 10 + 10 + 4 =
7. 10 + 5 =
8. 5 x 5 =
9. Reverse the digits in 53
10. How many days in 9 weeks of school? (hint: school is only 5 days per week)
11. A palindrome between 45 and 65
12. You have a quarter. You spend 8 cents on a piece of candy. How much do you have left?
13. Count by nines 3 times
14. One yard plus one inch =
15. 9 x 5 + 2 =
16. What number comes in between 56 and 58?

Figure 9.2 We use math vocabulary and terms we know to create the puzzles.

But where do you find enough activities to introduce a concept to a multiage group all at once? My response is, "All around me." The *Arithmetic Teacher* magazine is a good source, as are math resource books, and ideas from my colleagues. Sometimes I dream them up, and the kids suggest some humdingers.

Joey loved doing origami. He often had a workshop set up for his classmates so they could try some of the forms he showed them. One day he made a cube and blew air into it to open it up. He asked me if I thought he might be able to make some of the other geometric shapes we had been studying. With his help, our class made hanging mobiles of many geometric shapes.

Sharyl brought in a small plastic bag from home filled with peastone from her driveway. We had been trying to find a million of something that we could look at. So far we had started collecting grains of sand and we had hung a million dots of paper in the school cafeteria. Sharyl estimated that her very long driveway must have a million stones. She and her dad had measured a square foot of it and provided us with information about the size of the driveway and the depth of the peastone. We were able to calculate together approximately how many stones the entire driveway must have. Yep. More than one million. So we all walked up to her house one day and viewed a million of something.

In *A Collection of Math Lessons for Grades Three Through Six* (1987), Marilyn Burns, an author and presenter of wonderful math suggestions, offers a chapter entitled "Exploring Multiplication with Rectangles." It is a perfect example of the "individually all at once" approach. I use one of her ideas with my multiage class. I give the children in randomly chosen groups a paper plate with a number on it from one to thirty-six. I also provide graph paper and scissors. Each group is to cut from the graph paper as many rectangles as necessary to represent their number. If their plate has the number twelve on it, they could cut a rectangle, also known as an array, that is three squares by four squares, two squares by six squares, or one square by twelve squares. After each group has cut out their array, I ask them to tape their cutouts onto our bulletin board, which has numerical headings, under the appropriate number.

We discuss the patterns we see. For example, one group might have cut a two-by-eight and an eight-by-two rectangle and discovered that they were exactly the same. Some numbers—prime numbers—have only one rectangle. We can talk about multiples; we see math facts right in front of us. Square roots pop right out at us every time a square is posted, four-by-four or six-by-six.

We do the bulletin board all at once, and then over the next few weeks I will refer to it and use it in individual and small group work. Some students in my multiage class are ready to move on to factoring, common multiples, and prime numbers. Others are at the stage of identifying multiplication patterns and beginning to learn math facts. But we all make use of the same common activity.

Cuing is another extremely helpful strategy. It provides children with real experiences that they can apply in new ways as they move on to more abstract math concepts. Sitting in a circle and counting from zero to twenty-five to take attendance and see how many students are absent is one way to do this, especially at the beginning of the school year. After a few weeks I begin one morning with "Let's count for attendance today. I'll start, but let's count by tens. What number will we reach if all twenty-five are present?" Together we decide it will be two-hundred fifty and we begin. Over the next few weeks we continue to count attendance by tens, fives, threes, twos, and so forth. Then I take it one step further. "Let's count for attendance today counting by tens. I'll start with seven." After a lot of baffled looks someone always comes up with seventeen and then twenty-seven, thirty-seven, forty-seven, fifty-seven, and so on. This exercise establishes numerical patterns that can cue the children for future work on multiplication tables, base ten and other base operations, large number concepts, and mental math.

During Explore Time I like to present interesting math materials, challenges, and games. Using parent volunteers for enrichment during this time is a marvelous way to tap their expertise and strengthen the partnership needed to educate a child. One father came into our classroom every Thursday morning before he went to work to present a math challenge for the week. Once he helped the children figure the height of Mount Mansfield—a mountain we can see from our classroom window. A mother taught chess during Explore Time. A parent who works as an engineer brought an example of his work to class and explained it to us. A merchant marine brought in depth maps. An older sibling did an internship one day a week offering tutoring in math through games.

We share the results of our math work by surrounding ourselves with it, just as we do for other subjects. Bulletin boards, presentations, discussions, projects, and big books all contribute to an accumulation of keepsakes that celebrate what we have learned and provide a summary, a conclusion. Children who are not quite ready for something are exposed to it anyway. Often they surprise me by their grasp of that knowledge. Students also find new and creative ways to present what they've learned.

Charlie and Noah created a math game for the class. Amy, Michael, and Evan put on an original play called *The Flat Family Visits Three Dimensions*. Sue, Nancy, Judy, and John used Tangrams to tell stories.

As I think back to Erin and Mark's planning for our math chat, the image of an hourglass seems to explain my approach to teaching math:

I broach a math topic with the entire class in math
chats, "individually all at once presentations,"
and Explore Time activities. I cue kids
through everyday, routine activities.
Experts in the community come in to
share their relevant experience or
challenge our math thinking.
I form flexible groups to
work on specific concepts
and skills as needed. Children
practice or pursue enrichment
activities individually while I do
one-to-one work with a few. We all meet
to share what we have learned and sometimes come up with a summarizing project,
mural, book, or game we can create together.
If we approach math more like we do reading and writing, it will come
alive for kids. Talk about it. Put it in a meaningful context. Make connections
to prior knowledge. Find as many everyday chances to use it spontaneously
as possible. Take the time to make it real.

ANNE BINGHAM: WHEN YOU NEED TO INDIVIDUALIZE

JASON brings the basket of Base Ten Blocks to the table where he and Adam
have placed their math folders. Inside the folders are some practice pages
they started yesterday. Yesterday they worked with Mrs. B., but today she has
asked them to continue on their own. Jason takes out the paper and looks at
the first problem: 38 + 46. He selects three tens rods and eight little cubes.
Underneath he places four tens and six ones. Adam looks at what Jason is
doing. "Hey that's not what I have." They look at Adam's paper. His problem
is different. "I'm going to watch you do one, OK?" Jason gathers all the ones
cubes together.

"See, I have more than ten, so I have to trade." He puts ten ones in the
basket and pulls out a ten rod. Then he puts all his tens together.

"Oh yeah, I remember now," says Adam, "but I forget how you're supposed to write it down." Jason shows him.

Jason is seven and Adam is eight. Some younger children are working
with similar materials, Cuisenaire rods:

"Four and five make nine. Which rod is nine?"

"Use the squares at the bottom of the page to figure it out."

"Oh yeah, blue." Chuck and Cindy each place a blue rod on the graph paper/puzzle sheet they have. "Hey, you know what I think it's going to be? A face!"

This is a fairly typical math time in Room A. Many children are working alone or with a partner. If this day's math had concerned something like graphing or measurement, the whole group would have been involved together or worked in small, heterogeneous groups with a similar assignment. We might have been immersed in a math mini-theme such as mapping the room, graphing the number and kinds of pets owned by children in our class, or measuring and weighing Halloween pumpkins and counting seeds.

Instead, on this day children are working alone, with partners, or in small groups focusing on different skills. Their particular work represents the place on the math continuum where I know each one needs to be, practicing or learning something new. Time like this is essential when the age range in a class is three or four years. Expectations for six-year-olds and eight-year-olds diverge considerably.

Individualized work need not mean working alone. Partners may be sharing similar work or one child may be helping another who is working at a different level.

What other activities were taking place in Room A on this particular day?

Jill and Anna were creating models of two-digit numbers with Unifix cubes, matching them to number cards they selected from a small basket. Kent and Suzie were playing a game called "Take Ten," practicing combinations that make ten. Mike was practicing harder math facts at the computer using a game involving a math maze. Alex and Wendy were working together using a hundreds board and Unifix cubes to work out the four and six times tables, recording them in small math booklets. Several children were working with practice pages of addition or subtraction at various levels, some using counters. I was sitting on the rug with a group of five.

"LET'S see three hundred fifty-six," I say. The seven- and eight-year-olds in a circle on the rug around me dutifully tap calculator keys and show me the results. I'm surprised to see that Kate, age eight, is still not sure how to show three-digit numbers. This time she shows 30056 on the calculator. Jerry is working with a good deal of hesitancy, too, and their errors tell me they are not ready for the activity I have tentatively planned for this group. After modeling some three-digit numbers with Base Ten Blocks and using number cards to identify each set—hundreds, tens, ones—I send Kate and Jerry off to practice building other three-digit numbers with the blocks. Later they will have an empty hundreds square in which to write numbers from 301 to 400.

The other three children remain with me on the rug to watch me demonstrate addition with three-digit numbers on the easel. Then they return to their chosen work space—at a table, desk, or with a lapboard on the floor—to practice.

On my desk is a weekly math planning sheet on which I have jotted down goals and expectations for each student, grouping those who are working together on the same skill.

I don't always have an instructional group. Much of the time I circulate around the room helping children who request it, checking on progress, and observing how children solve problems. I often plan group instruction on days when I have a parent helper in the room.

Materials for Individualized Math

What are some of the materials needed for this individualized work in math?

Manipulatives are the most important component of the math program, whether for individualized work or for carrying out a whole class math activity. Teachers must constantly seek ways to use concrete materials, from pinecones to Geoboards, to help lay the groundwork for mathematical concepts. The challenge is to reflect our knowledge about how children learn and to accommodate what society expects from school math. We must also consider what kind of materials to present and the sequence in which to use these materials in teaching situations in order to move children from the concrete to the abstraction of numbers on paper.

It is important when using manipulatives for math instruction to make sure that children have had time for some free exploration of the material. I have already spoken of Explore Time. In addition, after free exploration students need experiences that give them practice in using the materials in the specific ways they may be expected to use them for math. Jason and Adam played trading games with the place value blocks before they linked this trading to abstract number work.

Chuck and Cindy have already made their own designs with Cuisenaire rods. They have built towers and played a game called "Rodney Rod." They did some of this on their own during Explore Time and I directed some of it during math. They are familiar with the structure of the materials and also with the convention of giving each rod a number name.

What other materials support individualized achievement and accomplish the goals of a math program? The examples just presented also include games, paper-and-pencil tasks, and math folders. The papers Chuck and Cindy were working on were photocopied from a book of Cuisenaire rod puzzles intended for that purpose. Jason and Adam each had my handwritten pages, and they will go on to some practice pages from a workbook. But all the paper work comes only after demonstrations and practice with real objects.

Workbook pages are one tool among many that may be used for math practice. If you are experienced in teaching math entirely without a workbook, you will certainly be able to make the transition to multiage teaching without them. On the other hand, if the children joining the class are at the upper end of the age spectrum, it may be that some readily available paper-and-pencil practice would be helpful. The children usually enjoy doing workbook pages when they represent one of the resources of the math program but not the only one. Some workbooks now make extensive reference to manipulatives and expect children to use them along with the workbook. Make sure children are ready for the paper work you give them through your group or individual assessments.

Not all the pages in a workbook need to be used; indeed, they should not be. Don't use workbooks for measurement. Measure real objects in the room. Graphs, sorting, patterns, time, money, and fractions are also better done outside of workbook pages. Workbooks also provide far more computation practice pages than many children need, all of which makes them a costly use of financial resources.

What are some alternatives? In the New Zealand schools I visited, children used small notebooks for their pencil-and-paper math work. The pages of the books designed for math had graph paper grids instead of lines. The squares provided an easy way to organize work with numbers. I saw six-year-olds use tiny three-by-five-inch books to practice number writing and to write simple equations. Most notebooks were seven-by-nine inches and were used for recording all kinds of number work. I watched one child complete an assignment from the board—to draw lines of various lengths—in her book and label them carefully. Photocopied materials were used occasionally, but not workbooks.

Sets of cards are also available for use in problem solving. The story problems they include can be challenging. They are often related to real-life situations and provide examples of the kinds of stories we can then make up ourselves.

One year we had a Halloween bulletin board with a huge haunted house full of ghosts, black cats, and other spooky characters. We celebrated the holiday by making up our own story problems related to the bulletin board: "In the Halloween picture there are 14 jack-o-lanterns, 5 ghosts, and 3 black cats. How many does that make together?" "If you have 14 pumpkins and 5 ghosts, how many more pumpkins are there than ghosts?"

Math folders, as a way to organize individual student assignments, are something my team has used for years. Each child has an individual pocket

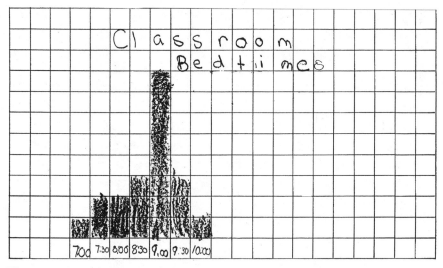

Figure 9.3 Graphing is part of the math folder.

folder, which I file in a plastic dishpan near my desk. There they are available for me to work with after school. The children pick them up at the beginning of math time if they are going to be using folders that day.

What else might go into a math folder besides practice pages and problem-solving cards? Some examples would be: a hundreds square in which children write numbers one to one hundred or beyond; a booklet in which children record equations as they work them out with manipulatives, dominoes, or dice; a booklet for recording times tables after children have been introduced to multiplication with manipulatives and such things as arrays, or one used to record the solving of story problems presented on cards; a note suggesting a particular game or computer program; graph paper for creating a graph or demonstrating area.

Planning for an Individualized Math Program

I organize individual work using a planning sheet that lists all the children's names down one side. I always have a file folder of class lists available on which I have separated the children's names with lines. I use these to keep track of all sorts of things, from whether they have returned field trip permission slips to what projects they have completed during a theme. I prepare them on the computer and can print more as I need them.

After the year is under way and I know the children better, I create a new list for math by rearranging these names on the computer so they are clustered by where they are on a math continuum. These become my math planning sheets. I rearrange the names again on pages I use for planning reading

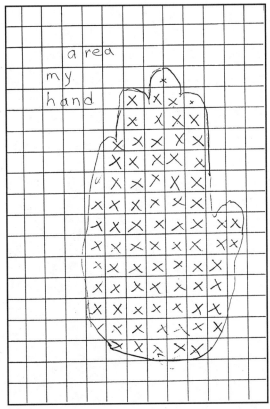

Figure 9.4 Math folders may also contain samples demonstrating area.

and writing. Even if groupings change during the year, I can easily make changes on the computer.

I print out a number of these sheets and use them to jot down plans for each week. As the work is completed, I place a check mark on the page, using this as my guide to plan the next week's work. I drop these dated sheets into a folder in my file during the year. They have now become a record as well as a plan, and I can refer to them during reporting periods and parent conferences.

Groups as Part of Individualized Instruction

Let's look at some issues concerning group management. When I introduce a new concept in math, I usually work with from two to five children, depending on who is ready. In order to pull together a group of children who are ready for the same instruction, I may give a few individuals enrichment work while one or two others "catch up."

Math Planning — Week of March 3

* = groups with me

Anna, Jill: C-rod / addition practice — Thurs: work with Carol — counting bags (nuts, shells, stones) — count backwards under 12 & "take away"

Ted, Chuck: practice / subtraction facts 7–10, with counters — *Wed: with me counting back using number line — Thurs: Miriam rules for zeros, doubles

Suzie, Cindy: ____

Kent, Betsy, Patty: subtraction practice pp. Mon / Mon/Tues addition practice — *Tues: work with me — place value unifix cubes / compute games pp — Wed: Trading game with Betsy & Betty who need reinforcement — Thurs: practice pp place value / *Thurs: work with me introduce 2 digit +

Mark, Jerry: enrichment activities — fractions with pattern blocks

Stacie, Ron: practice pages 2 digit + — Thurs. choose game w. partner

Emma, Jason: subtraction practice 2 digits using Base Ten Blocks

Adam, Mike: X — multiplication patterns with 100's boards & unifix cubes — color patterns on paper — record 3X to 6 or 7X

Mac: same, but working on 6X – 10X

Wendy, Alex: Work with me *Monday — concept of ÷ → ÷ with beans & paper cups → easy practice on paper

Friday: Groups finish graphs based on class surveys last Friday.

Figure 9.5 Math planning sheet.

"MARK and Ron, I have tucked in your folder a list of activities from which you can choose for the next few days of math. You might want to put your heads together, because some of these are things for which you might need a partner."

Later, in checking with these two, I find them building pattern block designs on nine-by-twelve-inch construction paper. Mark is putting the finishing touches on a second design that pretty well fills the page.

"Could we have that scorecard now?" he asks.

"It's right in plain sight on my desk," I tell him. "Help yourself." The card in question assigns a score to each pattern block shape. They will count each shape in a design, record it on a chart, and sum up using a calculator.

The list I gave them also included a choice of computer and board games, chip trading, and the suggestion that they make up story problems using characters in a book they are reading.

I try to use manipulatives and games in such a way that the child who is waiting for others to "catch up" is occupied with activities that do enrich, not just busywork.

In addition to gathering a group of children for instruction with the teacher, children can also work in groups on their own. I often assign a group to work on chip trading or to play some other math game for a day. Even when children are working in heterogeneous groups, their individualized learning moves forward. Planning for individualized work and for work on individual goals within heterogeneous groups requires a delicate balancing act. It depends on what individual students need at a particular time.

GROUPS are scattered around the room, counting. Children pile sets of ten seeds in small paper cups. "Two, four, six, eight—we need two more tens," Emma points out. When they get two more she dumps them all into a plastic margerine tub. "One hundred! Last year my pumpkin had more than five hundred."

Chuck takes one of the cups she has just emptied. "One, two, three, four," he drops seeds one at a time from a handful he holds.

Chuck is learning about counting and place value just by being a part of this group, listening to talk about tens, ones, and hundreds, and to Emma counting by twos. When he arrives at formal instruction in place value or counting by twos, these experiences will help the concept fall into place for him. He may even surprise me with what he has already learned from his multiage classmates.

Putting together a math program day by day is a little like choreographing an intricate dance. Many steps must be pulled together in coordinating the hands-on tasks and the pencil-and-paper-tasks, the manipulatives, the games: introduce, practice, and apply. Sometimes children work alone, sometimes together, but each child's part in the dance must be noted, the child's progress recorded, and the child's successes celebrated.

CHAPTER TEN

■

BECOMING LITERATE

Molly McClaskey and Anne Bingham

MOLLY McCLASKEY: LITERACY LESSONS

ETHAN moved like a Ninja, his legs and arms swinging, his grunts signaling his imagined power. He was nearly airborne by the time he reached me, holding a small paper book in his teeth, arms slicing the air. Luckily, no one was in his way. He cut through the already bustling atmosphere with a shout: "I can read this! I can read! Listen!" And we did. Ethan pointed to several words he had written on the first page of a blank wallpaper book he had found at the writing table. He pointed to the letters he used to represent words, "I LK NJ," as he read, "I like Ninjas." "Ms. McClaskey, I can read!" he said exuberantly.

"Yes you can," I replied excitedly. Six-year-old Ethan is learning to read through his writing, as many children do.

Planning Time
Today Ethan chose to work at the writing table during Planning Time (called Explore Time or Choice Time in many schools), a switch from the building and tactile activities he chooses on most days. He wanted to experiment with writing on his own terms, with no one watching. He is making the connection between the spoken word and print in slow, concrete steps, reeling in his literacy lessons from his experiences with labeling block structures, watching me write his words while he tells a story, singing and chanting a song or poem as someone points to each word, recording his findings at the science table, or reading a simple book in a warm lap with an adult who points to the words.

Print was beginning to make sense to Ethan. I could see the words coming to life for him. "He got it today," I happily reported to my husband when I got home. Ethan was gaining the control he desperately sought. I knew that, gradually, he would become an independent reader and writer, a step I had struggled to imagine for him when I first met him as a four-year-old two years before. (Most of my beginners are five, but a few are still four when they start school.) Now six, he was hearing and associating sounds with letters, connecting meaning with print, and making intentional use of letters to communicate his thoughts—and he was also motivated to practice and experiment with these new skills independently. Ethan was having a literacy breakthrough, making sense of what had previously been a confusing cacophony of sounds and letters.

Ethan shot back to the writing table, grunts and karate chops preceding him, to add more to his story, while I jubilantly jotted notes in my anecdotal records about his emerging skills. I left Ethan to his own devices. Observing his hard-won independence and success, I did not want to get in the way.

Planning Time is a sixty- to ninety-minute block of child-directed time at the start of the day. When the children arrive each morning, they sign their names in the check-in book (my way of doing attendance) and immediately go outside the door to "make a plan" on the large pegboard that is mounted on the wall and shared by the three classes in our multiage team. The pegboard displays labeled pictures of classroom areas such as blocks, drama, and sand, as well as of specific activities that change weekly, like a sewing, gardening, or problem-solving project. Parent volunteers often contribute extra hands and activities at this time. The children plan for the morning by hanging their name tag on one of the hooks under the picture of their activity. There are two to six hooks under each picture. If the hooks are full, they choose something else. Two days each week they plan an activity in any of the three classrooms; on the other days they plan to be in our own room. Children spontaneously make up their own activity, draw a picture of it, and hang it on the pegboard for other children to choose. Activities are often extensions of theme work.

Planning Time is orchestrated by the children. They take responsibility for themselves in pursuing their interests and passions. They move independently throughout the classroom, changing their plans when necessary. It is a rich and active time in the day. When I am not absorbed in an activity, I am moving among the children, listening, watching, and taking anecdotal notes.

Literacy is practiced independently and taught informally throughout Planning Time. I can observe how they apply literacy skills during this self-directed block of time. The writing center in my classroom encourages literacy practice through communication and interaction. The writing center is

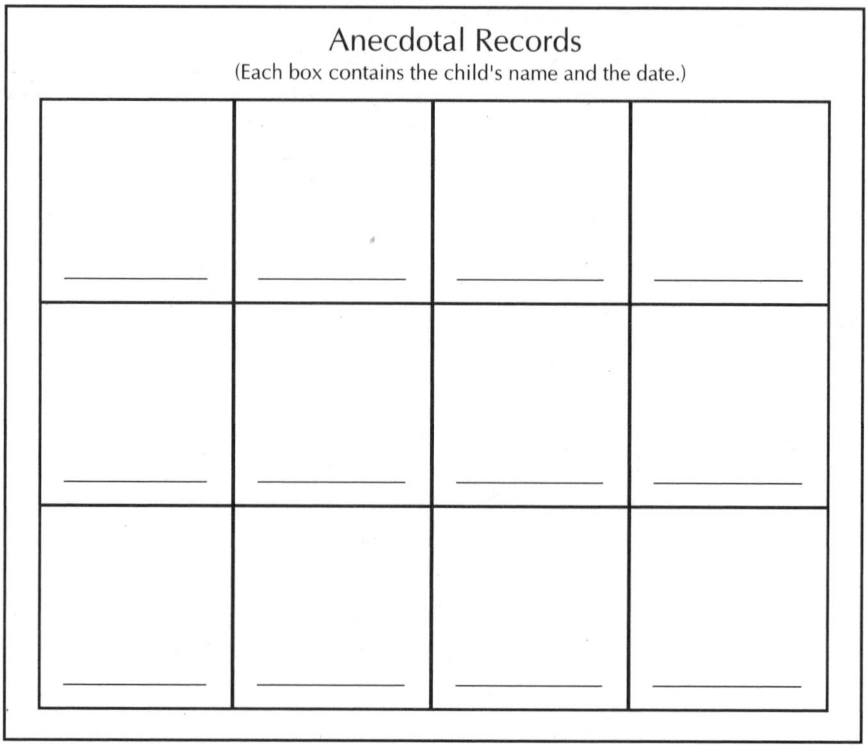

Anecdotal Records
(Each box contains the child's name and the date.)

_____	_____	_____	_____
_____	_____	_____	_____
_____	_____	_____	_____

Figure 10.1 Anecdotal records keep track of each child's emerging skills.

equipped with blank books of many shapes and sizes, colored and regular pencils, rubber letter stamps, rulers, glue, tape, and paper. Envelopes, wildlife stamps, and a variety of other materials are added during the year to encourage different kinds of writing, to draw in another child, or to extend the theme we are studying. Children might go to the writing table often and for several days in succession or, like Ethan, rarely choose writing for their daily plan. Some children choose areas in the room where literacy skills are practiced more subtly, like the science corner, block area, or art table.

In the block area, children record their work in "The Block Book" and write about their structures or represent them in pictures. They make signs to define buildings or villages and indicate who built it and how many days it has been standing.

While harvesting our class garden this fall, the children become fascinated with worms. We filled the sand table with soil and they brought in worms from the garden and made a list of rules about caring for worms. Later they wrote their observations in booklets.

Every Friday a parent helps several children plan the next week's snacks. The children write menus, make a shopping list, and shop for food. The cook of the day follows a written recipe or sets out a simple snack with parent help.

Children in the drama area are working at an "architect's studio," an outgrowth of our study of community and homes. They are creating documents in a cardboard "blueprint machine" they have fashioned, making architectural sketches at the drafting table, and labeling the rooms and parts of the buildings they design to look like a drawing they saw on a field trip.

Children inadvertently discover their need for literacy competence. Literacy is woven into everything we do in school, just as it is in the "real" world. The children practice reading, writing, speaking, and listening skills throughout the morning as natural ways to participate, create, and communicate. Planning Time provides concrete purposes for their literacy learning.

When the music comes on softly, children put away their Planning Time activities. One child takes the planning journals from their box on top of the math shelf and spreads them out on the floor for everyone to find when they have finished cleaning up. Children record their morning's activities with words and pictures. Ethan has a large space for a picture and a few lines under it on his journal pages. He writes, "I KN RD" (I can read) on his entry for the day and stamps the top of his paper with the date. His picture is a quick line drawing of him and Ely sitting at the writing table. Leo writes about the house he has constructed in the block area, with attached garage and a computerized alarm system that detects robbers. He writes with ease and the pages of his planning journal are fully lined, with just a small space for a picture at the bottom. Keith describes his work at the drama area, now an architect's studio, while Eliza tells about making butterflies from clay in the classroom next door, where a chrysalis has just opened. Each child records the morning's activity in a manner appropriate to his or her own developmental level. Some children fill two pages with writing, while others write two sentences, and still others draw a picture and dictate to a classroom helper. As the children complete their journals and read them aloud with me or a parent volunteer, they help themselves to a snack and visit with their classmates until everyone has finished and shared in the good food.

Now our morning meeting begins, and the children share their discoveries from Planning Time with one another. Ethan explains, "I learned to read today. I can show you," and he eagerly reads his one-line story. Keith has brought "The Block Book" to the meeting and shows the picture he drew of his structure. He reads the description of the complicated alarm system, explaining each part of his structure—spring, wire, and lever. The other children talk and listen in turn. They all learn from one another the many possibilities of each area in the room and are stretched by the provocations, innovations, and discoveries of their classmates.

Planning Time gives depth and purpose to daily journal entries and class discussion. It provides children with self-directed time for practicing literacy skills and applying them to their other learning.

Literacy Groups

RYAN roared like Frankenstein's monster through the classroom door, his outstretched hands dripping with clear art paste. He wore a man-sized maroon shirt buttoned up the back to protect his clothes. "You should see how big he is . . . he comes up to here," he blurted, holding a slimy hand to his chin. "Come see, Ms. McClaskey!" Most of the class had already left their small groups and were pushing through the classroom door to see the life-sized penguin Ryan's group was making. I followed the crowd. Indeed, the Emperor Penguin was nearly the height of a six-year-old. This was a tantalizing discovery!

Four literacy groups like Ryan's were working simultaneously in the room and in the pod, the common space outside the door that we share with seven other classes. The groups were at various stages of investigating a topic. Our team, then two classrooms, was studying Antarctica, and literacy groups had chosen subtopics to research. One group had gathered around books on seals, which were spread on the floor in front of them, and were reading to themselves and out loud. The assistant for two special needs children in this group was leading, asking questions and guiding the readers as they looked in the books for seals from Antarctica. She recorded their findings on large paper. Younger children in the group were paired with older or fluent readers. Other groups had finished gathering information and were either writing or planning their projects. The group studying whales wanted to make a book together. I watched as the student teacher skillfully paired emerging writers with more experienced authors. Then they began to create the text of their joint big book. Another group had started a small model of a glacier with me, and Ryan's group, assisted by a parent volunteer, had put a first coat of papier-mâché on its Emperor Penguin.

A parent volunteer, a special education assistant, and a student teacher from the University of Vermont work with small groups like these. Two children in my classroom share a full-time special education assistant. She integrates these children with the whole class through mixed-age and mixed-ability groupings for this kind of literacy work.

Literacy groups are a mixture of children from four to seven years with varying interests and strengths. The groups meet two or three times a week, depending on when parent help is available. They are one of the many ways children experience writing and reading in the classroom. The composition of these groups changes frequently in order to broaden the children's exposure to one another and to avoid stagnant groupings in which children associate themselves with a fixed reading level. At times students arrange themselves in groups based on the topics they have chosen. At other times the teacher arranges the groupings, taking into account need, range of reading material, content, and helpful pairing. Children are often paired to assist one another and model the reading process. The literacy groups stress content: children at every stage of the reading process are exposed to enticing stories and rich resource material. Some children crave fact and content; others are pulled in by a good story, but everyone wants to become a reader. Literacy groups provide children with an opportunity to delve into books with friends, so that they learn to read and to respect many points of view.

In these groups children do a variety of skill-strengthening work in the context of a book they have read together over several weeks. During that time the book is read many times in different ways: aloud, in pairs, and independently. The groups might read a big book together or multiple copies of the same book, and work on specific reading strategies, such as identifying words in a family, recognizing a repeated structural pattern, working with rhyme, practicing phonetic rules, and relying on meaning and picture clues. The teacher for each group bases mini-lessons on an element in the print that lends itself to instruction. One book might be a good example of story elements like voice, character, or plot, another better suited to discussion of rhyming or repeating phrases and prediction. A single book could be the focus of a group for a week or a month, depending on how right the book is in literacy lessons. Books are usually, but not always, related to the classroom theme and eventually lead to research and book-related projects. The groups typically move through several phases of research: posing questions, finding resources at the learning center, reading and recording information, planning, making, and finally sharing their work. The culmination of each group's endeavor is celebrated in a whole class gathering, where children demonstrate their expertise and learn from one another.

MRS. MONTRO listened during the literacy celebration while the groups made presentations on everything from Antarctic Leopard Seals to how glaciers are formed. She had been a weekly parent volunteer and worked with the group that had chosen penguins as their focus. She watched as each group of children in turn took their place and shared the information they had prepared. Abe talked about the vicious mother seal who would attack a penguin for food. Lee nervously read from a group pop-up book on whales, obviously intrigued by how far whales migrate each year. It was clear that all of them had something invested in their topic. An atmosphere of seriousness and respect filled the room.

Mrs. Montro shifted her weight as the penguin group moved to the front of the sharing circle. The children proudly carried the five-foot penguin, holding its flippers to keep it steady. Each child stepped forward to relate something about the penguins of the Antarctic. They told of the odiferous rookeries they had learned about from a naturalist who visited the class. They described penguin family units and eating habits, and how they shelter themselves during a storm, continuing for twenty minutes. No one interrupted their enthusiasm or challenged their belief in themselves as experts. After children had asked one another questions and praised each other, the groups dispersed to carry their projects to the pod, where they would be on exhibit. As Mrs. Montro helped children move the life-sized Emperor Penguin, she commented, "I've never seen young kids use books for information like this before. They really know how to look something up don't they?"

Quiet Reading

Sarah sat in the library space of our classroom with a stack of books. They ranged from *I Spy,* to a juvenile National Geographic book on animal homes to *James and the Giant Peach*. She spent a long time on each page of the nonfiction book, naming animals and working hard to decipher the text. She looked at it carefully and read some part of every page. Then she moved swiftly through the rest of her selections, giving only a cursory glance at some pages and missing others altogether. She read one page of *James and the Giant Peach* and put it down. After ten minutes she abandoned her small pile of books and foraged among the book bins, unable to settle on one. I had been watching this six-year-old choose books over many days, and I suspected I would keep watching all year. I was waiting to see if she would find her way and learn to choose a book that would keep her engaged. But I realized that it was time to review book selection strategies again.

During the year, particularly in the fall, I model book selection for the whole class, role playing a child going through the bins and baskets looking for a book. I articulate what the child might be thinking: "This one looks great, I'll read a little and see if it works. I missed too many words, I don't think I'll enjoy this one." One goal of quiet reading is to achieve reading independence, and mature book selection is a key to self-reliance. With enough practice and guidance, children will recognize text that is workable and of interest to them and become self-selecting, self-motivated readers.

I interfere as little as possible while children browse through books making selections; at the same time, I watch for children who might need guidance. Sometimes children will choose books they can read but do not yet have the endurance for. Or I see children taking a temporary break from challenging reading before returning to another long book. I also see children like Sarah, who lose their sense of direction altogether.

I SAT down on the floor beside Sarah. "What are you finding?" I asked quietly, respecting the hushed tone in the room.

"This." She proudly held up *James and the Giant Peach.*

"It looked as if you put that one down. Let's look at it together." We looked over the pages as I thumbed them slowly. "There aren't many pictures in this book are there?" I asked.

"Yeah, but I can read it, you know," Sarah responded defensively.

"I noticed you can. You have become quite a reader Sarah. Is it sometimes hard to find just the right book?"

"Yeah," she answered. This conversation felt familiar to her. She and I had been working on book selection every week since school started.

"Why do you think you didn't keep reading this one?" I asked, pointing to *James and the Giant Peach.*

"'Cause I got tired."

"That makes sense. It's long, and it has lots of words on each page. Let's try to find a book that you won't get tired with, maybe one you don't have to work quite so hard on so you can really enjoy the story." I chose five books, four in the reading range of Lillian Hoban's Arthur stories, and one an easy-to-read nonfiction book on insects. Sarah chose the nonfiction, of course. She has an appetite for nature books of all kinds. She also chose *Little Bear* (1986) by Else Holmelund Minarik. She settled in for the rest of quiet reading with a look of relief and contentment, having chosen her books in the end with a little guidance.

The room is hushed. Sarah is snug in a corner with *Little Bear,* two five-year-olds have exhausted their attention for independent reading and are listening to a book on tape, two others are working with *Stories and More* at the computer. The rest of the class is scattered around the room at tables, on the floor, nestled with the coats in the cubby area, and even under the easel, all in a place where they can enter the world of their book undisturbed.

I have assisted several children with book selection and made sure they have a private place to read. I review my clipboard with the parent volunteer and special educator who work in my classroom at this time to see which children need conferences and what strategies or skills to emphasize. We move around the room spending ten to fifteen minutes in a book conference with a child and keeping running records of each conference to note miscues, decoding strategies, and retellings. These daily assessments are filed in the child's reading folder. They are reviewed during each conference and aid the adult in identifying each child's specific needs. Running records also guide planning and provide information to report to parents. They are added to the child's portfolio each marking period, providing a continuous picture of reading progress throughout the year.

Book Talk

I put quiet music on the tape recorder and the children recognize the signal to pack up their books. Some children save out a book for Book Talk if they have noticed it is next on the daily schedule. Book Talk occurs one or two times each week. We gather in the meeting area to talk about books. "Who has a book they want to discuss?" I ask the chattering group.

SALLY is eagerly raising her book in the air. I call on her.

"I'm reading *Uncle Elephant* by Arnold Lobel. I'm actually reading all the books in the Arnold Lobel basket. This is my fifth one," she proclaims proudly.

"You must really like Arnold Lobel, Sally," I respond.

"Yeah, I do. Did you ever notice all his characters are talking animals?" Sally remembers our discussion about talking animals as main characters in our last book talk.

Jeff agrees, "Yeah, Frog and Toad talk."

"What would you like to tell us about Uncle Elephant?"

"Well, it's a sad story because the little elephant doesn't know if his parents will come back."

"That does sound sad. Can you read us that part?" I ask. Sally quickly flips to the beginning and reads. Several children raise their hands. She calls on Eben, whose freckled face is twisted with a worried look.

"Where are elephant's parents?" he asks.

"They're lost in a boat and his parents left him home 'cause he had a runny trunk. That was funny. Instead of a runny nose, get it?" Sally chuckled.

"I'd be scared. My parents would have taken me with them or called my baby-sitter," Eben said earnestly. Many hands shot up and a long discussion followed about the young elephant's dilemma and being home alone. After we had shared many points of view, we predicted how the problem of the story might be resolved.

The book was a perfect model for discussing story format—introduction, story problem, and conclusion. I asked the children who had already read the book to keep the end a secret while the others thought about the ending. Sally ended by asking, "Who wants my book when I finish it?" Nearly every hand went up.

Books that are talked about during Book Talk are always popular, and this one was exceptionally thought provoking. Sally gave it to Tara, who had not received a book from a peer for some time. It would be a "looking book" for her, but reading the story from the pictures would be easier for her now, after our lengthy discussion. Other children will ask her for it when she is finished, and it will circulate throughout the room, a "looking book" for some, a quick read for others, and a perfect reading level for many. Regardless of their reading level, Book Talk helps readers interpret what they are reading and gives books and authors special significance. All the children, regardless of age or stage in the reading process, are exposed to good literature and benefit from it on many levels. As the year progresses, a vital pipeline of interest and book exchange develops. A contagious love of literature fills the room.

Shared Language

I hang a chart from the easel as the children tuck their books from Book Talk behind them. It displays a winter poem carefully written in enlarged print. Rhyming words are highlighted in matching colors. I point as we read the poem together. We play with the beat and change our voices from loud to soft in places. I ask children to describe what they notice when they look at the poem. The diverse levels and developmental stages of our mixed-age class are obvious in children's unique views of aspects of the verse. Allison recognizes three *t*s in a row. Sam sees the repeating short vowel *a* in two rhyming words, and Ethan tells us that the *ing* makes a certain sound in a word and then makes the sound for us. Kevin is proud to find the word *was* throughout the poem. This shared reading time is another element in the literacy program: children discover, learn, and practice letter identification, sound-letter correspondence, phonetic rules, spelling patterns, language structure, and a variety of reading strategies. The skills they rehearse as a whole group in this setting are reinforced and practiced in the context of their individual reading and writing at other times during the day.

Writer's Workshop

Children glance up at the daily schedule posted on the wall near the easel. They know now why I put on the dancing music. We are getting ready for a quiet work time and need some body movement and stretching first. We dance, each moving in his own space. We often move around or sing a song with gross motor movements to make a transition from class meeting to work time. When the children seem stretched and ready, I hand out writing folders one by one, offering reminders or a bit of encouragement to each writer: "Ben, are you going to finish your fish story today?" "Keith, I like your description of floating like a balloon. I could picture that."

Val, a class member, recently moved away. She had been with us for two years and everyone was feeling her absence. The day after she left I asked the children to talk about their feelings in a discussion before writer's workshop. Their conversation was a rehearsal of sorts, a first run, preparing their ideas for writing. That day, some wrote letters, others made cards, and still others wrote books and dedicated them to her.

Writing is another avenue for teaching and practicing literacy skills. It is a tool for recording and communicating in math, planning time, science, language arts, music, the arts, and social studies. Twice each week we write in long, uninterrupted blocks of time for the pure sake of authorship and storytelling. This is Writer's Workshop, a space of forty-five to sixty minutes during which children write, hold writing conferences, illustrate, and publish their own work. Like quiet reading, it is an individualized work time. The teacher floats, facilitates, assists, and records each child's progress, taking care not to interrupt those who are immersed in thought and creating a story.

Writer's Workshop accentuates and models the author as personal storyteller. Mini-lessons occasionally precede the children's writing time. They might highlight an author's style, words that describe, or how stories begin. Or small groups might come together to look at one student's writing and discuss punctuation and other skills as the need arises or as good models emerge. I plan to discuss the use of metaphor with a group of fluent writers now that Keith has discovered it on his own. In another mini-lesson I share my experiences as a fledgling author with the class and talk about my participation in a "writer's workshop" with my peers. I show my rough drafts and point out revising and editing marks. The children are always amazed at all my errors and revisions. Once a five-year-old viewing my scrambled pages remarked, "What a mess. How do you read that?" Through this demonstration the children realize they, too, are practicing authors; they, too, are learning to edit and revise their work.

A hushed tone surrounds us as the children settle in to their work. They review their lists of stories to see which are unfinished. They reread passages or begin new pieces. Several children compose stories at the computers while others have dispersed to tables and the floor, finding a quiet niche. Two four-year-olds are drawing and talking quietly about their stories. An adult will transcribe their words below their drawings. A five-year-old at the same table has finished a picture and is making random letters at the bottom of the page. My student teacher approaches and writes the words of his story beneath his writing, accentuating each syllable and initial sound out loud. She involves the child in naming the letters he hears in each word as she writes it. Other children are making books and filling pages with their own writing. The children take this work seriously. Several children in the class are sure they will continue to be writers when they grow up.

Today, Toby, who is laboring to gain reading fluency, told a volunteer, "I don't really like reading. It's hard. But I love writing." Although the skills required in both reading and writing intersect, children do not always see the interrelationship. Fortunately, Toby sees himself as a strong author, while recognizing his difficulty with reading. Toby is another child who learned to read through writing, and it continues to support his reading.

I HUNCHED down next to five-year-old Ely to watch and listen to his writing process. He had drawn a colorful, detailed person in tall grass. He asked Sheila, the seven-year-old next to him, how to spell *run*. She said the word slowly, as I would have, so Ely could hear the sounds as they were elongated. He wrote "RN." "Is this right?" he asked her. Sheila replied, "Yup," without looking up. Then Ely reread his short piece aloud in order to find his place.

"I am run," he read. He added an *ing*, remembering this morning's reading of the winter poem. "Finished!" he announced to Sheila, who never acknowledged his remark. He grinned from ear to ear as he read it again, satisfied even without recognition from Sheila.

Quiet conversations like this one happen throughout writing time as children ask their peers for assistance and read their work aloud in order to hear it.

Sheila was absorbed in her writing project, a nonfiction book about houses and an extension of our class theme. I asked Sheila to read her work with me and we discussed various spellings and phrases. On a recording log stapled to the inside cover of her writing folder, I noted the skills we had worked on and those she was using independently. Her writing folder, like those of her peers, was full of stories written on different kinds of paper and in a variety of homemade blank books. Each child keeps a running list of stories and indicates when a story is complete. Teachers also note if a piece was edited and if a conference took place. This helps maintain some organization in the child's collection and allows the teacher to look over the work accomplished each day quickly. Sheila mentioned that she had completed four stories and was ready to publish. Together we checked her story list and made plans to have a reflective conference next time.

Children choose a favorite or best piece after they have completed four. Then they take part in a self-evaluation process with a parent volunteer. The assisting adult asks questions that encourage self-reflection: "What makes this your best work so far?" or "Why did you choose this story?" Sometimes the child writes her reflections on an "entry slip," which is attached to the original story and put in the child's portfolio for future comparison. Entry

Student Selected Writing Sample

This sample was complete on (date): _____

It was:
- ☐ done independently
- ☐ done with assistance
- ☐ dictated to an adult
- ☐ copied

It is:
- ☐ a revision
- ☐ a first draft
- ☐ student selected
- ☐ teacher selected

What makes this your best work? _____
_____
_____
_____

What did you learn from writing this? _____
_____
_____
_____

Figure 10.2 Self-evaluation by the students encourages self-reflection.

slips help explain to parents and future teachers each item in a child's portfolio. (See Chapter 11 for more information about portfolios.) A parent volunteer then edits the story with the child and types it on the computer in such a way that short pages are already in a book format. The parent makes a cardboard and wallpaper cover and the child adds illustrations. Like other pieces of the children's work, published books are shared with the whole class. The children have an opportunity to ask questions and offer feedback to the proud author. The author takes the book home where parents can share in the excitement of the published story. Children eventually bring their books back to school, where they are kept in a basket of student-authored books. These often become the most popular in our classroom library.

Family Reading

Regular reading at home is another component in the instruction and development of literacy. My teammate Janet and I were looking for a way to emphasize the role of reading at home and assist in creating a family reading ethic. We also wanted parents to be more aware of and involved in their children's reading development. We created "Family Reading."

Children pack up a homemade cotton book bag with a book they are reading, or want to read, along with their reading journal after Book Talk on Friday afternoons. Over the weekend parents and children read together in any way that suits the child and the situation. Parents write comments about each weekend's reading in the journal and look forward to a reply from the teacher the next week.

"Dear Molly . . . I feel the greatest problem Alan has with reading is losing his place. He just seems to stall. I try to get him to point or use a bookmark and he balks a bit, so I point . . . "

"Dear Joan, Keep up the great reading at home! We'll try introducing book marks at school for some so that Alan won't feel alone in keeping his place with one."

Teachers can also make suggestions to parents who ask about strategies for helping young readers.

"Julie is being instructed to point to each word, predict words that will come next, and watch for the beginning sounds of words. The one-to-one correspondence in pointing is very important at this stage."

The observations parents make also contribute to the teacher's picture of each child and provide opportunities to reassure parents who worry needlessly. One parent wrote:

"Jenny does well in her reading, but we are seeing a decreased interest. She becomes frustrated easily and has been choosing books that she read last year and that are quite easy for her now."

"Children's reading often fluctuates; Jenny is not unusual in this respect. I will keep an eye on her book selections and guide her to more challenging books if she does not return to them on her own. Children often take a break and fall back on familiar text after tackling a difficult book."

We observed an additional benefit: parents came to conferences more aware of and realistic about their child's reading progress.

Children also became intrigued with this family reading journal. During the first year of the program, they began to write in the journal along with their parents. When the teacher wrote back, the children were excited about having their notes read and answered. They were eager to keep the dialogue going—it was as thrilling as getting mail. They told their friends and now both parents and children write in the reading journal. Reading and writing at home have become a valued routine that builds a bridge between home and school.

Learning to read and write is a multilayered process that intertwines with every aspect of the classroom day. Rich content and open-ended exploration compel children to communicate their ideas. They read, write, listen, and discuss with genuine purpose:

- while responding to one another in conversation
- while discussing characters in a book
- while recording observations of earthworms
- while writing their own word problems
- while composing fiction and nonfiction
- while researching a trip to an architect's office
- while keeping data on color-mixing experiments
- while planning and building an imaginary community called Peace Town

This continuous, integrated practice leads to literacy competence, independence, and empowerment.

ANNE BINGHAM: PIECES OF THE LITERACY PUZZLE

Molly McClaskey has portrayed literacy as a thread that weaves throughout the school day. So many activities contribute to the development of literacy! Since I've already presented literacy in the context of Explore Time and thematic work, I'm going to concentrate here on what goes on during the afternoon block I set aside for language arts. How do we spend our afternoons in Room A—those afternoons when we are not totally involved in a theme?

The language block includes all the things that are a part of a whole language environment in combinations that vary from day to day and from one part of the year to another. The schedule might be:

12:20–12:45 Read-aloud story or poem
12:45–1:15 Quiet reading
1:15–2:00 Literature and instructional groups, writing, spelling, and handwriting
2:00–2:20 Shared reading or writing, singalong, or read-aloud time

The item on this list that varies most is the read-aloud time. After lunch and just before going home are both especially good times to relax and savor a story together, so this changes from year to year and sometimes even during the year. Quiet reading provides such a good opening for other language activities that it most often begins the block.

My Language Arts Work for This Week	
☐ Reading	☐ Conference
☐ Monday Journal	☐ Handwriting practice
☐ Writing Project	☐ Puzzle or word work in folder

Figure 10.3 An assignment sheet from a reading-writing folder.

After quiet reading, the children choose from a variety of activities: Some read aloud to a parent volunteer and talk about the story. Others work in a small group on anything from phonics to editing. At the same time, still other children write, have a writing conference, work on spelling, or practice handwriting. On another day some children might meet in a literature group, under my guidance or that of a parent, to discuss a book they have all read. The children usually choose their own activities unless they are meeting with a group, I initiate a conference, or I ask them to read to me or another adult. They also decide for themselves how much of an activity to do on any particular day. They might concentrate totally on writing a story for a day or two, as long as they have not neglected other expected activities over the week as a whole.

Their individual reading-writing folders remind them of some of those expectations. They contain the children's current writing projects, each child's personal wordbook or dictionary, small books for beginners, and an occasional puzzle sheet. They may also contain individual contracts, or assignment sheets, on which children can check off the activities they have done. In my class the older children use these during at least part of the year. The sheets list the language arts activities I expect the children to find time for each week. Occasionally I will give them a specific assignment, such as a story to read, but mostly they check items off on the general list.

We close this quite individualized session by coming together again to share our own stories, books we've read, a read-aloud, or a singalong with Rooms A, B, C, D, the classes that are a part of our team.

Individualized Reading

Individualized reading goes on all year as children make personal book choices during quiet reading. I monitor this reading through reading logs and conferences. Quiet reading time may begin as fifteen minutes and expand to thirty, sometimes more, as the year progresses. I will hear some children read aloud during this time and discuss a book with others.

Figure 10.4 Individualized reading goes on all year.

The older children, at the beginning of the year mostly eight-year-olds, make a dated entry in their reading logs at the end of quiet reading time each day. Later, most children are keeping some kind of record: some simply record a book title, others a paragraph about the story. This process is supported by brief conferences with me about their reading and about their choices.

Conferences are essential parts of the interactive process of teaching and assessing progress. They enable me to assess whether children are using a variety of strategies to recognize and remember new words, whether they are paying attention to meaning with self-correcting strategies, and whether they can summarize a story and discuss it. It may also be necessary to confer with some children about their book choices, as Molly McClaskey has so clearly illustrated with Sarah. Conferences in my classroom are usually short impromptu meetings, which occur as I circulate among the children or as they come to me for help.

"How's it going, Ron? Are you enjoying that book?"

"Yeah. It's pretty funny."

"How did you happen to choose *Fantastic Mr. Fox?*"

"Well, the kids talk a lot about Roald Dahl books . . . and I liked the one you read last year."

"*James and the Giant Peach?*"

"Yeah, that one."

"Would you choose a part you really like and read just a bit to me?"

"OK, I think I'll read about Farmer Bunce."

I have tried again and again to impose some kind of formal conference structure on my school week, scheduling whom I will see each day and how often I will meet with certain groups, but this quickly proves too rigid to allow me to respond to special and spontaneous needs.

I do keep records, however. Here I use my class lists again, this time ruled off in a grid that gives me a row of squares after each child's name, like a class record book. The days of the week are indicated across the top. I record my brief conferences as follows:

R reading conference or reading aloud
W writing conference
A work with a teacher aide
V work with a volunteer, another adult specifically asked
    to work with a child

A quick glance tells me if I have missed someone during the week. I also have a planning and anecdotal record sheet similar to the one I use for math (see Figures 10.5 and 10.6).

For all the reasons I have mentioned in discussing student decision making, choosing their own reading matter is an important experience for children. Interest and ownership are big factors in motivation. Beginners and children needing special help will often be reading books of their own choice during quiet reading time; at other times I will ask them to work with me and follow up by reading a story I suggest.

In addition, very capable readers often need to expand on the kinds of reading they do and the types of books they enjoy. Sometimes they seem to be stuck on one author or in one genre. That's OK for a while, but I also like them to have a variety of reading experiences.

That's where the "reading wheel" comes in. The wheel is printed on a piece of oaktag that fits into individual reading-writing folders (similar to math folders). In each section of the wheel I list a different type of book: a mystery story, a story set in another country, a story about someone who is handicapped, a biography, a story from America's past, a talking animal story, a story about friendship, a fairy tale or folktale. The categories change a bit from year to year. As children finish a book in each category, they color in that segment of the wheel (see Figure 10.7).

Usually I start a group by introducing one category, for which I have gathered a basket of books of varying lengths and levels. I expand on the categories of books as children work through the program, reading in a category of their own choice after our initial group start. They can also search for a book in the school library, and because they move through the program at different rates, one child may pass a particularly popular book on to a friend.

. . . .

	Dec 3 M	T	W	Th	F	M	T	W	Th
Jill	R	V		A	R				
Chuck	R		W	A					
Anna	V	R		A	R				
Ted		R		R	W				
Suzie		V	R	R					
Kent	V		R						
Patty		R		A	R				
Jerry	R	V	R						
Mark		V		R	R				
Cindy		W		R					
Stacie	V		W	R					
Betsy									
Ron			W						

Figure 10.5 Checklist for brief conferences.

For many children the reading wheel opens an entirely new door into the reading world. They encounter history through story; they are introduced to children of other countries or children coping with handicaps; budding athletes suddenly discover biographies of sports heroes.

Books available for quiet reading in Room A come from a number of sources. I have a large collection of children's paperbacks, which I've acquired over a number of years, including small, predictable books for beginners like the Story Box collection. I also bring in armfuls of books from our school library, especially easy-to-read books and short chapter books, which I sort into brightly colored plastic baskets, easy readers in a red basket, short chapter

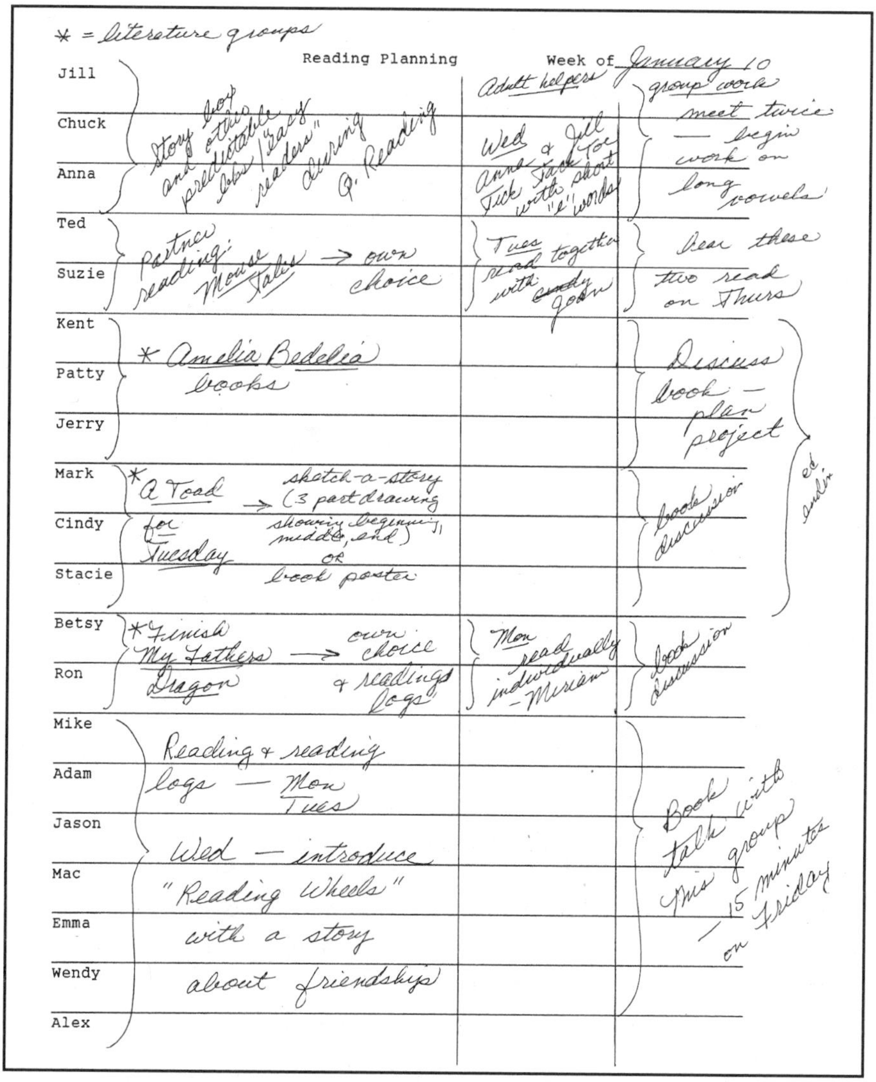

Figure 10.6 *Checklist for reading planning.*

books in a green one. Sometimes I sort them by author (Bill Peet), by topic (dog stories), or by genre (fairy tales). The commitment to teach reading in the context of meaningful language requires a careful look at the reading materials we use with children.

Children's literature offers a rich source of picture books, stories, and novels, but it is sometimes a challenge to find the right fit for a particular child. One of the most useful resources I have found in this regard is the blue pages at the end of Regie Routman's books, *Transitions* (1988) and *Invitations* (1994a). (*The Blue Pages* [1994b] are now available as a separate book.) They

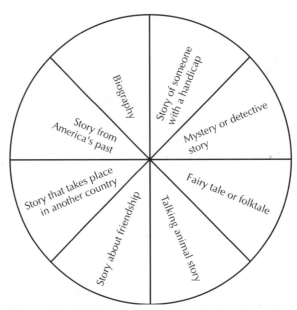

Figure 10.7 Children read a variety of genres from the "reading wheel."

list a wide range of stories classified by level of difficulty and literary style. Children reading longer books are also encouraged to select books from the school library. Our librarian always allows children to check out a book for quiet reading in the classroom in addition to the books they take home.

Some children need to work on sight words, while others do not need much help in this area since they gather new words easily from their reading. This kind of work is very individualized and occurs in one-on-one sessions, often with a parent volunteer. I like to use words from Don Holdaway's Bedrock Sight Vocabulary (*Independence in Reading,* 1980). Each word is contained in a sentence so that it can first be practiced in context. This format, however, can be adapted to any list of basic sight words.

"Reading Groups": A New Look

As I have noted, multiage classrooms rarely include fixed groups. A group will exist for a while for a given purpose, then change or disband. I enjoy literature groups. Discussion adds dimensions capable readers don't get when they read on their own: an understanding of a story from more than one person's point of view, critical assessment and comparison with other literature, the enjoyment of good books in the company of friends. Nancie Atwell (1987) has compared this in *In the Middle* to book talk around the dining-room table, something many children do not experience at home very often.

The children in a literature group read the same book and meet regularly to discuss it. The group allows them to develop a number of skills that a wholly individualized program does not. They share background information and make predictions, an important prereading process. They discuss character, setting, and plot. We look together at how stories begin, develop (often around a problem), and end. The children also share their opinions and reactions to stories, beginning to think critically about what they read. In the process, they learn to respect individual responses to literature.

IN *The Biggest Bear* some children were horrified that Johnny might be expected to shoot his friend, but the actual ending provoked an even greater response from Mike: "Zoos are very, very bad places for animals!"

"But some zoos take very good care of them," asserted Patty, "and it's good for people to see them, if they like animals and nature. Then they might worry about some of them getting extinct."

"How would you like to live in a cage?"

"But in the story," Jill pointed out, "it was better than getting shot."

Literature groups need not start meeting in September. Beginners need a lot of time and attention early in the year, so during that time the better readers choose their own books. When other work is under way and I have a handle on everyone's needs and reading level, we launch the groups. They don't have to meet continuously through the year, either. Some groups may meet for a month or two while the other children follow an individualized reading program. Later, these groups change places. Everything does not have to be happening to everybody all the time.

Literature groups can be formed in a variety of ways. Often I set them up myself, based on children's approximate reading level and likely ability to read the same book at about the same rate.

It is possible to set up groups on a different basis occasionally, to announce a selection of books and allow the children to choose their group on the basis of the book that will be read and discussed. Students who read more slowly will often rise to the occasion when given a chance to select their own reading matter, but they may also need extra time. The limiting factor is that difficult books cannot be offered as special challenges to better readers.

During a theme study, when children are reading nonfiction, it is possible to work on different reading skills: to establish a purpose for reading, to look for specific details, and to skim to locate information.

Some schools provide collections of children's paperback books for use with groups. These are often gathered in sets of about six and stored for teacher use. In our school, such collections are available in the library for the parent volunteers who work with book discussion groups throughout the school. If collections like these are not available, a teacher can gather—over a period of years—such sets for a classroom library.

In addition to literature groups, I arrange another kind of "reading group": the instructional group. As in math, I pull them together as needed for what I call "word work." Beginners work on such things as long and short vowels, story patterns, and word families. They gather on the rug in front of the easel and we use poems, stories, collections of words on large sheets of newsprint, and word games to focus on these concepts.

I meet more often with beginning readers than with children who have become more independent, but groups of all ages will do some "word work." With the older children this includes phonics, word structures, spelling, and word meaning. Some children need this work for spelling development, others for reading. Membership is fluid, although the core group may stay the same: some children are invited in for a week or two depending on the topic, and new topics come up when I see the need in children's reading or writing. If only one child needs the work, we handle it during a conference, but if there are several children, I pull a group together.

One activity I use in these groups is sorting into categories: for example, sorting *ow* words into one group that sounds like *cow* and one that sounds like *snow*. *The Reading Teacher's Book of Lists* (Fry, Polk, and Fountoukidis 1984) has been an invaluable resource for planning these activities. The children search storybooks for words that belong in a group, those with the inflectional ending *ing,* for example, or compound words.

" s e e the one I just found." Cindy shows me the word *peppermint* in a poetry book she is reading.

"Look at this. I knew I saw one in my library book on oceans." Ron points to the word *frogman.*

In fifteen minutes I'll call the whole crew together to see how many compound words they have collected. They are starting lists in the back of their personal dictionaries, which I call their wordbooks, and they will continue to add to them during the year.

Word searches and crossword puzzles are also favorite tasks for these groups, often in relation to a theme.

Instructional groups, like literature groups, need not meet continuously all year. During the fall of the year I sometimes have a flurry of such activity; then we take a break while I carry on as needed in individual conferences or partner work.

Writing

In a multiage classroom, writing is pervasive and varied. It may take place in conjunction with themes, since some projects are in the form of written reports. I do not have a separate writer's workshop; the writing goes on during the workshop atmosphere of the language arts block. Often the first thing the younger children do is pull out their personal journals, in which they write and draw. On some days a literature or instructional group might be meeting during the same time, or neighbors might be having a reading or a writing conference. There have been years when I planned separate periods for writing and reading, and an alternative would also be to emphasize writing on some days and literature on others. There will be times when everyone is concentrating on writing, and I begin the afternoon with a writing mini-lesson.

Mini-lessons are ideal ways to introduce a variety of genres, including poetry and letter writing, to the whole group. What Wendy, at age eight, will do in writing a letter to a friend will be quite different from Kent's one-liner to his grandmother, but both children will start with the same form. The group can brainstorm for ideas about what might go into a letter and talk about opening and closing conventions. Children will have an expanding number of possibilities for their own writing projects as they encounter different genres.

During mini-lessons we also discuss various aspects of the writing process. A multiage setting lends itself to the concepts of process writing because the choice of topic or genre can be so open-ended and the product so varied. Here are some of the concepts children need to understand, adapted to a wide developmental range:

Prewriting: We discuss some of the things writers do when they get ready to write: draw a picture, talk with a friend or an adult, brainstorm a list of details, make a "story map" or "web." All these options can be accommodated in a multiage setting and demonstrated to the entire group. Younger children will usually draw first, but they can also try activities older children may need to learn, such as creating a "story map." Encourage the older children to try appropriate new methods and to illustrate their stories after they are completed, instead of before writing them. If an older child needs to draw first, however, other children will also be doing just that, making it a comfortable option.

Drafting: The first words that are put on paper do not have to be perfect. Like clay they can be changed and reworked. One big difference between children of different ages will be the length of each piece of writing as well as spacing and handwriting. For the younger children, learning to form letters goes hand in hand with beginning writing. The youngest may start out using paper with no lines and lots of space for a picture. Older children, on the other hand, may need to be encouraged to stretch their thinking and add more details to their writing.

Responding: Learning to respond to each other's writing most often comes at this stage of the process, in connection with revision, when children share finished or in-progress stories with the whole group and have conferences with each other. We expect them to listen to another child's writing and respond in a way that will be helpful to that writer. These "kid conferences" have three essential steps: (1) find something you liked or that "works well" in the story and tell the author about it; (2) ask questions if there is something you didn't understand or if you need more information; (3) remember that the story belongs to the person who wrote it. He or she will decide whether or not to make changes.

These response guidelines can be modeled in class sessions when children read their writing to the group. Younger children become skillful listeners and responders, and responses from children of different ages make for a rich variety.

Revising: Most revising goes on in writing conferences with an adult and strategies can be adapted to fit each individual child. The younger members of the class can begin by making simple changes, such as adding or subtracting a word; older children can be encouraged to rethink, add, subtract, and rearrange at whatever level they show readiness. Writing conferences occur as I move around the classroom during language arts time, or I may seek out a child after reading what he or she has written. Like most of my reading conferences, these are brief and informal.

Some habits need to be encouraged from the beginning because they make revision easier: writing on every other line, rereading what you have already written each day as you begin, and asking the inevitable question, "Does it make sense?" The next question is, "Have I told enough?" Finally, there is the more difficult issue: "Are there parts I should leave out? Have I perhaps repeated myself too much?" In a multiage classroom children will be encouraged to ask the questions for which they show readiness.

Editing or proofreading: The last process before publication has less to do with meaning than with using conventions. Children should be helped to see that respect for those conventions indicates respect for a reader, a willingness to make the writing accessible. A parent volunteer will often edit for the younger children; older children can start editing on their own before working with an adult. They may also be sent to the dictionary to make some spelling changes themselves after they have met with the teacher. The intricacies of quotation marks, commas, and paragraphing are introduced as needed.

I post an editing checklist to help the children move into this process:

1. Find good stopping places and mark them with a period.
2. Begin each new sentence with a capital letter. *I* should be a capital.
3. Circle any words you think you need help spelling.

I have had a box in which children place stories for which they need an editing conference. Then, during the actual conference, we attend to a few things. It would be too much to teach everything a child needs to learn in one conference, so there will always be a certain amount of adult editing.

Publishing: I like to think of publishing as "making public," meaning any kind of group sharing, including oral sharing. The next step, obviously, is to make the written form available for others to read, which will involve copying the writing either by hand or on the computer. Some eight-year-olds write long stories, which they copy on their own. I type some of the younger children's stories for them, but find it too time-consuming to do this for everyone all the time. Sometimes a volunteer can help.

Publishing may involve putting the material between covers of colored oaktag to make a book and producing illustrations or putting the material in a class book. It may involve posting the finished product on the walls of the room in a display. Over the years, the children can explore a variety of forms of publication.

Writing Folders: As in Molly McClaskey's room, children revise, edit, and prepare for publication only selected writing, but all writing is saved. Filed in a wallpaper-covered box near the writing materials are folders containing all the writing that children have completed throughout the year, even abandoned projects in first draft. The published work may be displayed somewhere in the room or may even have gone home. Each folder does include, however, some final drafts (or photocopies of them) of pieces that can be pulled out when evaluating progress or to contribute to a portfolio. Children enjoy looking back at what they have done. They are proud of their growth.

Word-processing: Simple word-processing programs should be available. Since we don't teach keyboarding at this age in our school, the children's use of the computer in writing varies with age, interest, and experience. Those who have practiced writing on a computer at home will be more independent at school and may be able to help others.

Spelling

A personal dictionary in which the teacher may write some words children specifically need when they write or edit is useful. Children can get in the habit of looking up these words by finding the proper letter page. I don't use personal dictionaries with beginners, however, until they have formed the habit of sounding out and trying to spell most words on their own. I want them to be independent writers first and figure as much out for themselves as they can. Recently, my team purchased small commercial dictionaries for each child. These reference books list commonly used words on alphabetical pages and allow room for the addition of other words. Children can keep them throughout their three-year stay with us (see Appendix A for the source).

I include spelling here because of my experience with eight- and nine-year-olds. Many children develop from invented spellers to conventional spellers quite naturally. But not all children make this transition without help. Some very good readers continue to pay little attention to conventions in spelling. Invented spelling is important in the early learning process, because it enables children to develop the habit of looking carefully at words and thinking about letter sounds, becoming more fluent writers and readers. At what point invented spelling is no longer acceptable has been a matter for much discussion. For a seven-year-old whose writing is shaky, invented spelling is fine. When the child begins to develop fluency, he or she is ready to pay attention to conventions. In spelling, as in everything else, the multiage teacher looks at a range of developmental levels and needs.

I integrate spelling instruction into phonics instruction and editing. This is enough for six-year-olds and most seven-year-olds. I have come to the conclusion, however, that most children are ready for some sort of spelling program as soon as they begin to see themselves as writers, establish a writing flow, and begin to spell some common and phonetic words conventionally. In my class this usually includes most eight-year-olds and a few seven-year-olds. Midway through the year, of course, I have nine-year-olds as well, and that's when I start my spelling program.

For these children I make up spelling lists of commonly used words, drawing on "High Frequency Bookwords" in *Transitions* (Routman 1988) and *The Reading Teacher's Book of Lists* (Fry, Polk, and Fountoukidis 1984). These always include "outlaw words," my label for common nonphonetic words (*they, give, some*) that can be introduced and discussed. I also include some words from our current theme. The children love to have a word like *paleontologist* on their spelling list.

I send lists of words home for study and combine spelling with cursive writing practice for eight-year-olds, who are asked to write the words cursively as homework. Testing can be done in a small group session. Parents of children this age often begin to worry about spelling. It is necessary to point out the words in their child's writing that are conventionally spelled or they will see only the "mistakes." Lists like these seem to help them relax. Teaching a group of older students a few spelling rules can also be helpful: for example, talking about rules for adding endings to silent *e* words. This can also be covered in conferences.

I observed another model for spelling instruction in a multiage classroom visit I made some time ago.

JONAH and Peter were sitting opposite each other at two desks that had been pushed together. "*Thought*," said Peter. "I thought we would win the game last night." He was giving Jonah a spelling test. Other nine- and ten-year-olds were scattered around the room doing the same thing.

"*Exactly*. We won by exactly two runs." I wondered where the words came from, and when they were finished I found out.

"See this box here?" Peter pointed to a small file of three-by-five-inch cards. "Each of us has a card and Mr. S. puts words on the cards when we have a writing conference or if he's just, you know, reading our stories: words we have to fix in our story. Every week we pick twelve words to work on. We have to study words we miss on tests, too. Then on Friday we give each other tests." They also checked their tests together and started a new list of any words they had missed in their spelling books.

Mr. S. had a cluster of students around him as they finished. He looked over each test and recorded the score.

Enjoying Books

Enjoying books from an early age is one of the most important factors in building school success. Young children who enjoy books read often, giving themselves lots and lots of reading practice. I try to create an atmosphere in which this pleasure in books is nurtured. Literature groups contribute to this, as do book talks, in which we share some of our favorite "reads."

"DO SOME of you have a character in your story you would like to have for a friend? Someone you could have fun with?" I begin with a question I first heard in the classroom of my friend, Judy Allen, who introduced me to "book talks."

"Aldo?" Alex holds up *Aldo Applesauce.*

"Can you tell us why you might enjoy Aldo?"

"Well, he's just a regular kid . . . and he does things I like to do, like ride around on his bike."

"Can it be an animal? Morris is so funny in this book." Suzie shows us *Morris Goes to School.*

"If we're talking about animals, I'd like the mouse in *The Mouse and the Motorcycle,* or the kid." suggests Jason.

"You know who I wouldn't like. Alexander in this book," Cindy holds up *Alexander and the Terrible, Horrible, No Good, Very Bad Day.* "He's a grouch."

Betsy objects: "But he's funny, too, and he's probably not a grouch every day."

Many questions could kick off book talks: "Is your book a story that could be true or is it fantasy? What made you decide that?" "Is anybody reading a story in which animals act like people?" "Does someone have a problem in his or her book?" Any of these lead to engagement with books, and increased interest in reading.

Fun with books extends to reading aloud with the whole class, one of my favorite times of the entire school day.

TWENTY-TWO children are gathered. Some lean against the bookcase. Some are sprawled on the rug. Stacie and Emma sit on a bench. It's 2:20 P.M. I glance at the clock, wondering if I'll have time to finish the chapter, and then read on:

> "You shall not die," said Charlotte, briskly.
> "What? Really?" cried Wilber.
> "Who's going to save me?"
> "I am," said Charlotte.

"I know how," Jerry offers.

"Don't tell," says Emma. "Even if you know, don't tell!"

"Can you keep it a secret, Jerry?" I ask. He nods. I glance at the clock again and close the book. The children groan, but our time is up. We'll get back to *Charlotte's Web* tomorrow.

Now I dismiss the children a few at a time to get their coats, backpacks, and lunch boxes. The buses are lined up outside the door and it's time to say good-bye until tomorrow.

CHAPTER ELEVEN

MAKING ASSESSMENT AUTHENTIC

Molly McClaskey and Justine O'Keefe

MOLLY McCLASKEY: OLD SHOES IN A NEW BOX

Assessing and Teaching—One Continuous Cycle

THE ROOM buzzed with the murmuring voices of young children reading to themselves. It was quiet reading time and I was having conferences with individual children. Abby read aloud in a low voice from *George and Martha Back in Town* (Marshall 1984). I noted her phrasing, her miscues, and the strategies she used to pronounce unfamiliar words. When she came to a logical stopping place, I asked her to tell me about the story and took notes about her retelling, recording in places her exact words so that I could revisit them later. Abby paused in her detailed explanation and looked at my quick running record sheet and the nearly illegible scratchings I had made in her reading folder.

"What are you doing?" she asked.

"These are my notes about your reading. While you read I write down what you are doing, like how you figure out new words."

"Oh." She quickly returned to her description of Martha, who jumps off the high dive.

Abby and I became engaged in a discussion about why Martha jumped off the high dive when she had said she was afraid of heights. Abby's remarks lead me to see her deeper understanding of this book: she recognized the intimacy of the friendship between George and Martha.

"Martha really cares about George so she's helping him out. All the people will watch her so that George won't have to be embarrassed in front of everyone. He's really the one afraid," she explained. "See," she pointed to the illustration. "He's sneaking back down the ladder because he is so scared."

I noted her detailed explanation and then asked, "What would you have done if you were Martha?"

"I don't know. I would want to help if it was my best friend Chelsea, but I'd be too afraid to go off the diving board. Martha was really brave. I think it was stupid for George to go up there in the first place since he was so scared."

I had one last question for the well-balanced Abby. "How was this book for you—hard, easy, or just right?"

"Well, it wasn't exactly easy. It was medium."

"What makes it medium?" I asked, encouraging her to reflect on her reading.

"Some words were hard and some weren't. The ones that were hard I could figure out myself," she reasoned.

"I see. Will you be able to find more books like this when you finish this one?" I asked, checking to be sure she could maintain her independence when she completed the book.

"Yup," Abby confidently answered, her nose already back in *George and Martha Back in Town*. "Now, can I keep reading?"

Conferences are sometimes an unwanted interruption for eager, independent readers. I attempt to stay out of the way as much as I can yet still find some time with each child during the week. Some children need frequent reading practice with an adult, while for others a reading conference every day would be an unnecessary intrusion. I individualize assessment and instruction during reading conferences.

We both keep records in a daily reading folder: I record my ongoing assessments and anecdotal notes from the reading conference on one side of the folder, and the child records the books she completes on the other. This "tandem" or "side-by-side" folder, along with the reading conference, is one of many forms of authentic assessment used throughout the day (see Figures 11.1 and 11.2).

Because it blends in with other classroom activities, teachers often think they are not doing enough assessment. In fact, authentic assessment looks a lot like good instruction. It is imbedded in daily practice, in listening to Abby read and talking about her interpretation of the events of the story.

While I listen to another child read a story he has written, ask questions, and instruct him about spelling patterns, I am simultaneously assessing that child's progress. I notice which skills he applied and which he did not. I assess, instruct, and record, all in one continuous cycle. These daily interactions immediately inform what I plan and implement for each child.

Writing and reading conferences lend themselves to an ongoing review of children's work, as well as questioning, conversation, and record keeping,

Daily Reading Running Record

Name _____

Date _____ Title _____

		sample miscues:
Easy Medium Hard	Retelling-	
Liked	Inferred	
Disliked	Reflection / personal response	
	Oral Reading- word by word phrase	
	Observations-	

Meaning	Visual	Phonemic	Structure / Grammar

-substitutes appropriate
  word
-prior knowledge
-reads on
-reads on / returns
-makes sense
-self-corrects
-predicts
	-directionality
	-1 to 1 finger pointing
	-picture clues
	-sight vocabulary
	-spelling patterns
	-focuses on print
	-focuses on picture
		-beginning sounds
		-ending sounds
		-middle sounds
		-blends sounds
		-little words in
		  bigger ones
		-rhyming elements
		-rhythm
			-sounds right or wrong
			-corrects tense
			-uses endings
			-uses punctuation clues
			-relies on repetition

Figure 11.1 Ongoing assessment is recorded in the Daily Reading Record.

all of which are at the very heart of authentic assessment. Such assessment is authentic because it genuinely reflects what the child has learned and is able to apply in the context of daily classroom life.

Writing is the simplest place to begin collecting children's work and practicing authentic assessment strategies.

JARRED was working on a self-made book about *The Littles*, based on the stories by John Peterson. He was enthralled by these families of tiny beings who constructed homes and furniture from toothpaste caps and thimbles. At Planning Time he played at the Littles' home, an area in the room equipped with an old stump the children had hollowed out. He and his companions moved small animal figures up and down the log and in and out of holes. Jarred and a friend sewed small pillows and bedding for the minute families. Another child built a sign at the work bench, "the ltls," and nailed it to the log. Furniture was created from acorns, pine needles, bark, and small pieces of wood.

A group of children were reading every book they could find about the Littles. Jarred was taking his ideas further through writing.

"Can we have a conference?" Jarred asked shyly during writer's workshop. "I wrote a book."

Name				

Books I Am Reading!

Date	Title	Author	with adult	without adult
	easy medium hard			
	easy medium hard			
	easy medium hard			
	easy medium hard			
	easy medium hard			
	easy medium hard			
	easy medium hard			
	easy medium hard			
	easy medium hard			

Figure 11.2 Each child has a personal reading log.

"Sure," I said. We found a quiet place and seven-year-old Jarred read from his book about a tiny imaginary family and their world.

When he was finished he commented. "See, it has characters and they have a problem to work out." During a recent prewriting lesson I had emphasized the problem element in stories and their resolutions.

"I see that your story has a beginning and a middle. Does the problem get resolved?" I prodded, not seeing the outcome.

"Yeah. The dad found a spring from a pen and put it on the door and it stopped banging," Jarred explained. Children usually have an ending in mind but do not always have the endurance to write it.

"What an ending! Now everyone can sleep," I remarked. Jarred was pleased with his book and skipped off to the writing-publishing table to quickly write the ending before he forgot what he had said. Later he found the colored pencils and started the illustrations.

I took Jarred's writing folder from the box and recorded his progress on the sheet stapled onto the left side. The recording sheet reads, "I am learning to . . ." and "I can . . ." in two columns. I noted that he was consistently using punctuation and the appropriate uppercase letter. He was using vowels correctly except for *e*; vowel blends needed more practice. I wrote briefly: "Story includes beginning and middle, needs help with endings." I made a note in my planning book that a group of children were ready for work with vowel blends. When writer's workshop was over, Jarred recorded his new story on his own "writing list" record sheet on the right side of his writing folder (see Figures 11.3 and 11.4).

Portfolios—A Work in Progress

A few years ago my teammate, Janet, and I began a series of conversations about assessment. We had always saved the children's writing and shown it to their parents at conference time. We had also kept daily running records of children's writing and reading. Gathering all the pieces—teacher notes and the children's lists and work—in an organized and meaningful manner was another matter. Our efforts often seemed fragmented. We needed a way to pull the pieces together so that children and teacher could more easily review and respond to work as it accumulated over the year.

We liked the idea of a portfolio: a picture of an artist's folder holding precious works came to mind. Something about keeping everything in one place, preserving work, and helping children see the value of it appealed to us. One summer, Janet and I gathered up the necessary materials—oaktag and extra wide book tape—and spent hours fashioning our first portfolios. They were large, eighteen-by-eighteen-inch multipocketed versions hooked together at the spine. At that point we envisioned several pockets, each holding two subject areas: writing and reading, math and science, social studies and theme work, as well as a pocket for child-selected work. Finally, however, I settled on four pockets: one for a collection of work to go home, one for the child's selections, one for teacher choices, and the last for large theme and art work. We exceeded our oaktag and book tape quota for the year by a wide margin. "What are you doing with all of it?" the supply-room administrator inquired nicely.

We presented the crisp, new, pocketed portfolios to the children in the fall and discussed our version of an artist's portfolio, a folder of treasured works that would tell each child's story. We talked about how artists save their work in order to take care of it and look back on it from time to time. The children were excited about the idea and set about the task of decorating and personalizing the covers. While coloring her cover, Abby commented to Kyla: "It's like my photo album at home. It goes all the way from when I was a baby to now. I look at it a lot."

As the children completed their covers they brought them to me one by one. I watched as the children fumbled to get their short arms around the

| Name _____ |
| Reflecting on Writing |

I am learning to...	I can...
Date	

Figure 11.3 Record sheet for the writing folder.

huge square shapes with brightly colored covers. With five in my arms the pile was awkward to carry. "Where will they go?" Susan asked innocently. Everything in the room had a place. Surely these would, too. But they were too big—too big for a shelf, too big for the floor, too big for the children to comfortably carry across the room, and too big for me to tote home!

"What have we done?" I asked Janet, half laughing, after school that day.

I finally found a cardboard box long enough and deep enough to hold the new portfolios. Partway through the year it burst. Then we tried laying the portfolios flat on a bottom shelf, but that made it difficult to take out one specific portfolio without hauling out all twenty. Size, shape, and accessibility were serious factors. We would have to reconsider them next year.

The fall was as hectic as usual. It seemed to evaporate into Halloween, then, in the blink of an eye, Thanksgiving. Parent conferences came, but the portfolios had rarely left the large detergent box. We explained their purpose to parents and said that we hoped to have more to show by the April conference. The parents liked the idea. January came and we scurried to find several pieces of work by each child to put into the portfolios. We chose work because it seemed significant and because it was available, but we were not

Name _____				
Writing List				
Stories I am working on:	dates	editing conference	finished	published

Figure 11.4 Record sheet for the writing folder.

sure what it showed once it was collected. April came and we scrambled again, finding a few more pieces to add. This time the parents appreciated seeing the work, but it struck me that, aside from writing, which is a natural indicator of progress over time, we were comparing apples saved in January with oranges saved in April. It was difficult to assess growth using the collections we had created. Each piece stood on its own rather than overlapping with the previous one to illustrate the child's progress. We could see that collecting and selecting were other elements we would need to refine.

Colleagues heard that we were trying something new and stopped in from time to time to see how things were progressing. I was embarrassed to show them the oversized pastel pockets and their meager contents.

The portfolios themselves were in such good shape at the end of the first year that we decided to use them again rather than request more supplies. I told the seven- and eight-year-olds that the contents of their portfolios would go to their new third-grade teachers, and the new four- and five-year-olds in our class would then use their portfolios covers next fall. Five- and six-year-olds staying in our class could use their same portfolios another year. As Eliza, who always had good ideas, suggested, "We could make new covers over the old ones so they seem new. Once my mom put my big sister's pink sneakers in a new box and gave them to me for a present. They almost seemed new."

Another child noted that he wears his older brother's clothes all the time and commented, "Some are really gross." We talked about recycled clothes and books until the children seemed content to start next year with last year's still crisp portfolios. Deep inside, I knew the folders should have been well worn by this point in the year, like a favorite pair of old shoes with indentations for each toe. Maybe next year.

Janet and I sat down over the summer to assess our fledgling efforts. We laughed a lot. We had started the portfolio process. That was the good news. But the children were not involved in looking at their work and hardly used the portfolios. That was the bad news. As we talked, we were flooded with our own questions and these have guided the portfolio project in subsequent years: what is the difference between a daily work folder and a portfolio, and how do you manage these folders, for writing or math, along with portfolio collections? When and what do you put into a portfolio, and who selects the work? Whom is the portfolio for? How can we involve children in reflection and self-assessment? Where do we begin in the fall?

Help was on the way. This same summer the teaching staff of our school had decided to investigate authentic assessment. Two professors from the University of Vermont, already collaborating with the school, designed a course based on our interests. After two weeks of reading and talking, Janet and I realized we had barely dusted the cover of the subject.

We also realized we could not go back to assessment as we once knew it—the kind of assessment you do only at the end, when everything is finished, the kind you never look back on, the kind that can make kids cry, the kind you are glad to have over.

Although we felt we were just beginning, we had reason to be encouraged. Teachers I talk to often feel they fumble with assessment and hope an appropriate package will come along to solve the problem. As it turns out, we have been doing wise and reliable classroom assessment all along. No one, including ourselves, recognized it as such. It is the old pair of shoes, the ones we have worn day in and day out, the ones that fit each unique bump and bunion. The packaging has changed, but good assessment still involves the teacher's recordings and anecdotal notes, which are customized to fit the children and the curriculum in each classroom. Daily evaluation techniques—observing, listening, asking questions, and recording—are the tools of authentic assessment. They can be varied to fit different projects and different approaches; they can also be adjusted minute by minute for each child and activity. These practices, integrated with instruction and learning as they unfold in the classroom, are the purest form of assessment. Assessment will never be a brand-new package. We simply have to get better at what we already do.

As the staff worked that summer, we talked about collecting information. What data is valuable, and why? We found that discussion of assessment is also discussion of philosophy, instruction, and curriculum. As a group we committed ourselves to a new method of reporting and collecting information and to a year-long investigation and implementation of literacy portfolios.

It was a vigorous and tumultuous year of study, one of disagreement and consensus building. It could not have moved forward without the inspiration and steady hand of our two university mentors, who guided the staff and community into new waters. They met regularly with us—in and out of classrooms; before, during, and after school; individually and in small groups. We updated our knowledge of running records, anecdotal observations, story retellings, and other ongoing assessment strategies. We shared teacher-made record-keeping ideas and invented new formats. The portfolio project Janet and I had started moved forward, overlapping with the staff project throughout the year. We discovered practical solutions to many of our problems and to many others we had never even considered.

Portfolios and Daily Work Folders

Portfolios are different from daily work folders. They are collections of the children's work culled specifically to draw attention to the child's progress and application of skills over time. Children save finished and unfinished work in daily folders. At the end of each marking period I go through this work, looking for good examples for the portfolio. Work is either sent home or deliberately chosen and labeled for the portfolio. The children also select pieces for the portfolio.

Some classrooms save daily work in something called a "collections folder" and periodically pull materials from it for the portfolio. (Teachers in Washington state call this process "weeding.") When portfolios seem too bulky teachers and students review them and weed.

Portfolio Selections

Portfolio pieces must have a purpose. Janet and I saved too much the second year, making up for our lean results the year before and yielding more papers than we could possibly deal with effectively. After that experience we became more selective and taught the children to choose samples wisely.

The staff agreed upon core items or "common tools" to include in every child's literacy portfolio throughout the school and to collect them three times during the year. We identified core items that created a whole picture of a child's literacy development. We chose to document growth in sight-word recognition, reading strategies and word attack, comprehension, independent reading, and writing. Now we could make comparisons and observe growth over time.

Whom Are Portfolios For?

The portfolios serve several audiences. Janet and I created those original oversized portfolios because we wanted the children to reflect on their own work. But teachers and parents also reap rich benefits.

Rather than saving random selections of every child's work, we now have a concise portfolio with specific work by each child over time. A child's progress and difficulties stand out in such a sequenced collection, so that it is easier to draw conclusions, summarize, and plan the next steps. It is also easier to write reports to parents when the evidence is gathered in one place.

Portfolios also serve parents. In a staff-conducted survey, parents' responses showed they were pleased to have examples of their children's work demonstrating their growth. The portfolios allowed them to see much more clearly what the classroom goals were.

At the conclusion of one marking period, I realized, too, that the portfolios show parents far more than a teacher-written report could. Now the written report could return to a more workable length and not attempt to redescribe all of the work in the portfolio.

Portfolio Visits

That second year, Janet and I were still learning how we could best use portfolios with the children. We reused the oversized portfolios from the first year, but this time we found large boxes early on and reinforced the corners with tape. We also went from too few items to an abundance. We saved everything. At the conclusion of each marking period we had so much to go through that we spent full weekends slogging through piles of children's papers. We wrote about each entry and color coded them all with small stick-on dots so that science papers, all green dots, could be distinguished from writing or math by children and parents. We used jumbo paper clips to keep papers in each subject area together.

The process was doomed when we invited the children to look through their portfolios. They eagerly took apart and mixed together each carefully clipped, color-coded bundle. We had never noticed before that young children do not know how to use a paper clip. The "Jumbo Gem Clips" were bent, flung, lost, and made into chains. Before long the color-coded dots had fallen off and the papers were shoved back into portfolios every which way. All I could see were the hours of reorganizing and color coding that lay ahead. How to organize papers by subject in a user friendly and accessible manner was another practical issue we needed to solve. There had to be a better way.

We saved several pieces of each child's work from the portfolio and in June, sent the unwieldy pastel pocket portfolios home. Good-bye! Then we purchased twenty nine-by-fifteen-inch brown accordion folders, and legal-sized, colored file folders to hold each subject area. Now in their third year of using portfolios, the seven-year-olds have work dating back to when they were four in folders they can manage themselves. And we found ways the children could really use the portfolios to examine their own progress.

CARL was the first to notice the new title on our daily schedule. One of his jobs as this week's morning meeting leader was to read the schedule for the day. "Portfolio Visits," he read aloud. "What's that?"

I explained. "It seems as if I know more about your portfolios than you do since I collect your work and file it inside." I had asked Carl if I could use his new brown accordion portfolio as an example, and I had it beside me with two samples pulled from his blue math folder. "When I think about how you are learning, I compare your work. Here is a math paper Carl did in September" I held it in one hand. "Here is another he did a few days ago." I held it in my other hand. Each paper contained several word problems that he had written and solved. "When Carl's parents come for the parent conference I will compare the September paper with this one from November to see what has changed. Can anyone see changes or differences in the two?" I passed them around the circle. Everyone looked at them for a few minutes.

"He wrote more words in November," commented Elizabeth, "and he used higher numbers."

"He subtracted on this one," Zack pointed to the November piece, "and only added in September."

"I think you have the idea. That's exactly the kind of information your work can show you, your parents, and me. I compare your papers like this before I write your report cards, so that I can see what you are good at and what needs more practice. But there is something missing. I am wondering what you think of your work and what areas you think are easy and hard."

"I get it. This is what the portfolio visits are. We look at our work ourselves," Leah said. "Then we'll know everything instead of just you."

"They're our portfolios anyway, right Mrs. McClaskey?" Josh asked.

"Right," I responded, pleased that they understood the purpose. "Once each month we will have a portfolio visit. You will spread your work out, look it over, and see what you are learning." (I was being idealistic. I've missed quite a few months this year.) "Today you are going to visit the blue section of your portfolio."

"That's math," shouted Evan, who never speaks softly.

"Next month we will visit another section," I said.

"What if the paper in November wasn't your best job and the one in September is better?" Ely blurted, always one step ahead.

"That's a good question, Ely. If a piece from November is not your best then that's what you will have learned about yourself, that you worked harder in September than you did in November. Now I want to show you how to visit your portfolio." I wanted to demonstrate and establish a few routines.

I opened Carl's blue math folder, one of the six file folders that together make up the portfolio. I spread his math papers around the center of the circle of children. "This is what you will be doing with a partner when you leave the circle. Your first job will be to put your papers in order." Together we arranged Carl's math work in chronological order from September through November according to the date stamped in the corner of each paper.

When we had finished, I posed several questions for the children to think about. They would use them to critically examine their work and write about their reflections.

As we practiced portfolio visits, we developed a regular set of questions that became part of our routine throughout the year. Each question was printed on a separate slip. Children answered the question in reference to a selected piece of work in their portfolio and stapled it to that piece. These entry slips helped children think about their work and helped their parents interpret the collection in the portfolio.

The reflection questions we used that day went something like this: "Find a piece in your math portfolio that shows the most difficult problem you have ever solved. What made it so challenging?" Another reads, "Which piece of math shows your best work? Explain why." The third question was, "Find a math paper that shows something that has become easy for you. Why do you think it is easy?"

A final question stands alone in each folder of the portfolio, unattached to a specific piece. It encourages children to set goals for themselves: "What area in_____[math in this case] needs practice now? What is your favorite kind of_____[math] work?"

TOGETHER we assessed the work in Carl's math folder, reading each reflection question and discussing various pieces of Carl's work. In this way, I modeled a portfolio visit.

The children left the circle in carefully matched pairs—old with young, leader with follower, drifter with organizer. Each pair took their portfolios from the oversized milk crates where they are kept and found a work space. Several pairs worked in the pod, the common space outside our door.

Soon the floor was a maze of math papers, sorted and organized in piles by date. Conversations among children focused on finding dates, which month came first, October or November, and which number came first, twenty-seven or seventeen. Children shot up and down like jack rabbits from the wall calendar to their work spaces.

When they had accomplished the ordering task, attention shifted to the real meat of self-assessment: What does my work show? What have I learned? What do I think about my work? Entry slips with one of the three reflection questions were available on a central table. When the pairs were ready, they picked up a slip and began to assess their work.

I moved around the room encouraging the children to assist one another in reading the questions, thinking, evaluating, and then recording their thoughts. The time was productive and purposeful, a pleasant shift from last year's confusion.

Sadie, five, and Tyler, seven, sat at a table in the writing area. As they randomly scattered Sadie's work across the table they moved onto the floor for more space. Slowly a chronology took form, with Tyler frequently correcting Sadie's early sense of numeral recognition and value. "No Sadie, September 21 comes after September 12. Listen," and he counted to twenty-one for her. A few minutes later Tyler asked, "Sadie, where is all of your stuff from October?" Sadie looked confused. A small pile of her work was set apart from the line-up.

"What about this pile?" I asked.

"Those I forgot to put the date on," Sadie answered. "I missed a lot. Now I know why we put dates on everything." Tyler left the small pile and resumed ordering the math papers.

I moved on to observe other groups and returned when Tyler and Sadie were working with their second entry slip. "What does it say?" Sadie asked, looking up at Tyler.

"It says, 'Which math piece shows your best work? Explain Why.'" Sadie immediately lifted a colorful graph from her paper parade. She had already spent considerable time reviewing each piece while putting them in order and was ready for this question.

"Is that the same one you would choose from Sadie's work?" I asked Tyler.

"Yes," he said. "Look at how careful it is. Everyone in our class likes dogs best. I remember when you shared that one." The graph was her own depiction of favorite pets among class members. She had drawn several kinds of pets across the horizontal axis on large graph paper, and put numbers on the vertical axis. Vertical columns of squares indicating how many children in our class liked each pet were neatly colored in fluorescent crayon. Her title read, "Fvt Patz." A written interpretation was stapled to the graph: "Mos kdz lk dgz, Ls kdz lk canaries" (someone had helped her spell that one).

"What should we write, Sadie? Why is this your best?" Tyler pushed on to complete the task.

"'Cuz I like canaries and I worked my hardest on it." Tyler asked Sadie to say it again more slowly as he wrote down each word. They stapled the entry slip to the graph project and went to the table for the third question.

I have noticed that children go through developmental stages in self-assessment just as they pass through maturational benchmarks in writing or math concept acquisition. The youngest children in the room talked about their work in terms of favorite topics, pictures, or colors. As children mature and become more experienced with self-assessment, they compare, evaluate, and reflect on whether or not they have met their own expectations. While the four- and five-year-olds described their work as fun or pretty, the sixes discussed execution and effort. "This is my best because it is my most careful work," or "These are my neatest numbers." The sevens and eights, with several years of experience and feedback under their belts, compared their work and thought more analytically about the quality of their pieces: "I think I am better at solving math problems in my mind." "Now I can solve problems with two digits and many numbers at one time." "I solved this problem by counting by twos and that was a different way to do it. I am good at that now." I ask the older children to ponder the creativity, concepts, and skills they have applied.

I have discovered that three questions are enough for any single work session. Beyond that the children's responses become repetitive and they lose their sense of purpose. I found some wonderful ideas for self-reflection questions and entry slips in *Putting the Pieces Together* by Bonnie Campbell Hill and Cynthia A. Ruptic (1994). I also write entry slips for the work I choose for the child's portfolios, indicating the purpose of the selected item and what it shows. Not all pieces in the portfolio have entry slips, but those that do aid parents and future teachers in interpreting what they see.

IT WAS a whole hour later when the groups completed their first portfolio visits. Papers were returned to the proper folder and portfolios were neatly stored. The children lined up at the door to go to gym. "What do you think about portfolio visits?" I asked the group.

Above several "cool"-, "great"-, and "OK"-type comments, Eliza piped up, "I really like it. Now I know about my portfolio."

"Yeah, I feel like I know myself," added Anna.

Portfolio visits bring portfolios alive for the children, integrating the collections of their work into the life of the classroom. The children and I save pieces that have personal significance, pieces that describe learning from a project or theme, pieces that offer comparison to an earlier work, pieces that show a particular strength, and others that demonstrate a weakness. By reviewing them regularly, children find meaning in their work and reflect on themselves as learners. In this way portfolios are more than a documentation and assessment tool for the teacher; they also have relevance for the children to whom they really belong.

A Portfolio Celebration

We thought we should celebrate. We had portfolios with work tucked inside. The children were involved and had ideas to communicate about their work. We thought parents would appreciate spending time with their children reviewing the year's work, seeing the portfolio in its entirety, and hearing their child's reflections. Eight teachers and I planned a portfolio event for March 31 and April 1, replacing our regular parent-teacher conferences. Our school has two days set aside for conferences in fall and spring. Notes home explained that this would not be like the usual parent-teacher conferences they were accustomed to, that it was designed instead to showcase the child and the child's work, to give them an opportunity to see their own child's work through the child's eyes. Each child would guide parents through the portfolio. The note included several key points:

- Our desire to include children in the portfolio process stems from readings and research about the importance of children's ability to reflect on and communicate about their own progress. Your child's work and the discussion between you and your child will be the primary focus of the visit.
- Your child will be reviewing his portfolio with you. He will also show you around the room so that you can view the current theme study and other work in progress.
- When you come to the Portfolio Celebration you will be given a list of questions you might ask your child and tips about how to "visit" the portfolio.
- We will be asking for your comments and feedback after the portfolio visit. Our staff has been studying portfolio assessment for a year. We are still engaged in the process of learning and refining our practice. Thanks for helping us fine-tune!

The children and the teachers spent over a month preparing: organizing, gathering, labeling, and writing about chosen work. The children also did

Name _____	Date _____
Portfolio Reflections on Reading	

When I read I used to...	Now I know how to...

Figure 11.5 Record sheet for the children's own reflections on their reading portfolios.

additional self-evaluations intended to help them think and write about favorite and difficult parts of the year.

We asked children to think about their growth as readers by responding to the phrase, "When I read I used to . . . Now I know how to . . ." Keith wrote, "wen I usd to read I only red sum books ovr and ovr. Now I can red al the books I pik."

A similar page encouraged children to think about their growth as writers. Sally wrote, "When I rite I used to hav the techer rite for me. Now I rite by my sef, and i no how to spail."

The children also worked on reflections specific to the social studies and science themes we had studied. "I lkd papr mashey best cuz its big and gooshee," wrote six-year-old Ellen, describing her favorite part of our extended study of Antarctica. She is a tactile learner, needing gross motor activity. She had worked on a life-sized model of an Emperor Penguin.

"I lrnd the mos frum the man who cam frum Antartica and shod slids," wrote Ethan, a visual and auditory learner. Photographs of completed three-dimensional projects were attached to each child's self-reflection. The chil-

Name _____	Date _____
Portfolio Reflections on Writing	
When I write I used to...	Now I know how to...

Figure 11.6 *Record sheet for the children's own reflections on their writing portfolios.*

dren had really thought about their projects and portfolio selections and were ready to share.

Five families assembled in our classroom at 8:30, on the morning of March 31. An easel propped at the classroom door welcomed them to the Portfolio Celebration: "Help your child find his/her portfolio. Each child will be in charge and guide you through the work. Your questions and supportive comments will help the portfolio visit. Find a quiet space in the room and make yourselves comfortable." A list of tips for the parents was clipped to the front of each portfolio (see Figure 11.7).

Families were clustered in niches all over the room, with siblings clinging to parents' backs and grandparents trying to get comfortable in child-sized chairs. I watched as children opened one folder at a time and spread their work across the floor, just as we had practiced. The children discussed each piece, reading entry slips, showing what they thought was their best work, and responding to questions from their parents. The parents were attentive and engaged. They offered praise and support, creating an atmosphere of mutual interest and respect.

How to Visit Your Child's Portfolio

We are excited about the opportunity you have to visit and review your child's work collected and chosen throughout the year. We hope you have a pleasant experience with your child. We make the following suggestions:

- help your child guide you through the portfolio.
- find a quiet space in the room and make yourselves comfortable.
- look at similar things at the same time, so progress can be noted.
- refer to entry slips or dates on children's work.
- compare seasonal samples.
- help your child reflect on what they see by asking questions: Why was this (project, writing sample, photo, etc.) chosen for the portfolio?
- encourage self-evaluation by comparing similar items and asking, Are there changes that you notice?
- have your child select a book they have read recently or are reading to share with you.
- explore with your child their points of interest in the classroom.
- take as much time as you need to fully explore your child's portfolio and environment.

Figure 11.7 Tips for parent's portfolio review.

Steven read a question from a self-reflection sheet: "What has been the easiest part of learning this year?" "Understanding stories, building, and science experiments," his answer read. Steven is an oral and auditory learner, fascinated by stories and discussion, eager to respond and think about the deeper meaning of a story. He is a keen abstract thinker. He is drawn to blocks and water, where he can test his theories, draw hypotheses, converse with peers, and easily move his body. Steven is also a kinesthetic learner. He is in motion while doing all tasks, from block building to writing. He reads standing up.

Steven continued to read to his parents as he rocked back and forth. "What has been the hardest part of learning this year?" "Solving problems. I don't know what to say," he continued, "and I can't stay still. I can't help it."

Steven's mother's eyes were wet. "Steven, I'm impressed that you recognized this and wrote about it. Now we can help you deal with it." I'm not sure which was more powerful, his sheer honesty and knowledge of himself or his parents' realization of the depth of his difficulty in settling his body.

Steven's father asked, "What do you think we should do about it?" A spontaneous goal-setting conference ensued. Steven and his parents talked about ways he could calm himself, about quiet areas in the room where he could go to work and sit apart from buddies at work times.

"It happens mostly when I don't want to do what I'm supposed to do," he commented. They talked about learning.

Steven's mother remarked, "Think of how hard reading used to be. How did you get better at it?"

Steven thought for a few minutes and said, "Just by doing it a lot. I'm good at writing now too."

"I guess it's worth sticking it out, even when it's hard," his mom continued.

"Yeah," he said with a smile. Steven knew how much he had grown. He knew he was being heard and that we all understood his unique learning style.

It was a satisfying experience to watch the parents scattered about the room, discussing learning successes and challenges with their children. The process seemed to reward everyone.

I worked my way around the room, video camera in hand, observing and listening. Occasionally I paused long enough to give children tips or reminders, but I stayed at arm's length. I wanted parents to focus on their child rather than on me.

When Rachel spread her math work across the table, her father perked up and asked all kinds of questions about how she had derived various recording sheets. Rachel leaped up and got the bins of bears and Unifix cubes to demonstrate. When I returned a while later, Rachel and her parents were stretched across the floor playing dice games. Most family groups were finished with the portfolio visit in forty-five minutes. Rachel and her parents stayed for a full two hours until a new group of five families arrived. Rachel's hands-on demonstration in math is an idea I will remember for the future.

Several weeks after the Portfolio Celebration, our pod members sent a survey to parents to get feedback. Parents reported that they missed having one-on-one conference time with the teacher. At the same time they raved about the Portfolio Celebration. They saw it as a valuable and meaningful process. "My child was empowered and in charge. I was surprised at how confident he seemed and how much he knew about himself," wrote one parent. Another wrote, "I saw the whole curriculum and how you teach it. I've never stopped to give all my child's work a careful look before. It really worked to compare it." Every parent saw benefits and felt they were better informed. We plan to return to the April parent-teacher conference this year and will include an evening Portfolio Celebration for families in May.

Parent conferences and report card summaries took on new meaning when we could look at children's comparable examples saved throughout the year, sorted and labeled in their portfolios. Report cards and conferences provided more revealing, realistic, and informative reporting than in previous

---

Parent Reflections

How do you feel about your portfolio visit with your child?

Did you gain information from the portfolio that you cannot get from other assessments?

Is this the most informative time of year for portfolio celebrations?

Do you have suggestions that would enhance portfolio celebrations?

Thank you for your time and thoughts!

Sincerely,

Figure 11.8 Parents get a chance to respond to the portfolio review with their child.

years. In fact, our entire school changed its reporting format from written reports four times each year accompanied by two parent conferences, to a schedule in which we use written reports in January and June. In November and April we meet with parents and look at the children's work in the portfolios together.

Portfolio assessment, the ongoing review and evaluation of children's work as it is collected and saved over time, has proven itself a worthwhile classroom activity. All of us—children, parents, and teachers alike—can vouch for that. This kind of assessment is inextricably related to the ways in which children and teachers learn and work. It offers a true picture. It portrays children and their learning authentically.

JUSTINE O'KEEFE: ASSESSING READING THROUGH TRADE BOOKS

Throughout my long tenure as a multiage teacher I have found my greatest challenge not in the education of young children, but in the education of their parents. Teachers and schools who strive to deliver education in a nontraditional way must continually explain and reiterate to parents what we do, why we do it, and how it will benefit their children.

Even when parents become accustomed to math manipulatives, invented spelling, and integrated themes, they continue to ask, "What grade level is my child on?" For teachers of multiage classes, those of us concerned with developmental levels and the progress of individuals, that question is outdated at best and threatening at worst. But ask it they will and answer it we must using our professional judgment and available assessment tools. Several years ago my colleagues and I embarked on a quest to locate a reading assessment that answered the grade-level question for parents, reflected the goals and methods of our literature-based reading program, and assessed the growth of children six through ten years old.

Searching for an Assessment to Meet Our Needs

Several people on the staff had been using a commercially available assessment tool, which we agreed to try for the midyear reports as a way to standardize the reading levels reported to parents. After using this instrument in January and again in June, it became clear to us that it was not an appropriate way to assess our students' reading ability. The word lists presented words out of context, the passages were in typed form with no pictures, the comprehension questions were low level, and most important, children who were just beginning to read could not meet with success on even the earliest passages. A group of us were frustrated by the inadequacies of the tool and asked Marge Lipson of the University of Vermont to help us locate an assessment more appropriate to our methods and goals.

We began by outlining our program, in which reading instruction is individualized and the teacher confers one-on-one with the children. Beginning readers use controlled vocabulary and predictable texts, while more mature readers choose trade books from the school and/or classroom libraries. We teach decoding skills through the children's use of invented spelling and flexible, informal phonics skills groups. We place strong emphasis on the value and enjoyment of reading, and a half hour or more of quiet reading is part of each school day. We read aloud to children from storybooks, nonfiction, and ongoing chapter books.

Students are involved in many activities that extend from books they have read or hear read to them. They study authors, produce and perform plays and puppet shows, make big books and murals, and become literary characters. Our emphasis is on understanding the motivations and actions of main characters, appreciating the importance of time and setting, and responding to the book in a personal way.

After describing our program and reaffirming our commitment to it, we began to meet regularly with Dr. Lipson to discuss elements and procedures of reading assessments. We formed a committee to synthesize the information we were gathering, and after looking at a variety of assessment tools, concluded that the one we needed was not among them. Thus, we decided to write our own, an assessment that would address the specific needs of our literature-based reading program.

Creating Our Own Assessment Tool

Together we discussed the elements necessary to our assessment. We agreed that the major goal of reading is to gain meaning, so comprehension was the critical factor. But it was also necessary to address children's miscues and word recognition. Those of us working with beginning readers felt strongly that the tool should measure the reading growth of very young children: those at the prereading, preprimer, and primer stages. With these expectations in place, the committee began to meet regularly to develop our reading assessment.

As we reviewed the many instruments Dr. Lipson made available to us, it became obvious that we would benefit from using elements of several of them. For instance, one assessment contained a section in which a question was asked of the child before the child read the passage orally. The question was of a general nature and meant to give the teacher an idea of the child's prior knowledge of the subject. It made sense to us that, if a child was to be assessed reading a passage about hang gliding and had no idea what hang gliding was, the child's ability to comprehend the text would be limited.

Because children are expected to read quietly for an extended period each day, it was important to include a silent reading component in our assessment. We decided that it would begin with an observation of the child engaged in practicing the passage independently. We would look for the degree of concentration exhibited by the child as well as behaviors such as pointing, reading in a whisper, and lip movement.

During the child's oral reading, the teacher would note miscues. The miscues we chose to record included substitutions, omissions, insertions, repetitions, reversals, and mispronunciation. Later, other staff members suggested that a child's refusal to tackle an unknown word was an important diagnostic clue because it indicated an inability or an unwillingness to employ decoding strategies. So we added refusal to pronounce.

In working with Dr. Lipson, we had become convinced of the value of retellings as a way to determine the child's understanding of a passage. It would give us clues as to his or her ability to remember details in sequence and the child's facility or difficulty with oral expression. The retelling and related questions made up the comprehension component of the assessment.

The committee agreed that word recognition should be left until after the child had read the words in context. Since gaining meaning from text was our goal for reading, it was necessary to test children on words they had first seen in a meaningful context.

We now had the elements of our reading assessment. Silent reading, free association, oral reading, retelling, comprehension questions, and word recognition. These six factors represented the areas being stressed in our classrooms. We had come a long way toward developing an instrument tailored to our beliefs about and our methods for teaching reading.

But we had one more crucial decision to make. What passages would the children be given to read? This proved the most difficult decision thus far. Most inventories we looked at used basal passages, but our children read trade books. Some used passages written by the assessment's authors, but writing all our own text was a task too demanding to be undertaken by busy classroom teachers. Besides, we wanted children to develop relationships with books. We wanted them to use illustrations to understand the story, to appreciate the style and tone of the author. How could we assess children on these points unless they were indeed reading from books? That was our answer. We would develop a list of books at various reading levels, some of which children would read for assessment.

Choosing the Books

As a committee we presented our ideas for the assessment instrument to our colleagues with some trepidation. We had spent many hours on our proposal and we believed it was sound, but we also knew that it would necessitate working long and hard to accomplish our goal. Every teacher would need to contribute, and compromise would be essential if we were to agree on which books to use and what reading levels to assign to them. We were not disappointed by the reactions of our colleagues. They were in agreement with the components we had chosen and enthusiastic about using the books children were actually reading for the assessment text.

In the following weeks, we participated in a series of book-sharing sessions that exposed us to new books and gave each of us a closer look at our colleagues. Those meetings were invaluable in developing our understanding of one another as teachers, since the books we brought to them provided a window for knowing each other in new ways. Exhausted after a day of teaching, we relaxed as we laughed at the antics of Frog and Toad, discussed the complexity of the Frances stories, and read favorite passages aloud to one another. To our delight, we realized that we were exhibiting the kind of involvement with and loyalty to books that we wanted to instill in our children.

Choosing appropriate books for our assessment proved much less difficult than the thorny problem of assigning grade levels to them. We had the least trouble with books for beginning and emerging readers because of the obvious progression of their limited, controlled vocabularies. But the levels for chapter books for third and fourth graders proved more elusive. We tried a number of readability formulas but found that the results varied too much for any of them to be considered reliable. The publisher's grade levels were often as much as two years beyond that of the children actually reading them. Did that mean that many of our students were significantly above grade level in reading or were there other factors to consider?

We decided that the length, complexity, and content of these books meant that they could be read on a variety of levels with varying depths of understanding. That is, the degree to which a nine-year-old comprehends the action and meaning of the story might vary considerably from that of a twelve-year-old, though both children could read the words fluently and follow the book's plot. To accommodate the many variables presented by chapter books and avoid inflating the levels reported to parents, we agreed not to indicate more than one year above a child's assigned grade.

Our attempts to determine reading levels reaffirmed what we knew all along: that "grade level" is a slippery concept. A book's reading level is relative to its content, the number of pages and presence of illustrations, the voice of the author, and the knowledge and experience of the reader. It is not an absolute. We were determined to strive for consensus as we undertook the task of assigning reading levels to books.

After determining a beginning list of books, we wrote a word list for each one of ten to fifteen words, depending on the difficulty level. Trial and error taught us to choose some words particular to the book's content and some words from basic sight vocabulary lists.

In our work with Dr. Lipson, we had engaged in lengthy discussions about the kinds of questions we should ask students. By now we were all acutely aware of the necessity of asking appropriate, high-level questions in order to determine the depth and breadth of the child's understanding. We decided to include at least one question from each of the following categories: main idea, detail, sequence, cause and effect, inference, and vocabulary. Rather than try to write six to ten questions for each book in our inventory, we held sessions in which we practiced developing the main idea, and inferential and cause-and-effect questions. We realized that even mature readers have difficulty articulating the main idea of a passage, so it was inappropriate to ask it of a six-year-old. We agreed that questions about the main character's behavior and personality would be easier for young children to understand.

Recording Assessment Data

Next, we developed an assessment form beginning with silent reading and free association, with a space for comments on each. For the oral reading pas-

Reading Assessment

Name _____ Date _____

Selection _____ Level _____

1. SILENT READING - comments:

2. FREE ASSOCIATION -
   What do you think of when I say _____?
   comments:

3. ORAL READING -   comments:

Type of Miscue	Tally
Substitution	
Omission	
Insertion	
Repetition	
Reversal	
Mispronunciation	
Refusal to pronounce	
TOTAL	

4. COMPREHENSION -
   a. Retelling: b.

Type of Questions	Number of Questions	Number Correct
Main Idea		
Detail		
Sequence		
Cause/Effect		
Inference		
Vocabulary		

5. WORD RECOGNITION -

Number of Words	Number Correct

SUMMARY:

Oral Reading	Comprehension	Word Recognition	TOTAL

Comments:

Figure 11.9 Reading assessment form.

sage, we listed types of miscues, with space to tally errors. We also made room for remarks about the child's fluency and expression. The comprehension section had two parts, a section in which to comment on the student's retelling and a grid listing types of questions asked, the number of each type, and the number correct. In the word recognition section, the teacher would tally the number of words the child read correctly.

Finally, there would be a section in which to summarize the student's performance in the oral reading, comprehension, and word recognition sections. Here we calculated percentages for each section based on the number of miscues, questions answered, and words read correctly and then averaged them to arrive at an overall figure. We determined that a score of 80 percent to 90 percent would show the child's instructional reading level, while anything below that would indicate frustration and a score above 90 percent would be the independent level. We realized that these were approximate figures and that teachers would need to rely on their own judgment about the individual child, the particular passage, and other relevant considerations.

After more than a year's work, our assessment was ready. We had a data base containing the inventory of titles, authors, levels, and word lists as well as an assessment form. We were fortified with many hours of instruction and discussion on the assessment of reading. The reports due in January had to indicate a reading level for each child. It was time to pilot our assessment.

Piloting Our New Assessment Tool
Shakily at first and then with growing confidence we met individually with each child, usually during the regular quiet reading time. Each assessment took one quiet reading period, so we spent several weeks in completing our first round. Because the assessment was closely aligned to daily reading instruction, the children were comfortable with the conferencelike format. They diligently practiced their passage silently, read orally with fluency, made detailed retellings, answered the comprehension questions thoughtfully, and worked their way through the word lists with care. We all felt that the children exhibited a greater degree of confidence and comfort with our assessment than they had with the commercial assessment we had tried earlier.

For the youngest readers, the assessment was especially useful. Unlike other instruments that presented beginning readers with full pages of typed text unaccompanied by illustrations, our tool allowed them to read from their own reading books. Their familiarity with these books contributed to their success on the assessment and their feeling of pride in their reading progress. Jamie's experience with the assessment illustrates this point.

In my first-, second-, and third-grade classroom there were children at all reading levels, including Jamie, the youngest student, who in September had not yet learned letters and sounds. Throughout the semester, children read to Jamie during quiet reading and listened to him practice alphabet books and predictable readers. He read and reread DLM's (Developmental

Learning Materials) tiny *I Can Dig* and *I Fly*, and then moved on the *The Little Red Hen* and *The Zoo*, both Ladybird Books. With determination and the support of his teacher and peers, Jamie was reading preprimers by January.

From group discussion at read-aloud time, I knew that Jamie possessed excellent listening and inferential skills. He could describe in detail the events of the last chapter to a classmate who had been absent and make insightful comments about the story's characters. He had many of the elements of a mature reader, but lacked facility with sound/symbol relationships and sight retention.

During a quiet reading period in January, we sat down together for Jamie's first reading assessment. The other children were reading alone or to each other in pairs, or quietly discussing information gleaned from a collection of books about the universe. They understood that we were not to be interrupted.

I had observed Jamie rehearse his book, *We Have Fun*. I asked him what he thought of when I said the word *beach*. He described a beach as a place where people swim, get a tan, and build sand castles. I was satisfied that he knew about beaches. Then he carefully read the passage he had practiced. Because of his limited decoding skills, Jamie's infrequent miscues were characterized by a refusal to pronounce. He waited to be told the word.

I closed the book and asked him to tell me as much as he could remember from his reading. In a relaxed, conversational manner he told the story of Jane, Peter, and Pat's day at the beach in its proper sequence and in detail. He answered my questions thoughtfully and with confidence. It was obvious that Jamie was enjoying this opportunity to read and discuss a book at length with his teacher.

But reading words in isolation proved difficult for him. He only knew 40 percent of the word list, but when this was averaged with his high scores in oral reading and comprehension, he attained an instructional reading level of preprimer. Flushed with pride he asked, "How'd I do?" I felt that Jamie's success reflected our own. We had created an assessment tool that could measure the significant progress made by a beginning reader in the early months of the school year.

Throughout the following semester, Jamie practiced more preprimers, moved on to *Goldilocks and the Three Bears*, *The Elves and the Shoemaker*, and *The Pied Piper of Hamlin*. By June he was ready to be assessed on *Hansel and Gretel*, a selection in the books for the second semester of first grade.

As he became a more able reader, Jamie's miscues consisted of substitutions and mispronunciations, reflecting his growing knowledge of sounds and increased willingness to apply that knowledge to unfamiliar words. He continued to experience the most difficulty reading isolated words. During the questioning on *Hansel and Gretel,* I asked him what he thought had become of the evil stepmother at the end of the story. He suggested that she and the witch were the same person. That, he explained, was why the step-mother is gone when the children find their way home. After all, didn't Gretel push her into the oven before setting her brother free? I was delighted with Jamie's response, which illustrated his sophisticated ability to make inferences and draw conclusions.

It was a long journey from our dissatisfaction with the previous assessment tool to Jamie's successful completion of our new reading assessment. Along the way we had learned a great deal about the assessment of reading, about children's books, and about the motivation and ability of our students. We had accepted the challenge to create an instrument tailored to our program, flawed as all such assessments are. But most important, we had become better teachers of reading.

Now the components of our assessment inform our regular reading conferences with children. We routinely check for prior knowledge and ask for retellings. And we have improved our ability to ask questions that challenge our students to explore the depths of their understanding and gain greater meaning and enjoyment from their reading.

CHAPTER TWELVE

MOVING INTO MULTIAGE

Peggy Dorta

T H R O U G H O U T this book I have tried to provide snapshots that show what actually happens in a multiage classroom day-to-day, month-to-month and to include tools that help a teacher plan for such a multiage program. Yet a teacher planning to make the transition from single-grade to multiage classroom may wonder how to prepare for and proceed with such a change. The transformation need not be immediate and total; in fact, there are advantages to proceeding gradually. It is easier to gain the support of community members and parents if the change is not abrupt. Children and teachers may find gradual change more comfortable. Many teachers begin by teaming with another grade-level, sharing children for some activities and planning a theme study together. Some teachers begin with moving toward a whole language approach in reading and writing or introducing an Explore Time.

Peggy Dorta has counselled a number of teachers involved in such a transition. I asked her to reflect on the process of "Moving into Multiage." Her comments review and focus on some of the ingredients of change.

PEGGY DORTA

In writing about moving into a multiage classroom, I have felt slightly apprehensive. Is there really a way to present this idea and at the same time include all the issues and concerns involved in making such a structural change? Even a semester graduate course seems too short. A brief overview could easily become too much like a "recipe" describing a list of ingredients and offering a step-by-step procedure. But this seems too easy, too simplistic, too "surfacey." One is inclined to neglect to mention the reflections, expertise, experiences, and personal knowledge necessary to bring the ingredients together effectively.

A chapter about starting a multiage program, however, can be seen in a useful sense as a "recipe" in that it is the beginning of something, a way to set a course. It can inspire reflection and creative thinking. It leaves room for innovation.

Let me set forth some guidelines:

1. Each situation is unique but will share some common elements. The multiage classrooms described here and elsewhere in this book represent possibilities, but teachers will need to decide what fits their school and community.
2. Introducing a multiage approach does not mean starting from scratch. Instead it builds on past experience and expertise.
3. Clarification and communication are paramount. The school community—staff, administration, parents—as well as the community beyond the school, need to understand the change that is occurring and feel part of the process.

DEFINITIONS

The entire school staff should share a common definition of the multiage structure. Too often we start working with an idea before we have established a clear sense of what it entails. In the course I offer on multiage teaching, we start by defining and then discussing these key concepts:

multiage
curriculum
environment
schedule and routine
communication
assessment and evaluation
classroom management

The discussion often reinforces the importance of a common understanding of these ideas among everyone on the staff. Many multiage teachers work in schools in which the multiage approach is not generally followed. Even if all staff members do not entirely agree with such an endeavor, they do need to understand what it is we are trying to accomplish, and they will be more supportive if they do.

Clear and common definitions also help in communicating the multiage approach to the larger community—parents, school board members, and other interested parties—all of whom should be aware of what multiage teachers are trying to do.

IDENTIFY YOUR STRENGTHS

The next step is to identify strengths and analyze needs. What is already happening that will support the program you want to see? This reminds me of the time I sat with a close friend on the day she and her family were moving. We watched with mixed emotions as a large moving van drove up to the house and loaded up the boxes of familiar belongings—photos, trinkets, keepsakes, mementos—and they prepared for the move to a new home. The process of moving, the anticipation, planning, and the good-byes, had been difficult. But once they arrived in their new surroundings these familiar items would help them feel more settled and "at home."

Packing up the old to move to the new is a good analogy for beginning a multiage program. As I work with educators, I ask them to identify what is important to them in their teaching and to give it priority. Complete change is not the issue—things that work well don't need to change. But in focusing on what we already do well and building on it, we proceed with more confidence.

For me, Explore Time is at the top of the list. It seems to be the most productive, creative, relaxed yet intense time of the day. It's my favorite period, and I think it's what my teammates think of when they think of me. At the top of my friend Michael's list is reading good literature to kids. He describes it as the time of day when he shares his own love of books, builds cohesiveness, carries on wonderful conversations with children, and extends their metacognition for reading and language. Alvin exudes science. He is always setting up experiments and challenging kids to observe and question. Research is predominant in his classroom. Pricilla's practice time is paramount. She can make skill work interesting, self-motivating, and challenging in a low-key way. For Janice, the daily brain twister is the priority she would choose. It involves a lot of thinking, communicating, problem solving, and just plain fun. The kids frequently add to the collection of ideas that have been created over the years.

Each of us has a particular slant or a special time of day that seems to peak our interest and that of our students. We have developed routines that work well with all kids, regardless of their age or ability level. In moving toward a multiage configuration from a single-grade level, those things that work well should go along. They will be comfortable and successful within the new setting and easy to expand for a wider age range.

· ·

Along with the familiar parts of the classroom program that will make the transition to the multiage setting, there will be others that need to be changed. It would be helpful to make a list of those you plan to keep and those you would like to change.

You can investigate ideas for change as you (1) observe established multiage settings; (2) read and discuss research and writings; (3) take a course or a workshop; and (4) reflect on the information and ideas that come from such resources. Be selective. Ask, "Does this fit my community, my school, my own teaching style?"

You can try out some of the changes you identify as desirable before making the major change to a multiage class. Perhaps a different room arrangement would be more effective, or new ways of working with children in groups, or a revamped approach to one area of curriculum, or even teaming up in some new way with a colleague.

CURRICULUM

In my class for educators we explore various definitions and presentations of curriculum. Our study usually includes the graded curriculum guides that so many school districts use for reading and math, in which skills and objectives are in vertical, hierarchal steps according to grade levels. We try to rewrite these documents so that they will be more helpful and more in line with teaching a multiage group.

When Amy, a seasoned teacher, came to class she spread computer paper out across the floor in front of us. On it she had rewritten her school's graded curriculum guide horizontally, placing skills and objectives along the paper like a time line, a new way to envision curriculum. This arrangement helped us get away from looking at curriculum in vertical, hierarchical stages. It was also an excellent way to reinforce the fact that skills are repeated over and over again from grade level to grade level. Amy's multiage continuum addressed the same skills that graded curriculums do.

Being clear about what children really need to learn is an important element for curriculum development. I often ask people to think about the categories that Lillian Katz, an authority on early education, outlined at a conference when trying to answer the question, "What do children really need to learn?" These categories are knowledge (facts, concepts, ideas, vocabulary, stories), skills (small units of action), feelings (subjective emotional states), and dispositions (habits of mind or tendencies to respond to certain situations in certain ways). When we talk about curriculum, we usually find ourselves concentrating exclusively on knowledge or skills. Yet it is important to include feelings and dispositions as well.

Some of the common elements in a cross-section of multiage classes address all these categories: Explore Time, when students direct their own learning; class meetings led by the teacher or by children; an integrated approach to curriculum; activities that reflect multiple intelligences; and various rationales for flexible groupings that allow frequent changes in multipurpose groupings.

Certain methods and materials do work better with a multiage philosophy. For a group of teachers or an entire school to embark upon an exploration of "best practices" is a worthwhile goal. An entire school staff can and should look at such approaches and support their implementation.

A word of caution: do not draw a line between multiage and single grades where it is unnecessary. All of us as educators can benefit from identifying and using "best practices." It also gives us an opportunity to keep our involvement a *shared* endeavor and avoid fragmenting our efforts between multiage and single-grade classes within a school.

After defining curriculum, looking at different ways of organizing the sequence of skills development, and studying common multiage approaches and "best practices," you will be ready to design your own curriculum.

ENVIRONMENT

Another important ingredient in a multiage classroom is setting. What kind of environment do you want to offer to your students? One of a teacher's many hats is that of interior designer. The elements involved in setting up and sustaining the classroom environment are time, space, and general atmosphere.

Draw a floor plan of your classroom. The procedure I suggest is to list everything you think is important: You will need an area where you can all meet. Would you like to include a comfortable reading area and an area for the arts? What about storage of students' personal belongings and classroom materials? What about traffic patterns? Can you use the outdoors?

When you have made such a list, draw a floor plan that fits your needs. Write a rationale for your room arrangement and keep referring to it as the school year progresses. Does it need revision? Involving children in the planning often inspires them to think about the use of the room for the first time. Their ideas can be quite incredible!

In working with a group of teachers from one school district, I realized that thinking of themselves as interior designers was a new idea. We took extra time to work on setting up room environments. They dreamed and schemed. They became carpenters, building cubbies, lofts, and book display cases (or enlisting family and friends to get involved). The furniture moving resulted in a lot of sore backs, but these were forgotten in listening to stories of wide-eyed children walking in on a Monday morning, excited to find something new. They also brought back stories of wonderful new things happening just because their space was better defined, easier to work with, and more inviting. Their efforts were contagious, influencing classroom design throughout the school.

SET A ROUTINE

A concern that often stymies many teachers is how to deal with a preordained school schedule. I suggest making a real distinction in their minds between *routine* and *schedule*. What routine will best fit your students? Think about it first and then see how the schedule supports it or undermines it.

A routine can be defined as a broad arrangement of time that is predictable and expected by kids. "Yep, I know that today we have Explore Time, then meeting, then portfolio practice." The time frames so often attached, such as 9:02–9:47, are the schedule, not the routine. An effective routine will alternate between whole group and individual activities, between louder and quieter ones, between intense and more relaxed tasks.

What routines do your students need and how do you fit them together into a given schedule? Sometimes there is no good fit. Then you need to rely on creative problem solving. Sometimes a readjustment here or there will accommodate everyone's needs. Sometimes compromise is the best solution. Do the best you can.

CLASSROOM MANAGEMENT

So far, I have mentioned a number of management issues. By this time definitions are clear, strengths identified, and needs defined. Curriculum planning is under way, the room set up and organized, the routine established. Classroom management likewise requires forethought and reflection. It does not mean classroom control. I think of it as turning over as much of the responsibility and decision making as possible to the students. Of course, that doesn't happen overnight, but procedures and modeling allow the children to understand what is expected and what their role might be.

EVAN was one of those students we might call "a handful." One day he arrived with a bulging bag of gourds.

"Mrs. D., we can make rattles out of these, just like the Native Americans did." We were in the midst of an integrated study of the early inhabitants in our state.

"What a great idea, Evan!"

"Yeah, we can set up a center in the arts area called Native American Crafts. I bet other kids could think of things to do, you too, Mrs. D." Evan continued, "Aren't we lucky my dad and I grew all of these? There's enough for one gourd for everyone in the class."

As he talked, he tossed his jacket on a hanger, put his backpack on a hook, and headed for the arts area. Within fifteen minutes he had written out sequential directions for creating a gourd rattle on a gourd-shaped piece of oaktag and posted it for all to see. He displayed the gourds in a basket and set out other materials—pins, tape, markers—nearby.

Evan could see quite clearly how his garden gourds fit in with our study of early inhabitants. It made sense. The project effectively channeled his bossy nature, and focused his excessive energy, too often seen as distractible. It is evident that ownership of the classroom is shared with students.

What else contributes to a smoothly running classroom? Children share classroom chores. Both teacher and student can lead meetings. The classroom follows an established routine. The room has well-defined activity areas and expectations for appropriate behavior are clear. Children participate in making rules and they are clearly posted. High standards of work are expected of the children and examples of such are shared. Children understand work assignments and know where to put finished work. There are procedures for building trust and involvement. Children have a chance to practice decision making and take on responsibility. The teacher and class provide input into all aspects of daily work. Although classroom management does not mean control, it does mean thinking about the what, the why, and the how of things.

COMMUNICATE, COMMUNICATE, COMMUNICATE

Share your definition of a multiage environment with the school and the broader community through newsletters, informal discussions, and planned presentations. Parents in particular will need to understand why you are planning change, what exactly will change, and what will remain the same. It is important to provide many opportunities for people to ask questions and get involved. Invite a speaker to come and give background information on multiage classrooms. Follow up with a panel or workshop by in-house educators. But don't stop there. Involve parents and community members. Invite parents of multiage students to sit on an informational panel or to write about their volunteering experiences for a newsletter.

Communication can never stop. It is vital before you begin a new program, but it must continue. Train parent and community volunteers to do meaningful work in the classroom. Tap their expertise for enrichment activities. Keep everyone informed and involved in the process.

FREQUENTLY ASKED QUESTIONS

The following is a list of some of the most common questions I've heard about multiage classrooms over the past eight years. How would you respond to them? Try your hand at it first and then read the responses I have used. Please remember it is not important that our answers match, or even that we agree. It is important that you are clear and that you believe what you are saying. It is important that others hear your conviction. I have purposely left my answers brief, but hope I have said enough to spark some thought and dialogue. The purpose is really not to convince with these answers, but to state beliefs.

1. *What is your definition of a multiage classroom and how is it going to be different from the single-grade classroom I'm familiar with?*

My definition has two parts. Philosophically, it means assessing students' strengths and needs, fitting the curriculum to the child, not the child to the curriculum. If I stop there I'm sure you will think of many single-grade classrooms that fit such a definition. Yes, I believe many single-grade teachers use what I would call a "multiage philosophy."

The second part of my definition addresses structure. In a multiage classroom, a group of students of varied ages remain together with the same teacher for two or more years. That means that each year a new group joins the old group and part of the old group moves on.

2. *What will look different in a multiage classroom?*

A multiage classroom will be a showplace for what goes on there each day. The displays will be child created and unique. The materials will include many manipulatives, books, artifacts, and teacher/child-made items. The organization of furniture will allow for children's active participation and involvement. The atmosphere will be inviting and interesting. There will be evidence that people are "at home" there.

3. *How are decisions about student placement made?*

A multiage class should use the same placement procedures as any other class in the school. Any class needs to be balanced academically and socially, and to have both leaders and followers. In addition, in a multiage class ages should be represented as equally as possible.

4. What about report cards?

I prefer narratives that allow me to write a letter to the parents about what, why, and how their child does things. I also feel that it is important to include self-evaluation by the student. I set goals with parents and students at the beginning of each marking period. The reporting process addresses how the goals have or have not been reached.

5. Are multiage classrooms less teacher directed?

Multiage classrooms strive for student-directed learning. Sometimes the teacher is "up front" lecturing, but she also acts as a facilitator, supporter, and provider of materials, and is herself a learner.

6. Do you use formal peer tutoring?

Any parent who has more than one child can address this question with ease. We see natural peer tutoring happening all the time. The youngest child in the family usually walks earlier, is toilet trained earlier, and does many other things earlier than older siblings. They watch and learn.

In a multiage class learning takes place quite naturally. It is my role as a teacher to set up situations that nurture positive, natural peer tutoring and to observe and assess the process. I do not feel the need to use a formal peer tutoring program, since it goes on all the time without my direction or interference.

7. What are some advantages for the older students in a multiage class?

This question always seems to pop up. I can't stress my answer enough. Those students who have been with me for a year or more already—the "olders"—are the very ones I keep in mind as I plan for the coming year. When I order materials, I am thinking about what we've already done and what they need to do next. When I plan approaches to themes or skills, I think of their interests and expertise. When I give a whole class presentation, I remember how I have presented something in the past and try to take it in a new direction. As the teacher, I am constantly thinking about the "olders."

Another factor is a definition of mastery. Mastery includes performing a task and being able to communicate what you do. A student might be able to recite all the multiplication facts, but can that same student explain what multiplication is or why it is used? In a multiage class children have many opportunities to become masterful, as children assist each other.

8. What if the "chemistry" is not right between student and teacher or between student and student? They will be together for more than one year.

Often in life we have to deal with people whose chemistry clashes with our own. School can be a safe environment for children to practice working this out. Where else can they learn to deal with such an issue? But, as in any other situation, if the problem worsens or if the chemistry seems to be a parent/teacher issue, a class change might be the answer for the following year.

. . . .

9. *Do all multiage teachers work in teams?*

Teachers can feel very isolated if they shut the door and work alone. Most of us team up in one way or another. "Teaming" has as many definitions as there are people. It can mean sharing ideas and materials or sharing children. It can mean networking with other educators to develop or learn about topics. It can mean touching base with other teachers about problems or strengths. In some way or another most teachers team up.

I have discussed some of the ingredients of a multiage program. The important thing is to take it step by step, gradually and comfortably. Make sure you have enough good support. You need to have other teachers, administrators, parents, and members of the community working with you in this endeavor.

But this is only the beginning. Just remember to think about what you are doing, reflect on why you do it that way, and ask yourself how you might improve or change in order to do it even better. Keep asking those three most important questions: What? Why? How?

CHAPTER THIRTEEN

■

ANATOMY OF A TEAM

Justine O'Keefe

M O S T of the descriptions in this book reflect my own teaching experience. I have frequently mentioned work within a team, but as Peggy Dorta told us, teaming has many definitions. Many teachers work in multiage classes that are completely self-contained. Collaborating with other teachers in some way, however, provides valuable support and professional stimulation. Teamwork can happen in many ways: from two teachers in neighboring classrooms planning a joint theme or field trip, to teachers exchanging groups for a once-a-week project time, to teachers sharing space and students and even holding parent conferences together.

One school I visited was physically designed to support a team structure. The central core of the building contained offices, a library, and an art room, and classrooms were grouped together in "clusters" at the corners of the building. Using movable walls and furniture, teams of six to nine teachers defined how each cluster was divided. Usually there were several classrooms opening into a common area. Each teacher was responsible for a two-grade span and each cluster had children in grades one through six. This was a school of more than five hundred students and the clusters created a small school within a school.

Schools, like families, develop their own special traditions and terminology to describe teams and space. I have asked Justine O'Keefe to describe her team experience to us. In her Williston, Vermont, school, teachers are part of a multiage team and children stay with that team for several years. Justine's team spans ages five through ten, and she is primarily responsible for a two-year age span. Each team has a name and the space in which they work is known as its "house." The team we are about to visit is the Discovery Team.

JUSTINE O'KEEFE

The long, carpeted hallway is dark after the brightness of the summer day. On both sides loom the shadowy shapes of bookshelves and stacked chairs, file cabinets and overturned tables. The only sign of life comes from the principal's office, which I pass before turning right into Discovery House.

This is my teaching home, where I am to meet my team to work on a House description of who we are and what we do. The large semicircular space is dark, illuminated by windows only on the outside wall. On my left, the project room looks vaguely forbidding. The sand and water tables and easels are piled onto the long counters. The tables at which children create papier-mâché animals and work on dioramas are gone. The shiny tiled floor is free of the usual globs of glue and spots of paint.

The lights are off, too, over the kiva, the meeting area where our team of ninety children and four teachers gather daily for stories, performances, and instruction. Beyond, the empty computer screens and bare walls stare blankly at the four surrounding classroom spaces.

But light spills out from our small teachers' room to my left and I am drawn to the welcoming laughter of my teammates. Clutching coffee cups, clad in T-shirts and shorts, their smiling faces and animated voices are a sharp contrast to the dismal quiet of the rest of the house.

We greet each other warmly, catch up on the latest news, and then adjourn to one of the classroom spaces to set to work. Dan "fires up" one of the computers while we settle ourselves among the stacked boxes, bits of broken crayon, and lost Unifix cubes.

I pull a chair up to the computer. Dan sits to my left on a table. To my right sit Liz, our new kindergarten teacher, and beside her my longtime colleague, Martha, her six-foot frame barely contained by the tiny chair in which she sits.

One of our tasks is to write a statement for parents about how we assess and report on the progress of our five- through ten-year-olds. We agree that it is the most difficult thing we have to do and Dan suggests we do it first.

"OK, shoot," I say, hands poised over the keyboard. Together we craft each sentence, often starting with one person's suggestion and ending with another's. We search out loud for the right word and coach one another from cloudy thought to clear statement. Certain contributions are lavishly complimented while others meet with groans and hoots of derision.

Martha complains that I never type her sentences and Dan suggests that we revamp our assessment system to a simple thumbs up or thumbs down symbol. Liz, recently out of graduate school, drops finely worded phrases of incomprehensible jargon. At each new bit of foolishness our laughter builds. I stop to wipe my eyes on the hem of my long summer dress and fumble in my pocket for a hankie. Dan blows his nose loudly into his wrinkled handkerchief, and Martha lurches to the water fountain for a calming drink.

We are having a great time and miraculously giving birth to a rough draft that reflects our combined attitudes about the topic. Writing together helps us clarify to ourselves and each other the theoretical and practical reasons for what we do and how we do it. This process is time-consuming, but in the end we have completed the assigned piece of writing while reaffirming the philosophical basis for our work with children. Like our formal meetings and informal discussions, this writing activity furthers our goal of creating a learning environment with uniform rules and expectations and a common language for behavior and achievement.

This kind of teaming, which I think of as "total immersion," is a result of our unique personalities and experiences. I am, as Dan puts it, the "elder statesperson" of the team, followed closely by Martha. We have both worked at the school for many years, several of those as teaching partners. Liz came to public education after working in an alternative school, which she cofounded, and Dan was a full-time artist before entering teaching three years ago. Because of our many years as multiage teachers and our long-term commitment to the profession, Martha and I value the opportunity to act as mentors and coaches for our newer members. The enthusiasm and freshness of the ideas Liz and Dan bring to us help rejuvenate our tired blood and challenge us to try new things. We are all deeply committed to making Discovery House a place where adults and children grow and learn together in a rich and stable environment.

In addition, we share an acknowledged desire to know each other intimately. We do not limit our relationships to the professional realm but attempt to foster friendship as well. In this way, our team differs considerably from other teams of which I have been a member.

In my previous teaming situations we shared themes and rotated children through various related activities. We planned our themes together, maintained the same schedule, and divvied up tasks. We did not, however, communicate about the daily operations of our individual groups or work together on math and writing activities. I found this to be an altogether efficient teaming model that allowed me the kind of autonomy I have always valued as a teacher.

In contrast, total immersion teaming demands that we give up a measure of that dearly held autonomy. In exchange, we experience the stimulation of working with teachers whose methods and ideas we respect while enjoying the support and affection of peers. There is a wholeness to our teaming that is satisfying intellectually and emotionally, and allows us to enjoy the work/play combination modeled so well by young learners.

Teams are as unique as their individual members, but I believe that effective teams share three common characteristics: communication, collaboration, and recreation. All three require time and effort, and often take place simultaneously.

In order for team members to collaborate and have fun together, they must know how to communicate with one another. Vehicles for honest dialog about sensitive issues need to be developed and implemented. Just as we expect children to work out differences through a frank statement of their feelings, team members must also be willing to make their desires and needs known to one another. Kindness, diplomacy, "I statements," and support from guidance and administration are all useful in facilitating communication. It is important that time is available for team members to sit together at lunch, at meetings, and in the teachers' room after school to discuss and resolve issues as they arise.

Collaboration is working together, not side by side. It is not the parallel play of toddlers but the give-and-take of six-year-olds inventing a fantasy together. Collaboration creates a whole greater than the sum of its parts. When my team writes a piece together it is unlike anything any of us would do individually. Likewise, when we brainstorm a theme together or plan a production it has the unique stamp of our team rather than that of a particular individual.

Collaboration requires that team members share their pet ideas and activities rather than be protective of them. It is another piece of autonomy that teachers committed to their teams relinquish. It does not mean that individuals are not recognized for their strengths. Indeed, collaboration is the means by which each member's strengths are woven into a strong net that supports all the adults and children on the team.

Recreation is the component of effective teaming that allows its members to let the rough side drag. Our work will never be easy or stress-free, but we can make it fun. Maintaining a sense of humor is essential. There is very little we do as teachers that is life-threatening, but we often approach parental concerns and administrative deadlines as though they were. A walk around the track before an after-school meeting or a funny story told over a cup of tea can soothe our nerves and renew our spirits. Moments of recreation enhance our workday and increase our efficiency.

Our team makes a point of socializing. A few times during the year we have potluck dinners, to which we invite our families, and avoid talk of school. On inservice days we go out to lunch, and we have dinner together before evening meetings and performances. On a shelf in Dan's closet we keep a variety of goodies to share at meetings or give a chocolate boost to a rainy afternoon. And we are not afraid to be silly. We tease, joke, and play on words. We laugh about our successes and failures and celebrate our birthdays. We are serious professionals committed to furthering the learning of our children and to having a good time doing it.

If an army moves on its stomach, a team meets to keep moving. To me, it seems that we meet for every possible reason: some meetings are regular and formal, others are lunchtime conversations, and still others are so spontaneous they don't require chairs. Whether they last an hour or five minutes, their purpose is to advance the learning of our children through planning and reflection.

We have developed a useful structure for our regular meetings that fosters the engagement and participation of each member, including our special educator, whom we share with another team, and often the guidance counselor as well. Our meetings are led by a facilitator, who copies the agenda from an ongoing list in our Discovery House teachers' room and leads a discussion of each item. Another team member acts as a reporter and takes notes in our team log, and still another as a time keeper to move the meeting along. The task monitor (fondly known as the task master) keeps us from digressions and tangential debate. These roles rotate throughout the team, the facilitator usually being that person most desirous of getting the show on the road. We meet in a comfortable spot in the House and always share a snack.

When our team plans for an upcoming theme study, we begin by holding a brainstorming session on the topic. We invite as many support personnel as are available: the guidance counselor, the special educator, the enrichment teacher, and the librarian. From this session we develop areas of study and related activities. These become the basis for a series of hour-long, weekly workshops through which groups of children rotate. Because we are assisted by one or more of the support personnel, we are able to offer a greater variety of workshops to smaller groups of children. When the special educator teaches an origami workshop during a study of Japan, or the enrichment teacher helps children build a model of the arm muscles as part of a human body unit, they contribute to the education of every child in the House. Frequently attending our brainstorming sessions are the art and music teachers, who then work to integrate our theme into their regularly scheduled classes.

Involved in both planning and implementation, these support staff are integral to the success of our program. In addition to theme workshops, they conduct small group lessons, provide help with songs and drama activities, and enhance themes with arts and crafts. The children benefit enormously from the rich opportunities provided by these professionals.

In addition to our regular team and occasional theme-planning meetings, we hold weekly "instructional support team" meetings to discuss how best to meet the emotional, social, and academic requirements of children with special needs. Again, the special educator and guidance counselor are present as we discuss the child's strengths and needs, accommodation made thus far, and our concerns. Finally, we outline a plan for improving the child's program and set a future date for evaluating the success of the plan. These meetings are an occasion for all the adults who provide services to the child to work together in the child's behalf.

Finally, we meet for lunch each day during the luxurious twenty minutes the children are supervised by others. Our conversations are as likely to be about Dan's new house or my old dog as about an upcoming parent's night or Joel's math difficulties. But these few minutes provide the chance to tie up loose ends for an afternoon workshop or share information from the various committees on which each of us serves. Though the time is short, these daily lunchtime engagements promote communication that is open and timely.

Teaching is hard work and teaming does not make it easier. It does, however, give us the opportunity to share the triumphs and pitfalls of our profession with peers who respect and support us. Committing myself to my team through communication, collaboration, and recreation has enhanced my personal life as well as my school life. Through my team, I have become a better teacher and come to know myself better, too.

CHAPTER FOURTEEN

■

EXPLORING TOGETHER

Anne Bingham

"H EY DUM Diddly Dum, Hey Dum Diddly Dum." We filed into Room C for our weekly singalong, Liz Farman and the other children singing us in. It felt warm and comfortable, a predictable extended family time together. Four classrooms joined weekly for singing and sometimes other activities as well.

Singalong moved on with both old favorites and new songs. Finally it was time to practice our farewell song. We were getting ready for our June day camp, reliving annual traditions. There we would sing farewell to the children who would be moving out of our program into other classrooms next year. We would miss them.

Yet how fortunate we were to have had those years together. During most of the time I spent with Shelburne's multiage team, children remained with us for three or four years, entering for many years as five-year-olds and later as sixes.

Community became a very important aspect of our program—both the classroom community and the wider community represented by the four classrooms. Jason spent two years with me and then moved on to experience the strengths and leadership of other members of our team. But he and I continued to have a relationship. He would appear in my room during Explore Time to say "Hi," look up a friend, work in the block area, experiment with batteries and bulbs when I brought them out each January, and use the materials and space with which he was familiar. After watching him become a reader and writer during his sixth and seventh years, I continued to be aware of his progress and accomplishments. I also welcomed his little

Figure 14.1 "I remember when I was new to the class and I didn't know anybody and you were my friend."

sister, Jessie, to our multiage family as she joined us in Room A. In a sense she was already part of our community. She had visited the classroom often when picking Jason up after school or attending a play.

The time we have with children and families is truly a gift to multiage teachers concerned about creating a sense of community and helping children develop a sense of responsibility for one another.

What are the strands that weave together to achieve this fabric of community? It is not automatic or easy to achieve community just because we have a multiage environment, but that helps. I think, first of all, each member of the community must have a sense of self, know who we are, and second, a sense of being accepted and valued by the adults and children who make up the rest of the community. When we share our own stories in group discussion we discover who we are and we search for that acceptance. When we choose our own activities and define our own projects we also define who we are and discover our own special interests and talents. Using those talents assures us of success. We are also more likely to achieve success through a program that allows us to progress at our own rate. And when we feel successful we also feel more acceptable.

Before it can extend to others, community begins with the self, but it also requires successful experiences of collaboration. When we work and play together in groups we seek roles that are comfortable and give us a sense of accomplishment. Teachers make this possible through varied encounters with groups, large and small. Children need guidance in learning how to accept differences of opinion and practice the give-and-take of successful collaboration. These experiences are not created artificially; they happen within the natural flow of the day as children discuss books, help solve a math problem, play games, and plan projects together. Many of the skills involved are modeled when the whole class meets: listening to different opinions, giving and receiving positive feedback, planning together, solving social problems.

Another strand in the community fabric is the accumulation of shared experience and the development of traditions.

"COULD somebody explain Day Camp to those who haven't been before?" I asked.

Stacie raised her hand. "We all go someplace, like to the woods or the mountains . . . everybody in multiage. And we stay out all day. We have supper and we toast marshmallows."

"Last year we hiked up to a lake," Alex added. "Some of us caught frogs."

"Mike hid one in his backpack, but Mrs. B. found it." Jerry includes one of my less favorite memories.

"And we had a watermelon-seed-spitting contest," Mike contributes, nonplussed by Jerry's reminder. I remember the seed-spitting contest as supervised. We have learned to channel some activities through the years.

Traditions evolve. This one developed after two years of trying overnights with young children. One early October, the weather did not cooperate. It became so cold that every leaf and twig was covered with a thin coating of ice. We were afraid to keep the children out in the state park's lean-to shelters overnight, knowing that some families had not been able to provide warm enough sleeping bags and others had forgotten the wool socks and sweaters we suggested on lists sent home. We called the school and buses were sent to bring us home after supper. Reflecting back, we realized that we'd had a wonderful day out, despite the weather. When worried parents met the school bus, after an emergency call from our office, they were greeted by huge smiles, albeit muddy faces, as the children disembarked. So the next year we planned just what we had experienced the year before, a day camp.

Many parents have come to look forward to this tradition. We never have to search for volunteers to help on this trip. More than enough fathers and mothers tell us early in the year, "Be sure to plan on me for day camp. I wouldn't miss it for anything." Or they ask months ahead of time when day camp will be so they can arrange to take that day off from work.

Figure 14.2 Day camp is an event both students and parents enjoy.

Such special events are not planned in order to provide relief from drudgery as much as to fit into our belief that learning is and should be fun. One day I walked into the room after a quick trip to the teacher's room for tea, during a winter indoor recess, one of my colleagues having kept an eye on things in Room A along with her own classroom. I was greeted by large letters chalked across our old-fashioned blackboard, "I LIKE SCHOOL!" Of course I was thrilled. I believe that discovering the joy of learning, of work, and of friendship will give us the capacity to face hard times when they occur. School should be stimulating and exciting, warm and caring. When parents tell me it is difficult to keep sick children at home because they don't want to miss school, I think this tells us that we are doing something right.

Most children come to school eager explorers of their world. The least we can do is to nurture that eagerness at this early age. If we meet children where they are developmentally it's possible to explore together, year by year, what it is they need, and how to help them meet those needs and still to maintain that excitement. But if we focus only on what they need to be in twenty years and forget who they are today, we will fail them and society.

We need to help them continue to explore the world eagerly and to see that year by year they gain the tools they need for the task of growing in knowledge, skill, and community.

THE CHILDREN, all eighty-three of them, scurried across the grass picking up jackets, Frisbees, and jump ropes and shoving them into backpacks. Already a colorful line of backpacks were lined up along the ground near where we expected the school bus to materialize momentarily.

I stuffed lists for a "nature treasure hunt" into my own backpack and started counting balls into a large black plastic bag. Ron's mother, Carol, had organized a group to clean up any trash remaining from our picnic supper. Chuck's dad carried one of the heavy coolers up to the roadside and Marilyn made sure our fire was out. We were almost ready to "count noses."

Tired and sticky from marshmallows, some of the younger children would doze on the way back to school. The excitement, chatter, and singing of the bus trip out would give way to a more comfortable subdued atmosphere.

Another multiage year was near its end and, as always, while I looked forward to the summer, my mind was also on those children who would be returning in the fall. I was wondering what new materials might be found to help connect Jerry's talent for the spatial with his understanding of math concepts. How could I continue to support friendships for Kent? What books might be so enticing to Patty that they would draw from her the extra effort she needed to make progress as a reader? The multiage cycle was about to begin again.

APPENDIX A

■

CUBES TO COMPUTERS:
MATERIALS LIST

T HE MATERIALS in the classroom are an essential part of the curriculum. Their variety and accessibility are important to the success of
Explore Time and to math, reading, writing, and theme studies. I have gathered
the materials in my classroom gradually, over time. Small grants have provided
funding for some items, such as a small toaster oven. On the following pages I
will list materials I have used or observed in other primary multiage rooms. In
order to make this a more usable reference, I have grouped materials in categories, although many have multiple uses. The list is not exhaustive but it does
include more than most classrooms have. Selecting from the list, with attention
to all the various categories, will create a rich environment indeed.

What I cannot list here is the knowledge, imagination, innovation, and
sensitivity to children that is also needed. As John Holt reminds us in his
1970 introduction to Julia Weber Gordon's *My Country School Diary,* we can
find ourselves faced with "costly and elaborate disappointment." Gordon had
"very little money and only those materials she or her students or friendly
outsiders could make, or what she could get various educational services to
give or lend her," yet she succeeded admirably.

MATH MANIPULATIVES

Children use many of the materials listed here as math manipulatives in
other creative ways, including combining them with blocks in construction.
But they belong in this category not only because they are used in math
instruction but also because most of them are inherently mathematical in

structure. I have listed the uses to which children and teachers often put these materials, but again, the list is not complete. Included are some supplementary resources: books with ideas for utilizing the materials and additional concrete materials to enhance or extend the manipulatives. These supplementary resources may be found in school catalogs along with the manipulatives themselves. These catalogs, along with your teaching colleagues, are ideal resources for locating the most useful materials.

Many math manipulatives are expensive, but they represent a long-term investment since, unlike workbooks, they last for many years. They are worth the cost, too, because of their attractiveness and multiple uses. Since they have to be accumulated over time, I will suggest those I consider essential for starting a classroom collection. Minimally, you need an assortment of counters and Unifix cubes or Multilink Blocks, a hundreds board, and number lines. Base Ten Blocks are important for children age seven and above. Then you can add pattern blocks, Geoboards, Cuisenaire rods, and Tangrams.

Assorted Counters

Here, cost need not be a factor. There are many commercially available counters in attractive shapes, such as teddy bears or dinosaurs, but it is also possible to use many found objects you can collect yourself. These include natural objects, such as pebbles, nuts, and small shells; locally purchased materials, such as tiles from a hardware store and dried beans from the supermarket; and objects that children can bring from home: plastic milk carton caps, buttons, and bread tags.

Uses: counting (by twos, fives, etc., as well as by ones), categorizing, place value, adding, subtracting.

Unifix Cubes

Uses: Counting and as counters in addition/subtraction/multiplication/division; creating sets to represent a number; categorizing by color; creating linear patterns; making linear measurements; creating tens and ones for place value work; copying or creating two-dimensional designs. Children often add them to their block constructions.

Supplementary Resources: Additional Unifix materials, especially "Number Indicators," which can be attached to a tower to show number, "1–10 Value Boats," and "Unifix 100 Track." Children also enjoy using the "Unifix Operational Grid" along with "Pattern Building Underlay Cards" to create two-dimensional designs. (All these materials are particularly useful for five- and six-year-olds.)

Books: *Developing Number Concepts Using Unifix Cubes,* by Kathy Richardson.
Unifix Teachers Resource Book, by Lola J. May and Larry Ecklund.

Multilink Blocks

Uses: All the same purposes as Unifix cubes. In addition, it is possible to create three-dimensional shapes, which can be used to develop spatial visualization skills (in copying a design or a picture) and concepts such as symmetry, congruence, and volume. They are also popular in the creative construction of fantasy shapes, spaceships, and dinosaurs. In my classroom, children have combined them with teddy bear counters in many ways.

Books: *Multilink Exploration,* by Peggy McLean, Mary Laycock, and Lowell Hovis.
Multilink Apparatus Handbook, by Bob Stone.

Pattern Blocks

Uses: Learning geometric shapes; categorizing by shape and color; creating linear patterns; creating sets demonstrating number facts (for example, two squares and three triangles make five); fractions; measuring an area using nonstandard measures; demonstrating concepts of symmetry, congruence, tesselation; and creating designs.

Supplementary Resources: Pattern block stickers and posters showing large pattern block designs.

Books: *Pattern Block Activities,* by Barbara Bayha and Katy Burt.
Let's Pattern Block It, by McLean, Jenkins, and McLaughlin.
Exploring with Pattern Blocks, by Vincent J. Altamuro and Sandra Pryor Clarkson.

Geoboards

Uses: Naming two-dimensional shapes; counting sides and corners; counting the number of shapes ("How many triangles can we find in this design?"); showing fractional parts; developing concepts of area; creating designs; visualizing when copying another's design or copying a design on paper.

Supplementary Resources: Colored rubber bands, paper showing a Geoboard grid with dots representing nails (useful for planning and copying designs and in working with area).

Books: *Geoboard Activity Cards—Primary Set.*

Cuisenaire Rods

Uses: Counting; categorizing by size and by color; arranging sequentially by size; using different sizes and colors to represent numbers; playing trading games; learning the concept of centimeter and square centimeter; figuring area; working with place value; adding, subtracting, multiplying, and dividing.

Supplementary Resources: "Rodney Rod" a beginning game using the rods; Cuisenaire blocks, three-dimensional blocks in the same colors.

Books: *Idea Book for Cuisenaire-Rods at the Primary Level*, by Patricia S. Davidson.
   Picture Puzzles with Cuisenaire Rods, by Patricia S. Davidson and Jeffrey B. Sellon.
   Spatial Problem Solving with Cuisenaire Rods, by Patricia S. Davidson and Robert E. Willcutt.

Tangrams

Uses: Learning about two-dimensional geometric shapes; making puzzles; showing spatial representation; problem solving; working with fractions; measuring area.

Supplementary Resources: ESS Tangram Cards (available on three levels—Sets I, II, and III).

Books: *The Fun with Tangrams Kit*, by Susan Johnson.

Geoblocks

Uses: Block construction; learning about three-dimensional shapes (surfaces, edges, corners, vocabulary); looking at fractional parts; problem solving in three dimensions (copying a design, filling in a shape, constructing a given shape); studying the concept of volume.

Base Ten Blocks

Uses: Constructing numbers showing tens, ones, hundreds, and one thousand; demonstrating volume (metric); trading games, adding and subtracting with trading.

Books: *Games and Activities with Base Ten Blocks* (Book 1 and Book 2), by Rebecca S. Nelson.
   Hands-On Base Ten Blocks, Creative Publications.

Hundreds Boards and Number Lines

Uses: Counting; formation of numerals; counting on and counting back; making number patterns, such as counting by threes, sixes, and nines, as well as by twos, fives, and tens; adding, subtracting, multiplying, and dividing.

Supplementary Resources: Inch graph paper to make number lines and hundred squares; Unifix cubes or other counters to use on the squares to show patterns (such as the three times table); photocopied hundreds squares to color in patterns discovered while working with manipulatives on the hundreds grid.

Books: 100 Activities for the Hundred Number Board, Ideal Supply Company.

Math Balance

Uses: Discovering number patterns and concepts through experimenting with the balance (two weights on number five will balance one on ten for example) for use in developing an understanding of addition and multiplication.

Chip Trading

Uses: Trading games of many kinds, including working with bases other than base ten (such as trading three for one).

Supplementary Resources: Chips usually come with boards for trading games, a pair of dice, and a book describing games.

Attribute Blocks

Uses: Categorizing by attributes of shape, color, and size; forming a matrix or a "difference train" based on these attributes; games (choosing a block having one difference, two differences, or three differences from the one shown); and reasoning and logical thinking.

Supplementary Resources: At least two available sets of attribute blocks are available: (1) the ESS set has blocks demonstrating three differences—shape, color, and size; and has two other sets—"People Pieces" and small color cubes. (2) another set of blocks adds a third attribute—the pieces also vary in thickness. In purchasing books or activity cards, be sure to choose those that go with the particular set you have.

Measurement Materials
Inch rulers and yardsticks, metric rulers and meter sticks, tape measures, trundle wheels, a pan balance with English and metric weights, a small

kitchen scale and/or bathroom scale, small square tiles for measuring area, graph paper (inch and centimeter), inch cubes and centimeter cubes (borrowed from Base Ten Blocks or Cuisenaire rods), measuring cups and spoons, liter measure.

Materials for Studying Time and Money

Large Judy Clock (with movable hands and visible gears that can be used to demonstrate the differing rates of hour and minute hands and to illustrate and set specific times), small clocks with movable hands, clock face stamp, games involving matching digital and analog times, minute timer, calendars, real and play money, money games, tens and ones trading games.

Calculators

Calculators enable children to solve problems with numbers larger than they can yet handle with pencil and paper or long strings of numbers. Facility with calculators needs to be introduced early.

Other Useful Manipulatives

Dice
Dominoes
Pentominoes
Hexahedrons
Interlocking centimeter cubes
Games involving practice with number combinations

READING AND WRITING

The materials listed here reflect the kind found in all whole language classrooms. In a multiage classroom, however, the range of reading material will be broader. New predictable material for beginners and new children's books are constantly appearing, so I will merely suggest some of the kinds of materials to include.

The Wright Group of San Diego is one very good source for sets of beginners predictable books, including Story Box and Sunshine books. Rigby, in Crystal Lake, Illinois, is another source for such materials. *The Blue Pages* by Regie Routman, as well as the blue pages at the end of her other books (see Professional References), include comprehensive lists of children's literature categorized by both literary style (predictable, rhyming) and level of difficulty. Scholastic has packages of books in sets of six that are useful for literature groups.

Books

- Books emphasizing rhyme and repetitive word patterns
- Predictable books for beginners
- Easy reading books with controlled vocabulary
- Some simple books emphasizing phonetic elements, such as short vowel sounds
- Assorted paperbacks, including easy reading books, short and long chapter books.
- Sets of the same book for literature groups
- A changing assortment of hardcover books borrowed from a library
- Poetry collections
- Nonfiction books, including alphabet books, dictionaries, and other picture/word books, atlases, biographies, science books, jokes and riddles, drawing and craft books.
- Big books
- Tape recorder, earphones, and books on audiotape

Puppets

Puppets are useful for language development and are often used in relation to stories.

Letter and Word Cards

Common easy words or letters may be printed on plastic, wood, or cardboard tiles. They may be commercially produced or school-made and are fun to use for constructing words and sentences.

Writing Materials

- Pencils, erasers, colored pencils for illustrations
- Lined and unlined paper in assorted sizes
- Paper with spaces for pictures and lines for writing (assorted)
- Materials for book covers, which could include construction paper, simple oaktag covers, and cardboard covered with wallpaper. (One assortment I often made available included five-and-one-half-by-eight-inch sheets of paper prepared with the copy machine, some fully lined and some with lines on half the page, along with construction paper cut to the same size. As the children worked on these books they paper clipped the pages together in their folder until the book was finished and ready for a cover. Later, such student-made books might be published: typed and placed in sturdier wallpaper book covers.)

- Copybooks: small lined notebooks used as personal dictionaries, reading logs, journals, and for other writing
- Commercial or schoolmade blank books
- *Writing Dictionary* from Steck-Vaughn, a small personal dictionary with space to add words, one per child
- Reference lists of commonly used words
- Date stamp and stamp pad
- Folders for collected writing (I prefer legal-sized folders that are closed on each end), kept together in a box or file
- Schoolmade journals. (The "Monday Journals" I used were made with sheets of drawing paper in covers decorated by the children and laminated, all spiral bound at school. The younger children made drawings and labeled them, or wrote a few sentences without lines. Later, children wrote on lined paper that was pasted into the book opposite their illustrations using a glue stick.)
- Alphabets both on the wall and smaller folder-sized cards. These provide models for correct letter formation (manuscript and cursive). I also provide short poems and riddles on sheets of oaktag, as copywork for handwriting practice.

COMPUTERS

Computers belong in the classroom along with a printer and assorted software that includes a simple word-processing program. Although computers seem to have added a new curriculum area, they actually need to be viewed as a new multipurpose tool for learning. Computers belong with writing supplies, but they also provide math practice, problem-solving experiences, reading, and games. They cannot, however, replace hands-on experience for young children.

ARTS AND CRAFTS

Some arts and crafts materials should always be available; others, such as plasticine and watercolors, can be in the room for weeks at a time and then packed away to make space for other project materials. Still others come out only as needed.

- Crayons, plastic crayons that are erasable
- Magic markers, fat and skinny
- Pencils, erasers, colored pencils
- Colored chalk, oil pastels

- Scissors, stapler, staple remover, paper punch
- Tape, clear and masking
- Glue, glue sticks
- Tempera paints (also available in solid blocks)
- Watercolors
- Paint brushes in assorted sizes
- Sponges and cotton swabs
- Paper (assorted sizes of newsprint, drawing paper, colored construction paper)
- "Scrapbox" for collecting usable pieces of colored paper
- Special papers, such origami and metallic types
- Plasticine and clay
- String, yarn, pipe cleaners
- Paper fasteners, paper clips
- Paper plates and cups

In addition, all sorts of scrap materials are useful, whether brought from home or donated by local industry: fabric, ribbon, egg cartons, yogurt tubs, wallpaper books, wood scraps. (Often a parent volunteer will be willing to take charge of locating some of these materials and helping sort them for storage.)

CONSTRUCTION MATERIALS

Various construction sets are available (look in school catalogs), many very expensive and wonderful. Here are the basics:

- Blocks, large sets of hardwood blocks and special shapes, such as arches and triangles
- Found objects, such as turnings from factories
- Small cars and trucks, figures of animals and people, miniature traffic signs to be used with structures
- Marble maze
- Lego sets (some include cards giving step-by-step directions for constructing buildings and vehicles). My team also added the computer and used Lego-Logo with our older children, supervised by parent volunteers.

SCIENCE AND SOCIAL STUDIES

- Magnifying glasses and microscopes
- Magnets of various sizes, both bar and horseshoe types
- Prisms

- Pulleys
- Batteries, bulbs, wires, and accessories such as buzzers and small motors
- Mirrors
- Assorted jars
- Materials for planting: seeds, bulbs, cuttings, soil, recyled containers (yogurt tubs or small milk cartons)
- Samples of such things as rocks and shells
- Plants
- Small animals in cages
- Fish in an aquarium
- Maps
- Globe
- Items gathered for specific theme studies

GAMES AND PUZZLES

There are interesting board games and puzzles related to themes, such as dinosaurs or space, as well as games supporting math and reading. For example, there is a commercial version of the familiar word game, Hangman. Here are a few basic games:

- Checkers and Chess
- Othello
- Mancala
- Mastermind
- Battleship
- Connect Four
- Pictionary Junior
- Assorted memory or Concentration-type games
- Jigsaw puzzles, floor puzzles, easy puzzles, 500-piece challenges

SOME EXTRAS

- Cooking supplies: toaster oven and hot plate, saucepan, cookie sheets, nine-by-eleven-inch cake pan, measuring cups and spoons, mixing spoons, rubber scraper, paring knives
- Sand/water tables with assorted small toys and measuring tools
- Workbench and tools

(It is important to have volunteers available to supervise cooking and workbench activities. They require extra adult help.)

APPENDIX B

---■---

SCHEDULES

A F E W years ago, I was active in a network of multiage teachers, a group coming from many different schools in the area surrounding my own. Two of our most successful meetings were ones in which we all brought copies of our daily and weekly schedules to hand out to the group and discuss. We were all highly interested in finding out how others organized the school day, so I asked the teachers contributing to this volume to provide schedules that I might include. As in the network meeting, people responded to this request differently and therefore provided a look at some different options. My own schedule was already presented in Chapter 4.

Molly has provided us with a very detailed look at a week in her room. We need this detail because each day is different. You will notice that she makes use of many parent volunteers. At least once daily, and sometimes twice, a parent is on hand to help during part of the day. In addition to those shown on the schedule, parents help a group of children shop for snack food each week and cook once a week. Molly schedules math in large blocks on Monday and Tuesday, rather than in shorter daily periods. "Planning Time" is Molly's term for Explore Time, because the children plan their own activities for this time block.

Justine has given us a weekly schedule used by her team, Discovery House. On the Discovery House schedule, there are times when children are shared by the entire team and may work in various parts of the house or team space. These times are Choice Time, workshops during which theme-related activities take place, and Kiva (when the entire group meets together). "Work

	Monday	Tuesday	Wednesday	Thursday	Friday
8:15-9:30	"Planning" (Explore Time)	8:15-8:45 Classroom Choice		Town Meeting (3 classes together)	"Planning" (Parent Volunteer)
		8:45-9:15 P.E.	Morning Circle	"Planning" (Parent Volunteer)	
9:30-10:00	Journal/Snack	"Planning" (Parent Volunteer)	Music		Journal/Snack
			Snack		
10:00-11:30	Morning Circle Math Chat Math (parent volunteer)	Journal/Snack	Literacy Groups (Parent Volunteer)	Journal Snack	Morning circle Literacy Groups (Parent Volunteer)
		Morning circle		Learning Center	
11:35-12:05	R	E	C E	S	S
12:05-12:35	L	U	N	C	H
12:35-1:05	Music	Quiet Reading	Quiet Reading	Art	Quiet Reading
1:05-2:35	Quiet Reading	Math Groups (Parent Volunteer)	Writing: Writer's Workshop	Quiet Reading	Book Talk Shared Language
	Writing: Personal Journals Keywords, Spelling (Parent Volunteer)	Theme/Project	"Planning"	Theme/Project	Writing: Friday Letter Home (Parent Volunteer)
2:35	Ending Circle	Ending Circle		Ending Circle	P.E.
	B U S E S A N D J O B S				

(TEAM MEETING — vertical, Thursday/right side of chart)

Appendix B.1   Weekly schedule: Molly McClaskey

Times" are skills-related periods during which children work within their own class groups.

Peggy prefers to emphasize the daily routine. She makes a distinction between routine and schedule, feeling that the expected flow of the day is most important to children. She prefers to omit a rigid time frame except when necessary—lunch, special classes, and bus schedule.

PEGGY'S ROUTINE

Explore Time: The students arrive at school over a thirty-minute period. They do their own attendance, put their coats and backpacks where they belong, socialize a bit with me and their friends, read the morning greeting chart, and get started in some area of the classroom.

It is important for the children to start the day by making a responsible choice of an activity that really is of interest to them. Some kids need a time for the transition from home to school. Others might finish up something

	Monday	Tuesday	Wednesday	Thursday	Friday
8:20-8:50	Choice Time	Choice Time	Choice Time	Choice Time	Choice Time
8:50-9:05	Meeting	Meeting	Meeting	Meeting	Meeting
9:05-10:45	Work Time	Work Time	Work Time	Work Time	9:05-10:00 Work Time / 10:00-10:45 Friday Workshops
10:45-11:15	Quiet Reading	Quiet Reading	Quiet Reading	Quiet Reading	Quiet Reading
11:15-11:55	L U N C H A N D R E C E S S				
11:55-12:20	Read Aloud	Read Aloud	Read Aloud	Read Aloud	Read Aloud
12:20-1:00	Related Arts GYM	Related Arts ART	Work Time	Related Arts GYM	Related Arts MUSIC
1:00-2:00	Work Time	Work Time	Wednesday Workshops	Work Time	Work Time
2:00-2:10	Cleanup	Cleanup	Cleanup	Cleanup	Cleanup
2:10-2:20	KIVA and Dismissal	KIVA and Dismissal	KIVA and Dismissal	KIVA and Dismissal	KIVA and Dismissal

Appendix B.2 Weekly schedule: Justine O'Keefe (Discovery House)

from the day before so they don't feel "behind." This period also gives me a chance to have informal conversations with some of the children and to observe or meet individually with those I need to. The children work in one of several distinct areas of the room (planned with Gardner's [1993] theory of multiple intelligence in mind) or at a center I have prepared.

Morning Meeting: We always sit in a circle so that each person can see everyone else. This is an excellent time to reinforce communication skills and practice eye contact, listening, and responding. We start out with a greeting activity and then review the morning chart to see the plan for the day. The remainder of the meeting will fall into one of three categories: educational, problem solving, or open-ended.

Portfolio Time: For the next hour or so we work on writing/language arts or math. Some days everyone participates in a writing or math workshop. Other days whole group presentations are followed by small group or individualized work. Sometimes we just work individually on writing or math, addressing spelling and handwriting, and having writing and math conferences.

Theme Work: We work with a year-long theme and fit three or four sub-themes into each year. Much thematic work is also done during Portfolio, Explore, Meeting, and Reading Times.

Silent Reading: We read for up to a half hour. I model, often reading children's literature and other books that students suggest to me. I also model reading nonfiction materials, professional journals, and recreational reading.

Recess and Lunch

Reading Aloud and Reading Reactions: I read a book, usually a chapter book, to the group. We discuss it, do book projects (dioramas, murals, puppets), work in book clubs, write in reading journals, or just talk about reading.

Specials: Art, music, library, or physical education teachers take the class. As much as possible we try to integrate our current theme.

Closing Meeting: We gather to provide closure for the day by discussing our activities and making plans for tomorrow.

APPENDIX C

CLASSROOM LAYOUTS

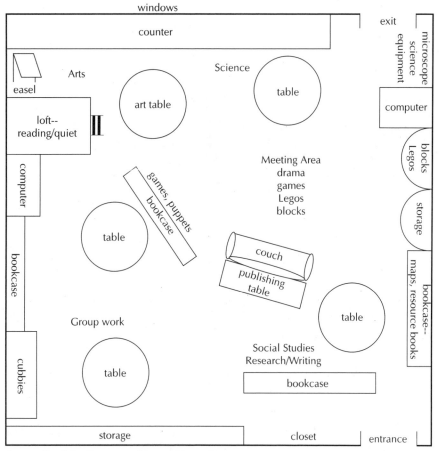

Appendix C.1 Classroom layout: Peggy Dorta

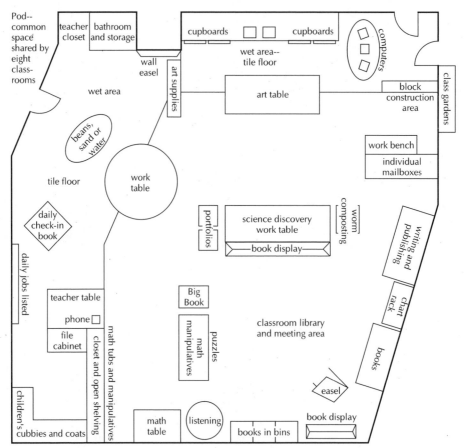

Appendix C.2 Classroom layout: Molly McClaskey

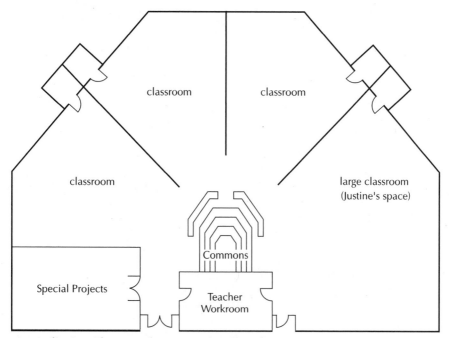

Appendix C.3 Classroom layout: Justine O'Keefe

PROFESSIONAL REFERENCES

Those resources that have been cited in the text are marked with an asterisk (*).

*Anderson, Robert H., and Barbara Nelson Pavan. 1993. *Nongradedness: Helping It to Happen.* Lancaster, PA: Technomic Publishing Company.

*Atwell, Nancie. 1987. *In the Middle: Writing, Reading, and Learning with Adolescents.* Portsmouth, NH: Heinemann.

*Baratta-Lorton, Mary. 1976. *Mathematics Their Way.* Reading, MA: Addison-Wesley.

*Barnes, Douglas. 1992. *From Communication to Curriculum.* Portsmouth, NH: Heinemann.

Baskwill, Jane, and Paulette Whitman. 1988. *Evaluation: Whole Language, Whole Child.* New York: Scholastic.

*Bredenkamp, Sue, ed. 1987. *Developmentally Appropriate Practice in Early Childhood Programs Serving Children Through Age 8.* Washington, DC: National Association for the Education of Young Children.

Bruner, Jerome. 1986. *Actual Minds, Possible Worlds.* Cambridge, MA: Harvard University Press.

*Burns, Marilyn. 1987. *A Collection of Math Lessons from Grades Three Through Six.* White Plains, NY: The Cuisenaire Company.

————. 1988. *A Collection of Math Lessons from Grades One Through Three.* White Plains, NY: The Cuisenaire Company.

Butler, Andrea, and Jan Turbill. 1984. *Towards a Reading and Writing Classroom.* Portsmouth, NH: Heinemann.

*Caine, Renate, Nummela, and Geoffrey Caine. 1991. *Making Connections: Teaching and the Human Brain.* Alexandria, VA: Association for Supervision and Curriculum Development.

*Campbell, Linda, Bruce Campbell, and Dee Dickinson. 1992. *Teaching and Learning Through Multiple Intelligences.* Seattle, WA: New Horizons for Learning.

Canfield, Jack, and Harold C. Wells. 1976. *100 Ways to Enhance Self-Concept in the Classroom: A Handbook for Teachers and Parents.* Englewood Cliffs, NJ: Prentice-Hall.

Centre for Language in Primary Education. 1988. *The Primary Language Record: Handbook for Teachers.* Portsmouth, NH: Heinemann.

Charney, Ruth Sidney. 1992. *Teaching Children to Care: Management in the Responsive Classroom.* Greenfield, MA: Northeast Foundation for Children.

*Chase, Penelle, Jane Doan, and Contributing Educators. 1994. *Full Circle: A New Look at Multiage Education.* Portsmouth, NH: Heinemann.

Clay, Marie. 1975. *What Did I Write?* Portsmouth, NH: Heinemann.

*Cochrane, Orin, Donna Cochrane, Sharen Scalena, and Ethel Buchanan. 1984. *Reading, Writing, and Caring.* New York: Richard C. Owen.

Cohen, Dorothy. 1972. *The Learning Child.* New York: Schocken.

*Cohen, Elaine Pear, and Ruth Straus Gainer. 1984. *Art: Another Language for Learning.* New York: Schocken Books.

*Dudley-Marling, Curt, and Dennis Searle. 1991. *When Students Have Time to Talk.* Portsmouth, NH: Heinemann.

*Eldredge, J. Lloyd, and John C. Weiss, Jr. Consultants. 1991. *Stories and More.* DOS Version 1.02. New York: IBM.

*Featherstone, Joseph 1971. *Schools Where Children Learn.* New York: Liveright.

*Fry, Edward B., Jacqueline K. Polk, and Dona Fountoukidis. 1984. *The Reading Teacher's Book of Lists.* Englewood Cliffs, NJ: Prentice-Hall.

Gamberg, Ruth, Winniefred Kwak, Meredith Hutchings, and Judy Altheim, with Gail Edwards. 1983. *Learning and Loving It, Theme Studies in the Classroom.* Portsmouth, NH: Heinemann.

*Gardner, Howard. 1983. *Frames of Mind: The Theory of Multiple Intelligences.* New York: Basic Books.

*_____ . 1993. *Multiple Intelligences: The Theory in Practice.* New York: Basic Books.

*Gayfer, Margaret. 1991. *The Multi-Grade Classroom: Myth and Reality, A Canadian Study.* Toronto: Canadian Education Association.

Gentry, Richard K. 1987. *Spel . . . is a Four-Letter Word.* Portsmouth, NH: Heinemann.

*Gordon, Julia Weber. [1946] 1970. *My Country School Diary.* New York: Dell.

Goodman, Ken. 1986. *What's Whole in Whole Language?* Portsmouth, NH: Heinemann.

Goodman, Kenneth, Yetta M. Goodman, and Wendy J. Hood. 1988. *The Whole Language Evaluation Book.* Portsmouth, NH: Heinemann.

Grant, Jim, and Bob Johnson. 1994. *A Common Sense Guide to Multiage Practices.* Columbus, OH: Teachers' Publishing Group.

*Graves, Donald H. 1983. *Writing: Teachers and Children at Work.* Portsmouth, NH: Heinemann.

Hansen, Jane. 1987. *When Writers Read.* Portsmouth, NH: Heinemann.

*Hill, Bonnie Campbell, and Cynthia A. Ruptic. 1994. *Putting the Pieces Together.* Norwood, MA: Christopher-Gordon.

Holdaway, Don. 1979. *The Foundations of Literacy.* Portsmouth, NH: Heinemann.

*———. 1980. *Independence in Reading: A Handbook on Individualized Procedures.* Portsmouth, NH: Heinemann.

Hornsby, David, and Deborah Sakarna, with Jo-Ann Parry. 1986. *Read On: A Conference Approach to Reading.* Portsmouth, NH: Heinemann.

*IBM. *Stories and More.*

*Katz, Lilian, Demetra Evangelou, and Jeanette Allison Hartman. 1990. *The Case for Mixed-Age Grouping in Early Education.* Washington, DC: National Association for the Education of Young Children.

Kreidler, William. 1984. *Creative Conflict Resolution: More than 200 Activities for Keeping Peace in the Classroom, K–6.* Glenview, IL: Scott, Foresman.

Labinowicz, Ed. 1980. *Piaget Primer.* Menlo Park, CA: Addison Wesley.

———. 1985. *Learning from Children: New Beginnings for Teaching Numerical Thinking.* Menlo Park, CA: Addison Wesley.

Maeda, Bev. *The Multi-Age Classroom: An Inside Look at One Community of Learners.* 1994. Cypress, CA: Creative Teaching Press.

Murrow, Casey, and Liza Murrow. 1971. *Children Come First: The Inspired Work of English Primary Schools.* New York: American Heritage Press.

*National Association for the Education of Young Children. 1988. "NAEYC Position Statement on Developmentally Appropriate Practice in the Primary Grades, Serving Five- Through Eight-Year-Olds." *Young Children,* 43, 2: 64–85.

*———. 1991. "Guidelines for Appropriate Curriculum Content and Assessment in Programs Serving Children Ages Three Through Eight." *Young Children,* 46, 3: 21–38.

Newkirk, Thomas, and Nancie Atwell. 1988. *Understanding Writing: Ways of Observing, Learning, and Teaching.* Portsmouth, NH: Heinemann.

Newman, Judith M., ed. 1985. *Whole Language, Theory in Use.* Portsmouth, NH: Heinemann.

Parry, Jo-Ann, and David Hornsby. 1985. *Write On: A Conference Approach to Writing.* Portsmouth, NH: Heinemann.

*Rathbone, Charles, Anne Bingham, Peggy Dorta, Molly McClaskey, and Justine O'Keefe. 1993. *Multiage Portraits, Teaching and Learning in Mixed-age Classrooms.* Peterborough, NH: Crystal Springs Books.

· ·

Rhodes, Lynn K., ed. 1993. *Literacy Assessment: A Handbook of Instruments.* Portsmouth, NH: Heinemann.

Rogers, Vincent R. 1970. *Teaching in the British Primary School.* New York: Macmillan.

*Routman, Regie. 1988. *Transitions from Literature to Literacy.* Portsmouth, NH: Heinemann.

* _____ . 1994a. *Invitations: Changing as Teachers and Learners K–12.* Portsmouth, NH: Heinemann.

* _____ . 1994b. *The Blue Pages: Resources for Teachers.* Portsmouth, NH: Heinemann.

Schwebel, Milton, and Jane Raph, eds. 1973. *Piaget in the Classroom.* New York: Basic Books.

*The Society for Developmental Education. 1993. *Multiage Classrooms: The Ungrading of America's Schools, The Multiage Resource Book.* Peterborough, NH: The Society for Developmental Education.

Trelease, Jim. 1989. *The New Read-Aloud Handbook.* New York: Penguin.

Wertsch, James V. 1985. *Vygotsky and the Social Formation of Mind.* Cambridge, MA: Harvard University Press.

CHILDREN'S BOOKS

■

Note: The books listed in Chapter 11 for Jamie's reading assessment are all Ladybird Books, Loughborough, England: Wills and Hepworth Limited. They are distributed in the United States by Merry Thoughts Incorporated, Pelham, New York.

Atwater, Richard, and Florence Atwater. 1992. *Mr. Popper's Penguins*. New York: Dell.

Bate, Lucy. 1988. *Little Rabbit's Loose Tooth*. Illus. Diane De Groat. New York: Crown Books.

Booth, Jack, Willa Pauli, and Jo Phenix, eds. 1984. *Good Morning Sunshine* (from the Impressions reading series). Holt, Rinehart and Winston of Canada.

Cleary, Beverly. 1990. *The Mouse and the Motorcycle*. New York: Avon.

Dahl, Roald. 1961. *James and the Giant Peach*. New York: Bantam Books.

———. 1978. *Fantastic Mr. Fox*. New York: Bantam Books.

de Paola, Tomie. 1983. *The Legend of the Bluebonnet: An Old Tale of Texas*. New York: Putnam.

Erickson, Russell. 1976. *A Toad for Tuesday*. New York: Dell.

Gannett, Ruth S. [1948] 1987. *My Father's Dragon*. Illus. by author. New York: Knopf.

Hoban, Lillian. 1972. *Arthur's Christmas Cookies*. Illustrated. New York: HarperCollins. Other *Arthur* titles available from HarperCollins.

Hoban, Russell. 1960. *Bedtime for Frances*. Illus. Garth Williams. New York: HarperCollins. Other *Frances* titles available from HarperCollins.

Hurwitz, Johanna. 1989. *Aldo Applesauce*. Illus. John Wallner. New York: Puffin.

Koller, Jackie F. 1990. *Dragonling*. Boston: Little, Brown.

Lobel, Arnold. 1970. *Frog and Toad Are Friends*. Illus. by author. New York: HarperCollins. Other *Frog and Toad* titles available from HarperCollins.

_____. 1978. *Mouse Tales*. Illus. by author. New York: HarperCollins.

_____. 1986. *Uncle Elephant*. Illus. by author. New York: HarperCollins.

Marshall, James. 1984. *George and Martha Back in Town*. Illus. by author. Boston: Houghton Mifflin.

Marzollo, Jean, and Carol Carlson. 1992. *I Spy: A Book of Picture Riddles*. Illus. Walter Wick. New York: Scholastic.

Mayer, Mercer. 1987. *The Pied Piper of Hamlin*. Illus. by author. New York: Macmillan.

McCloskey, Robert. [1952] 1976. *One Morning in Maine*. New York: Puffin.

Milne, A. A. [1926] 1970. *Winnie the Pooh*. New York: Dell.

Minarik, Else Holmelund. 1986. *Little Bear*. New York: HarperCollins.

Parish, Peggy, and Fritz Siebel. 1992. *Amelia Bedelia*. New York: HarperCollins. Other *Amelia Bedelia* titles available from HarperCollins, Greenwillow, and Avon.

Peterson, John. 1986. *The Littles*. Illus. Roberta C. Clarke. New York: Scholastic.

Slobodkina, Esphyr. 1987. *Caps for Sale*. Illus. by author. New York: Harper-Collins.

Travers, Pamela L. [1934] 1991. *Mary Poppins*. New York: Dell.

_____. 1991. *Mary Poppins Comes Back*. New York: Dell.

Viorst, Judith. 1987. *Alexander and the Terrible, Horrible, No Good, Very Bad Day*. Illus. Ray Cruz. New York: Macmillan.

Ward, Lynd. 1973. *The Biggest Bear*. Illus. by author. Boston: Houghton Mifflin.

White, E. B. [1952] 1974. *Charlotte's Web*. Illus. Garth Williams. New York: HarperCollins.

Williams, Jay. 1984. *Everyone Knows What a Dragon Looks Like*. Illus. Mercer Mayer. New York: Macmillan.

Wiseman, Bernard. 1983. *Morris Goes to School*. Illus. by author. New York: HarperCollins.

INDEX